Very "active"
in our 20's
love ~ M

SUBTLE ACTIVISM

SUNY series in Transpersonal and Humanistic Psychology

Richard D. Mann, editor

SUBTLE ACTIVISM

The Inner Dimension of
Social and Planetary Transformation

DAVID NICOL

STATE UNIVERSITY OF NEW YORK PRESS

Cover art: *Gaia Rose* by Bonnie Bell and David Todd, © 2012

Blue Marble image in cover art: NASA Goddard Space Flight Center Image by Reto Stöckli (land surface, shallow water, clouds). Enhancements by Robert Simmon (ocean color, compositing, 3D globes, animation). Data and technical support: MODIS Land Group; MODIS Science Data Support Team; MODIS Atmosphere Group; MODIS Ocean Group. Additional data: USGS EROS Data Center (topography); USGS Terrestrial Remote Sensing Flagstaff Field Center (Antarctica); Defense Meteorological Satellite Program (city lights).

Published by
STATE UNIVERSITY OF NEW YORK PRESS, ALBANY

© 2015 State University of New York

For information, contact
State University of New York Press, Albany, NY
www.sunypress.edu

Production, Laurie D. Searl
Marketing, Anne M. Valentine

Library of Congress Cataloging-in-Publication Data

Nicol, David, (date)
  Subtle activism : the inner dimension of social and planetary transformation / David Nicol.
      pages cm. — (SUNY series in transpersonal and humanistic psychology)
  Includes bibliographical references and index.
  ISBN 978-1-4384-5751-2 (hardcover : alk. paper)
  ISBN 978-1-4384-5750-5 (pbk. : alk. paper)
  ISBN 978-1-4384-5752-9 (e-book)
  1. Transpersonal psychology.   2. Human evolution.   3. Self-actualization (Psychology)   4. Consciousness.   I. Title.
  BF204.7.N53 2015
  155.2'5—dc23   2014036364

10 9 8 7 6 5 4 3 2 1

CONTENTS

ILLUSTRATIONS

ACKNOWLEDGMENTS

I wish to express my deep gratitude to the following people and organizations who have supported me, in a variety of ways, throughout this project.

First, I acknowledge the wonderful faculty and students of the Philosophy, Cosmology, and Consciousness Program at the California Institute of Integral Studies for providing the richly creative intellectual and spiritual container from which the ideas in this dissertation emerged. In particular, I thank Sean Kelly for his friendship and encouragement throughout the process.

I acknowledge Leslie Meehan, my close friend and colleague on the Gaiafield Project, for her love and support on multiple levels, including generous financial support that made this project possible.

The Gaiafield Council, especially Leslie Meehan, Myra Jackson, Claudia Weiss, Cynthia Jurs, Philip Hellmich, Bonnie Bell, and David Todd nurtured this work on the subtle realms for many years.

My beloved teacher and friend Florentin Krause guided my spiritual development throughout this project and beyond.

I thank my other spiritual teachers, Hameed Ali, Karen Johnson, and David Silverstein, and my Diamond Approach small group for their support at key moments.

Thanks to the people and organizations who provided physical spaces for me to write: Jon Rubenstein and Karin Swann, Lisa Tompkins, Ted Seymour, Leslie Meehan, and the Vedanta Retreat Center at Olema, California.

I give thanks to the production and marketing team at SUNY Press—especially Nancy Ellegate and Laurie Searl—for their warm encouragement and support throughout the process.

I acknowledge the many inspiring pioneers in this field: Dion Fortune, Maharishi Mahesh Yogi, Sri Aurobindo, David Spangler, and Marianne Williamson.

I thank my family in Australia and the United States for their unconditional support.

Last, but certainly not least, I thank my wife Kate for her fearless and steadfast love.

FOREWORD

Many good books are published each year but important books are harder to come by. One of the marks of a truly important book is that it challenges our deeply held convictions about what is real and what is possible in the world. It opens new intellectual horizons by showing us previously hidden connections. David Nicol's *Subtle Activism* is an important book, a very important book.

As a professor in a department of philosophy and religious studies all my life, I know firsthand how difficult it is for new ideas to dislodge deeply entrenched ways of thinking. Although a growing alliance of scientists has been demonstrating that wholeness and non-locality are inherent features of existence at multiple levels, this is still far from being the mainstream view in psychology and related disciplines. The Newtonian paradigm encouraged the emergence of an "atomistic" psychology that views minds as discrete separate entities, reinforcing our everyday experience of separateness. This vision continues to dominate our psychological thinking even after quantum theory and relativistic physics have radically changed our understanding of the universe. It seems easier to redraw our outer landscape than the inner landscape where we live and breathe.

This is precisely what makes Nicol's book so important. *Subtle Activism* invites us to rethink our entire inner landscape. It tackles one of the deepest questions we can ask about consciousness, namely, what are the boundaries of our mind? Where does one mind stop and another begin? I think this question is even more fundamental than the "hard problem" of consciousness—how does conscious experience arise from nonconscious biochemical processes? While not diminishing the significance of this question, I think the question of the boundaries of consciousness is more fundamental because it reframes how we interpret large bodies of data that bear on the hard problem itself. Most of the contemporary discussion about the significance of various neuroimaging technologies, for example, assumes the entrenched model that our minds are essentially separate entities. It assumes that minds and brains are paired in a one-to-one relationship and that our minds, like our brains, are isolated from each other.

Subtle Activism challenges this assumption. Through critically sifting research often ignored by mainstream thinkers, Nicol demonstrates the subtle interplay of minds at a distance and the emergence of collective fields of consciousness. He harvests what contemporary science is demonstrating but which many academics have been slow to accept—that our minds reach out and touch one other beyond the physical senses, that when intention is well focused, fields of influence arise, that group meditation can actually become a dynamic force in the world.

Those familiar with the history of religions know that these are not entirely new ideas. Wherever contemplatives have gathered, they have affirmed the view that collective intention can have far-reaching effects. What is novel in Nicol's book is the depth and breadth of evidence that he assembles for this hypothesis. His chapter on the scientific evidence that consciousness is a nonlocal phenomenon is the best I have seen, and I say this as someone who has tackled this issue in print himself. In my book *The Living Classroom*, I too marshaled the laboratory and clinical evidence for the existence of collective fields of consciousness, but Nicol's treatment is stronger than mine. His analysis of parapsychology, distant healing, the Maharishi Effect, and the Global Consciousness Project is more detailed and thorough. There is clearly more research to be done in this area, but Nicol has documented the tipping point we have come to intellectually. In this he has done serious thinkers a great service.

But the strength of Nicol's project goes beyond gathering the necessary evidence to give this hypothesis teeth, although that by itself would earn his book high marks. He embeds this discussion in a larger intellectual history, entering into thoughtful dialogue with Rupert Sheldrake, Edgar Morin, Teilhard de Chardin, Thomas Berry, Richard Tarnas, Sean Kelly, myself, and others. He carefully compares and contrasts his thinking with these authors, affirming common ground and marking differences. The scholarship is excellent.

Nicol goes on to place subtle activism in perhaps the most important social narrative of our day, the story of the emerging global systems crisis generated by our escalating desecration of the Earth. Here he aligns himself with those who believe that humanity has entered a century of increasing ecological and social instability, drawing us toward a critical bifurcation point that will decide our future for generations to come, perhaps even our viability as a species.

It is against the backdrop of these world events that Nicol argues that collective meditation may actually exert a positive influence in human affairs. Bridging the world of the social activist and the contemplative, he writes:

The more controversial proposal that I am making in this book . . . is that . . . certain activities of consciousness or spirit, which from the outside might appear to involve no obvious action at all, can be recognized as legitimate forms of social action. These activities can be understood to be subtle forms of social action because they transform (or so I will claim) what we might call the collective *psychic* or *spiritual* context out of which ideas themselves—and, therefore, decisions and actions—arise.

Acting on his convictions, Nicol, who is director of the Gaiafield Project, founded at the California Institute of Integral Studies, helped organize "WiseUSA 2008" and "WiseUSA 2012" which brought together thousands of participants in prayer and meditation around the 2008 and 2012 U.S. elections. He emphasizes that such initiatives are not a substitute for more overt forms of social and political action but a complement to them. Subtle activism provides "an expanded view of social engagement in which the inherent power of spirituality is recognized in and of itself as a legitimate component of an integral approach to social change."

These are ideas that deserve our careful attention. If we are not as psychologically isolated as we had previously thought, if our minds actually do meet in interactive fields of awareness as Nicol suggests, this leads to an expanded vision of the self and an expanded social agenda. Which brings us to perhaps the most important conclusion of this study. By helping us see our minds differently, Nicol encourages us to act differently. He has provided a powerful rationale for actively harnessing the collective potential of our minds in this time of humanity's great need.

Albert Einstein famously observed that, "You cannot solve a problem from the same consciousness that created it. You must learn to see the world anew." When the reader sees the world through David Nicol's eyes, he or she will truly see the world in a new way and hopefully act in a new way.

Christopher M. Bache, PhD

INTRODUCTION

I should not make any promises right now,
But I know if you
Pray
Somewhere in this world—
Something good will happen.

—Hafiz

This book suggests that spiritual or consciousness-based practices like meditation, prayer, and ritual, in addition to their positive effect on individuals, may play a subtle, yet crucial, role in supporting change in the world. It proposes that the intentional use of such practices for collective, and not merely individual, benefit can be understood as a subtle form of activism, or *subtle activism*. Subtle activism is a creative approach to social engagement that broadens the traditional scope of both activism and spirituality. On the one hand, it can be seen as a novel component of an integrative spirituality that aims to extend our spiritual attention to all aspects of our lives, including our participation in the social and political realm. On the other, it can be viewed as part of an integral approach to social change that seeks to address the underlying psychological and spiritual dimensions of sociopolitical transformation alongside outer actions. In straddling the worlds of spirituality and social change, subtle activism represents a bridge between the consciousness movement and the movements for peace, environmental sustainability, and social justice.

Although tales of yogis, shamans, and other adepts intervening on spiritual levels for the benefit of humanity are the stuff of ancient lore, this book constitutes the first comprehensive academic treatment of this topic. It proposes that the wider use of consciousness-based practices that focus on social or collective transformation has the potential to support a deeper integration of the positive dimensions of spirituality into modern public life, thereby enabling the public realm to become more permeable to such universal spiritual qualities as compassion, wisdom, and love. It argues that

1

the practice of subtle activism is an especially meaningful response to the contemporary global situation, offering both a stabilizing presence to help humanity through the multifaceted global crisis that looms before us, and a means for enacting the (re-)enchanted planetary awareness that a growing number of transpersonally oriented scholars regard as the basis for an alternative human future beyond, or around, the crisis.

By connecting the paths of inner and outer transformation, subtle activism stands in the lineage of spiritually inspired activism, or socially engaged spirituality, as exemplified by such inspirational public figures as Mahatma Gandhi, Martin Luther King, Thich Nhat Hanh, and Dr. A.T. Ariyaratne, and as articulated by contemporary scholars and teachers such as Michael Lerner, Andrew Harvey, James O'Dea, Joanna Macy, Starhawk, David Loy, Marianne Williamson, Kurt Johnson, Matthew Fox, and Donald Rothberg. Subtle activism is distinguished by its emphasis on the potential of spiritual practice itself to constitute a subtle form of action in the sociopolitical sphere. The use of spirituality as a source of renewal for overworked activists and of inspiration for wise outer action is vital for supporting creative and sustainable approaches to social engagement. But to *limit* spirituality to these roles in the context of social change work may be to reinforce the modern Cartesian divide in which mind or consciousness is seen as fundamentally distinct from—and usually subservient to—the "real" world of physical action. This proposal, in its strongest version, affirms the possibility that certain forms of spiritual practice might themselves subtly effect change in the social realm through the principle of nonlocal causality. Such an approach is not intended to replace more overt or direct forms of activism, or to deny the value of socially engaged spirituality as more commonly conceived. Rather it aims to maximize the potential of a typically overlooked, but possibly crucial, dimension of support in the context of a more integrative approach to social change.

Subtle activism is an umbrella term that describes a wide variety of spiritual or consciousness-based practices intended to support collective transformation.[1] These practices could include a broad range of traditional practices from the world's major spiritual traditions (e.g., meditation, prayer, chanting, drumming, ritual, ceremony, mindful movement), various psychotherapeutic and healing modalities (e.g., trauma-release work, dramatherapy), certain transformative forms of art and music, and creative syntheses of these and other similar practices. Although these practices are normally used to support individual growth, they all can be creatively adapted for the purposes of collective transformation, and thus constitute what I mean by subtle activism. Chapter 2 provides many historical and contemporary examples of subtle activism, such as the following:

- The (admittedly exceptional) claim by Indian sage Sri Aurobindo to have successfully wielded advanced yogic powers in psychic warfare with the Nazis from his bedroom in Pondicherry, India.

- The "Magical Battle of Britain," a project led by esoteric teacher Dion Fortune to strengthen the will of the British people during World War II through the practice of esoteric visualization techniques by a small London-based focalizing group and a wider national network.

- The "Big Ben Minute," another initiative intended to provide moral and spiritual support for the Allied war effort in World War II. The Big Ben Minute involved the daily practice by millions of people of one minute of silence during the chiming of Big Ben on BBC radio immediately before the nightly 9 p.m. news.

- The series of massive peace meditations organized in Sri Lanka in the 1990s by Dr. A.T. Ariyaratne and his Sarvodaya network to help facilitate a peaceful resolution to the Sri Lankan civil war.

- The WiseUSA initiative, convened by the Gaiafield Project (an organization I helped found), which brought together dozens of socially engaged American spiritual teachers and thousands of participants for a series of online meditation and prayer events intended to support the emergence of wisdom and compassion in the context of the 2008 and 2012 US electoral processes.

- The "Be The Peace" event on September 21, 2014 (the United Nations-designated International Day of Peace) that linked more than one thousand meditation gatherings in fifty-nine countries worldwide in shared intention to support a shift to a planetary culture of peace.

As these examples demonstrate, subtle activism can be practiced by individuals, small groups, and sometimes, in the case of mass or global meditation events, very large groups. It can be applied to all scales of social organization, from local communities to cities to nations to the whole human species or all life on Earth. It can be used to address various aspects of collective transformation, such as healing collective traumas from the past, providing support during sociopolitical crises or natural disasters in the present, or holding positive visions of a collective future.

As with all definitions, the lines that one might draw to differentiate subtle activism from other kinds of activities tend ultimately to be somewhat fluid. Although the term highlights an identifiably distinct phenomenon (namely, the use of consciousness-based practices for collective transformation), in practice subtle activism represents an expression of a way of understanding and engaging with reality that can be applied across all areas of life. For example, although I use subtle activism primarily to refer to practices that connect spiritual awareness with sociopolitical realities, one can easily imagine the application of similar practices to support scientific activities, such as a group that meditates or prays for scientists working on a cure for cancer. And such principles can obviously also be used for the purposes of individual healing and transformation, as in the case of distant healing practices for personal friends or relatives, or practices that focus on one's own healing and growth. Subtle activism is thus best understood, and practiced, as a creative component of an integrative spirituality that aims to encompass all domains of human experience.

It is especially important to recognize that the processes of individual and collective transformation are profoundly intertwined. The work an individual does on herself not only enables her to become a purer and more effective instrument for healing the collective, but, at deeper levels, can itself be a source of transformation whose effects extend beyond the individual. Jungian scholar Marie-Louise von Franz (1985) expresses this idea as follows:

> Whenever an individual works on his own unconscious, he invisibly affects first the group and, if he goes even deeper, he affects the large national units or sometimes even all of humanity. Not only does he change and transform himself but he has an imperceptible impact on the unconscious psyche of many other people. (17)

Conversely, whenever an individual engages in a practice ostensibly intended to support collective transformation, he himself is also inevitably transformed. By participating in the practice, he contacts a source of healing wisdom that cannot help but positively affect his own consciousness.

AN ANCIENT APPROACH, REVISITED

Subtle activism is really a modern name for an age-old practice, adapted to the structures of contemporary society. Spirituality was an integral part of all aspects of life in indigenous and ancient cultures, including their systems of governance and collective decision making. By many accounts, the rituals, prayers, and trance journeys of ancient shamans and seers, although sometimes applied for individual healing, were primarily intended to maintain the balance between the human society and its wider ecological and cosmic matrix. Their divinations were a vital source of guidance for tribal leaders and ancient monarchs on issues of societal importance, such as where to hunt for game or whether to go to war. Religion continued to play a dominant role in European political affairs throughout the medieval period through the influence of the Church. With the arrival of modernity, however, spirituality became largely divorced from the political decision-making process. A series of powerful and sustained critiques of religion and spirituality was fundamental in shaping the very structure of modernity. These critiques, and the scientific and political revolutions they helped spawn, created space for the scientific study of nature and the political development of democracy and human rights to proceed according to rational principles, free from the restrictive influence of religious dogma and the control of religious authorities. Religion and spirituality became effectively excluded from meaningful participation in the modern public realms of science, democracy, and social justice, leaving them little choice but to withdraw predominantly to the private domain of individual subjective experience.

This differentiation of modern society into relatively distinct spheres of activity has obviously brought innumerable benefits to humanity through the development of the positive dimensions of science and technology, and, to a lesser degree, through the (uneven) progress of democratic governance and human rights. But, as many have pointed out, our technological progress has come at a profound cost, most notably in the loss of humanity's sense of belonging to nature and the cosmos. In our times, alarming signs of the catastrophic trajectory of modern civilization have created a widespread awareness of the need to re-evaluate even the most taken-for-granted tenets of modernity. For a growing number, this awareness includes challenging the assumption that spirituality has no substantive role to play in helping to shape affairs in the public realm. Ecologically minded observers have argued persuasively that, by regarding nature as a "collection of objects" rather than a "communion of subjects" (to quote ecologist Thomas Berry), the disenchanted worldview of scientific materialism has shaped a culture in which the exploitation of the natural world for human gain has become standard practice. Social theorists have long commented on the dangerously lopsided character of modern development, in which our scientific and technological sophistication has far outstripped our ethical progress. Our path ahead, if determined by the same root assumptions that have guided modern society up to now, appears to lead inexorably toward a global crisis of historic proportions, symptoms of which are already clearly visible on multiple fronts. From climate change to the ongoing menace posed by the existence of nuclear and biological weapons of mass destruction, from the mass extinction of species to the calamitous loss of topsoil, from exponential population growth to the instability of the global financial system, from water shortages to the end of oil, humanity confronts a modern day Hydra, an encounter with any of whose monstrous heads threatens to trigger widespread systemic collapse. The scale of such a disaster (or series of disasters) might well dwarf all prior human experiences of tragic loss.

At the same time, with the growing understanding that modern civilization appears to be approaching a kind of death, our moment also represents an unprecedented opportunity for something genuinely new to be born. An awareness of imminent death is transformative, no less so for societies than for individuals. The precariousness of our situation has, in fact, spurred an extraordinary flourishing of creative activity at the grassroots level to develop alternative social, economic, and ecological solutions to the world's problems. Although commercial media outlets have largely ignored this remarkable social movement, environmentalist Paul Hawken (2007) calls it the largest in history. The acuteness of the threats has also engendered a planetary ecological consciousness at the highest levels of government, evidenced by the gatherings of world leaders in Rio in 1992, Kyoto in 1997, and Copenhagen in 2009 to attempt to develop coordinated international responses to these issues. And the emergence of the Internet has clearly revolutionized our capacity for grassroots collaboration in countless spheres of life, while supporting the development of a planetary awareness that transcends national identities.[2] Nonetheless, this movement for fundamental change has not yet matured to the point where it has been able to mount a serious challenge to the dominant paradigm of global capitalism and mechanistic materialism.

We find ourselves in a liminal period of history. The decline of the existing order is already apparent but the form of the new world is yet to fully take shape. Such a context is ripe for the re-emergence of spirituality beyond its modern confinement to the private realm of individual development. The resources of spirituality may be uniquely capable of providing both a crucial soothing presence to counterbalance the chaotic forces likely to be unleashed in the transition ahead and a foundation for the emergence of a planetary wisdom culture. It is largely in this spirit that a number of transpersonally oriented writers (e.g., Rothberg, Loy, Wilber, Lerner, Harvey, O'Dea, Macy, Johnson and Ord, Bucko and Fox, Vaughan-Lee, Spangler, and Williamson) have called for a more active engagement of the public sphere by various mature and nondogmatic forms of spirituality. To be clear, none of these proposals supports a return to public influence of the dogma of institutional religion, nor aims to subvert the principle of the separation of church and state. It is vital here to distinguish more superficial or conventional expressions of religion that emphasize adherence to orthodox belief from the deeper essence of spirituality which, whether found at the mystical core of the traditions, or beyond any tradition, centers more on the direct experience, realization, or enactment of spiritual realities. In this regard, it is noteworthy that, as Buddhist scholar Donald Rothberg (1993) points out, the main critiques of religion that resulted in its rejection by modernity (such as those made by Voltaire, Hume, Marx, Freud, and Nietzsche, among others) almost exclusively targeted the dominant canons of institutional Christianity. These critiques, in their dismissal of all religion and spirituality, did not tend to differentiate between institutional Christianity and other, less dogmatic, forms of spirituality, elements of which might have been easier for the modern sensibility to accommodate. We may thus question whether, in breaking free from the yoke of religious domination, modern societies may also have needlessly blocked their own access to legitimate sources of spiritual wisdom. Recovering a connection to these sources could bring to the notoriously alienated modern psyche a timely awareness of our underlying unity and connection to the whole. Such a move need not be viewed as a retreat to a naïve prescientific awareness, but as a postmodern integration of certain aspects of premodern traditions that have been dogmatically rejected by modern materialist science.[3] *Subtle Activism* argues for an expansion of the role of spirituality in society beyond the restrictions imposed by modern thought. It envisions the emergence of postmodern or integral expressions of spirituality that help to re-establish links between nondogmatic forms of spiritual consciousness and modern public awareness—not through overt action in the sociopolitical or even intellectual arena, *but via actual practices that enact the connection at subtle levels of consciousness.*

SCIENCE AND CONSCIOUSNESS

Science is increasingly coming to embrace the notion that consciousness and world, or mind and matter, are complexly interrelated. In the seventeenth century, Descartes specifically excluded subjective qualities of mind from the scope of modern science through his pivotal conceptual division between mental and physical realities. However, this split eventually could not be sustained in light of numerous scientific developments that have demonstrated an inextricable connection between mind and matter. The discovery in physics that the act of measurement appears to codetermine the outcome of events at quantum scales was pivotal in this regard. But science has come to acknowledge a complex link between mind and matter for a wide range of phenomena. The well-established placebo effect in medical science, the emerging field of psychoneuroimmunology, and research on the physiological effects of meditation are but a few examples.[4] Although orthodox science has thus become increasingly willing to assign a more active or causative role for consciousness in the shaping of physical reality than previously thought, it continues to be governed by the reductionist assumption that consciousness is produced by, or even equated with, neural events in the brain.

Yet arguably the clearest outcome to emerge from the explosion of scientific interest in consciousness in recent decades is the recognition that empirical science has very little idea how to explain how consciousness emerges from the neural activity of the brain and may not even in principle be able to do so. Although it is evident that conscious experience in human beings in some way depends on neurobiological processes (because their destruction almost always results in a loss of awareness), it has been consistently pointed out that these processes are not the same thing as the subjective experience itself. As philosophers like Thomas Nagel, David Chalmers, K. Ramakrishna Rao, and John Searle have persuasively argued, no amount of mapping the neural correlates of conscious experience will ever sufficiently explain the inner, subjective, qualitative states of awareness that are fundamental to that experience. This gulf between physical matter and subjective experience is known as the "explanatory gap," and it shows no sign of being adequately bridged by current empirical approaches. Furthermore, physical reductionist accounts of consciousness do not satisfactorily explain transpersonal and extrasensory aspects of our experience and are inconsistent with widespread and deeply felt human spiritual needs and convictions. Although most Western scientists continue to presume that consciousness will eventually yield to a neurobiological explanation, this confidence increasingly seems unwarranted, and based primarily on preexisting metaphysical commitments to materialism. In reality, the question of consciousness can be regarded as very much open.

To the extent that scientists take seriously the subjective aspect of consciousness, consciousness research represents a challenge to purely objectivist epistemologies, since the topic under study unavoidably includes the researchers themselves. For this reason, a number of scientists and philosophers have pointed out the need to complement traditional third-person methods with first-person phenomenological research to develop a more comprehensive science of consciousness (see, e.g., Wilber 1997a; Varela and Shears 1999; Velmans 2000; Rao 2002). In some scientific circles, this approach has corresponded with a greater willingness to consider alternative models of consciousness, especially those associated with Asian meditative traditions like Buddhism and Vedanta, which have accumulated vast stores of knowledge from centuries of systematic, first-person exploration of subjective aspects of consciousness. In these traditions, consciousness is typically seen as an autonomous principle that underlies and permeates all reality. There is no denying that this perspective has spiritual associations that are alien to the materialist assumptions of modern science. However, a sincere (although not uncritical) consideration of models that regard consciousness as an irreducible feature of reality may be necessary to allow us to gain a more complete understanding of this most basic yet complex and elusive phenomenon. In this spirit, chapter 4 examines (among other things) the "Theory of Vedic Defense" developed by Maharishi Mahesh Yogi, founder of the Transcendental Meditation (TM) movement and one of the most important figures in introducing the principles and practices of Eastern spiritual traditions to the West. The Theory of Vedic Defense draws from contemporary developments in unified quantum field theories and understandings of consciousness from India's ancient Vedic tradition to offer an explanation for how the widespread practice of meditation might increase social harmony.

In addition to looking to alternative models of consciousness from Eastern thought, we would do well to also examine analogous proposals that have been developed in various disciplines within the Western intellectual tradition. Leading attempts that have been made within the framework of empirical science to describe nonphysical dimensions of reality that underlie and influence the material world include David Bohm's theory of holomovement and the implicate order (physics), Rupert Sheldrake's hypothesis of formative causation and theory of morphic fields (biology), and Carl Jung's notion of the collective unconscious (psychology). Chapter 4 also considers these models in some depth in the context of exploring theoretical foundations for subtle activism.

EMPIRICAL EVIDENCE

The question of empirical evidence for the effectiveness of subtle activism is a tricky one. Given the complexity of modern social systems and the subtlety of consciousness-based practices, it is debatable whether the instruments and methodologies of empirical science are capable of adequately capturing the effects. The primary loci of action for subtle activism practice are subtle planes of consciousness. How the effects might translate from subtle to manifest levels of reality seems irreducibly mysterious. A standard view in many esoteric traditions is that the interaction of phenomena in subtle dimensions tends to be governed more by principles of resonance and affinity than by mechanical notions of cause and effect. From this perspective, the distance between two entities on subtle planes is determined less by quantitative measures of time and space than by qualitative factors such as the extent to which they resonate with each other. An example of this principle from everyday life is the common experience of feeling close to someone we love even when that person may be physically far away. This notion finds support in the parapsychological research literature, where it has been consistently reported that psychic experiences occur most frequently and vividly between emotionally bonded couples (parent–child, twins, married couples, etc.; e.g., Duane and Behrendt 1965, L. Rhine 1981 Dunne 1991). If this is true, it may not be appropriate to expect subtle activism to behave as a purely mechanical force that radiates out from its source in a linear fashion. For example, the effect might not necessarily manifest in observable changes near the location of the practice in time or space, but in events occurring far away, or later in time. Given the inherent challenges of measuring empirically these kinds of nonlocal correlations, recognizing them may inevitably require a certain degree of interpretation or intuition.

Nonetheless, several ingenious empirical attempts *have* been made to measure the social impact of consciousness-based practices, and with encouraging results. The most prominent of these is the series of studies on the so-called Maharishi Effect undertaken by scientists associated with the TM movement. The series comprises more than forty studies–more than twenty of which have been published in peer-reviewed academic journals–that consistently demonstrate statistically significant correlations between the presence of large groups of TM practitioners and improvements in indicators of social harmony (like crime rates) in nearby cities.[5] Another relevant study is the Princeton Engineering Anomalies Research (PEAR) laboratory's Global Consciousness Project (GCP) developed by psychologist Roger Nelson. The GCP examines correlations between events that capture the world's attention and the output of nonrandom data from a global network of random-number generators. The cumulative data suggests that focused collective attention produces a subtle increase in physical coherence in the world. More general support for the principle of nonlocality can be found in the large body of work associated with the fields of parapsychology and distant healing research, which offer substantial empirical evidence of nonlocal mind-to-mind and mind-to-matter interactions from over a century of scientific investigation.

Needless to say, these are controversial areas of research. If widely acknowledged, empirical evidence of paranormal phenomena would directly undermine the materialist paradigm of orthodox science and immediately constitute a prima facie case for consciousness being a fundamental and irreducible feature of reality. With so much at stake, results tend to be contested with the intensity of a holy war. The debate between proponents and skeptics of psychical research frequently resembles less a scientific conversation than a highly charged political battle. Yet the evidence for paranormal phenomena appears to be increasingly strong according to conventional scientific standards. I discuss these lines of research and their relevance for subtle activism in chapter 3.

DIRECT "VERSUS" SUBTLE ACTIVISM

One of the most exciting possibilities of subtle activism, in my view, is its potential integration with creative forms of social and political engagement. In my own work with the Gaiafield Project, our most compelling projects have been those that have connected the practice of subtle activism to social and political actions occurring in the world. For example, our WiseUSA initiatives linked subtle activism with the US presidential elections in 2008 and 2012, our WiseClimate project focused on the Copenhagen climate change conference in 2009, and our Occupy Gaia series in 2011 supported the then burgeoning Occupy movement. Yet, in my experience, the most strident opposition to the concept of subtle activism often comes from the ranks of traditional direct activists, particularly those on the political left. The typical complaint is that subtle activism represents a kind of middle class or new age cop-out that diverts valuable energies from the less comfortable but more productive activities necessary to generate real change. The unscrupulous powers that be, so this line of criticism goes, would like nothing more than for the people to believe that their salvation lies in meditation and prayer, as these practices could give people the feeling that they are making a difference while leaving the world open for continued exploitation. Far from being seen as a revolutionary force, spirituality is considered from this perspective to be a pacifying agent that serves to maintain the status quo.[6]

The possibility of subtle activism being utilized as a form of psychological defense is a legitimate concern. Although subtle activism is precisely intended to counter the tendency of spirituality to be otherworldly and escapist by connecting it to sociopolitical realities, some people could use it as an avoidance of, rather than an engagement with, the difficulties of the world. It is important to reiterate, however, that subtle activism is not proposed as a replacement for outer action, but as a method that ideally supports and amplifies more direct forms of intervention. Individuals who practice subtle activism should be encouraged to also participate in commonsense outer actions like community organizing, voting, signing petitions, and so forth. In fact, some spiritual teachings maintain that the power of subtle work is itself amplified by taking actions in the world that embody the ideals of the practice, especially when those actions entail an element of personal risk or sacrifice.

On the other hand, as a complement to direct action, subtle activ-ism has the potential to elevate social movements by infusing them with a psychological sophistication and spiritual depth often lacking in traditional approaches to activism. A common downfall of conventional activism is its tendency to devolve into a tribal mentality of "us versus them," which can weaken the moral power of a movement to enroll broader social support. The practice of subtle activism can provide a social movement with a cru-cial sense of coherence and discipline, and offers the possibility of a more profound mode of engagement with the "opposition." Although a sense of outrage at social and environmental injustice is natural, the indiscriminant acting out of rage can obscure the righteousness of a cause. Subtle activism creates spaces that invite the emergence of deeper levels of collective wis-dom about sociopolitical realities. This process supports participants in being able to hold social issues in greater complexity, beyond superficial notions of right and wrong. It can also inspire creative practical interventions that transcend more predictable reactionary responses. In general, the danger for traditional activists is the tendency to become so intensely engaged with the suffering of the world that they lose contact with the joy, love, and peace in themselves that is needed to facilitate authentic transformation. The danger for spiritual or subtle activists is to overly identify with the bliss and the light to the degree that they become disconnected from the realities of injustice and suffering. Ultimately, the optimal balance between inner and outer approaches to social change is likely to emerge from a process of honest dialogue and collaboration between open-minded representatives of both perspectives.

SKEPTICISM

Regardless of how convincing we might find the empirical evidence for nonlocality, the idea of subtle activism might still provoke the skeptic in many of us. The proposed force is so subtle that, in contrast with more overt forms of action, it may appear inconsequential as a factor in shap-ing events in the sociopolitical sphere. We cannot see the results with our own eyes. We therefore have to trust that our subtle actions are having an impact on the world. Yet we have been deeply conditioned by our modern scientific culture to doubt the reality of unseen or nonphysical dimensions. Having received a comprehensive modern education, including degrees in law, science, and philosophy, I have certainly not been immune to these doubts myself.

Personally, I have found it valuable to examine carefully and critically the voice of skepticism within my own psyche. Part of this voice seems to serve the constructive purpose of challenging truly naïve or inflated notions I or others may have about the power of consciousness-based practices to effect change in the world. It helps to keep the vision real and grounded. Even if acknowledged as real, the social effects of spiritual practice are deeply mysterious. Our knowledge in this area is rudimentary at best. Our efforts are still relatively small-scale and the world is a very large place. I consider this aspect of skepticism to be a healthy expression of intellectual and psychological integrity.

But I have noticed another side of the skeptical voice within me that seems much less rational. It is characterized by a dogmatic refusal to consider evidence of nonphysical dimensions of reality, even from my own direct experience. This part, on closer examination, seems clearly fear-based. Beneath its scornful exterior, it appears frightened of permitting any experience that lies beyond the bounds of consensual reality. Its stance toward reality is not one of genuine curiosity, the supposed hallmark of the scientific attitude, but ironically more like that of a devout believer—a believer, that is, in the dominant ideology of mechanistic materialism.[7] Whereas the first skeptical voice is like an alert, clear-eyed sentry, appropriately protecting the borders of the realm against charlatans and hucksters, the second resembles a corrupt and prejudiced customs official, belligerent toward anyone who appears different from the cultural norm.

Distinguishing between the rational and irrational aspects of my skepticism has helped me to be substantially more open to the truth of my experience. It has freed me to approach the practice of subtle activism not with the faith of a true believer, but with a radical openness to reality that transcends the categories of belief and doubt. In that expanded perceptual space, I find myself in contact with a mode of knowing that is both rational and intuitive. From there, I feel increasingly confident in the perception that the practice of subtle activism produces meaningful shifts in the subtle matrix that underlies manifest reality. I cannot specify exactly what outer changes follow from these interventions. But personally I find it sufficient to know that I have participated in bringing forth a source of blessing into the world and to trust that good things will flow from that action. In this respect, I find myself in agreement with Hafiz: "I should not make any promises right now, but I know if you pray, somewhere in this world, something good will happen."

MEANING

In early 2008, I was driving down to Santa Cruz from my home in Berkeley, California when I heard a report on the radio that Kevin Rudd, then Prime

Minister of my homeland Australia, had made a comprehensive public apology on behalf of successive white Australian governments for their historical
mistreatment of the Aboriginal people. The apology was made uncondition-
ally, and delivered sincerely. Aboriginal elders received the apology in person
inside Parliament House in Canberra. Thousands of Aboriginal people had
traveled to the capital for the occasion. Schoolchildren across the country
watched the event on live television, and large crowds gathered in major
cities to view it on specially erected big-screen monitors. Hearing excerpts
of the apology played over the radio, my heart leaped out of my chest.
Prime Minister Rudd's words had brought healing to a centuries-old division between the white and Aboriginal peoples of Australia. As an Australian, I carried the sorrow of this separation somewhere deep in my psyche.
Now the wound came rushing up for release. Much more would need to
be done, of course, to address the terrible social and economic conditions
experienced by most Aboriginal people. But the apology seemed crucial in
setting something right at the very foundation of the relationship between
white and indigenous Australia.

I know I was not the only Australian who cried upon hearing the
news. Similarly, many around the world wept openly when Nelson Mandela
walked free from Robben Prison, or when Barack Obama became the first
black president. These are sacred tears, tears that reveal the heart's word-
less knowing of our purpose together here on Earth. Although our political orientation might affect our emotional reaction to events like these to
some degree, there is something universal in the human heart that responds
with profound happiness when we witness the resolution of an historical
injustice. The elation we feel emerges from the depths of our being where
we care very deeply about each other and for the fate of our world. These
feelings might frequently become buried beneath sophisticated psychological
defenses as we go about our daily lives, but they can burst forth in tears of
joy on those rare occasions when we bear witness to events on the world
stage that fulfill the soul's private longing.

Subtle activism can be understood as a set of practices that allow us
to connect, in the depths of our being, with our love for the world and our
longing for it to reflect the highest potentials of human nature. Although
being in touch with our hope for a more loving or peaceful world can make
us more vulnerable, it is also the most powerful force for change we know.
Subtle activism represents the intention to cultivate this force as a transformative presence in the world. Although countless concrete initiatives will
of course also be needed to restore our planet to balance, underlying and
informing all of these actions is a shift in consciousness involving a deeper
awareness of our essential interconnectedness. That shift can, and indeed

must, take place in a very subtle way in the depths of the human psyche. Those who feel called to engage directly in the transformation of human consciousness, especially through the practice of what I am calling subtle activism, may thus have a crucial role to play in helping to establish the foundations of a planetary culture of peace. This book is dedicated to the success of those efforts.

CHAPTER ONE

THE INNER DIMENSION OF
SOCIAL AND PLANETARY
TRANSFORMATION

In early April 1988, in my late teens, I experienced a profound shift in perspective that radically disrupted the trajectory of my life. After several years of intense striving for academic and sporting success, something broke through my awareness about the futility of pursuing happiness that way. Nothing dramatic had happened to me in the external world. I simply had started to notice that no matter what I achieved, the resulting happiness and contentment would be remarkably brief. For example, I had spent months studying with driven intensity for final law exams and had been elated when I scored a wonderful result, yet the satisfaction had lasted for only a day or two before I noticed myself feeling vaguely restless and empty again, needing to move once more toward another horizon. I started to realize that I felt a subtle anxiety in relation to *everything* in my life I had previously assumed was necessary for happiness: friends, family, external achievements of all kinds. They were all fleeting. I could not hold on to any of them for even a moment without knowing they were simultaneously slipping away through the inexorable flow of time. One otherwise unremarkable Monday evening this realization about the impermanence of things entered my mind as a very big thought that seemed to burrow its way down into the foundation of my very identity. Time and death would take everything away. This was real. In light of this existential fact, I could no longer feed my inner hunger for meaning with any mere temporary fix from the world. In an instant, my motivation for external success utterly withered. For more than two weeks I could hardly eat. I could not watch television or read a book. All external pleasures seemed like mere tranquilizing diversions from the profound but disturbing reality of impermanence. I thought I was going crazy.

Yet amid the dissolution of my old achieving identity, I began to encounter some very interesting experiences of peace. Moments came when, out of despair, I simply gave up my efforts to salvage meaning or happiness from the world. In these moments I was surprised to discover the despair slowly transform into a simple but wonderful state of restfulness. I was still here, without any effort to create myself. And there was something intrinsically significant about this state of just being. I began to read teachings about Eastern mysticism and was amazed to find many descriptions in them that corroborated my experience. Thus began my (ongoing) journey on the "pathless path" of spiritual realization and personal healing.

The incident I have just described was the first of many initiations into deeper dimensions of being that I later experienced. At first I regarded the process as entirely personal—the outcome of my personal trajectory and relevant primarily to my personal life. In time, as I increasingly came to experience myself as part of something larger, I became more and more curious about the extent to which my personal journey might also be an expression of a collective evolutionary development occurring all over the world. Since I was a child I had been fascinated by the great saga of human history, that tale of the dramatic currents of collective public life, shaped by key individuals who seemed propelled by a mysterious force of destiny. Like many others, I was deeply stirred by those rare instances when men and women of courage—a Mahatma Gandhi, a Martin Luther King, or a Rosa Parks—made a stand in the public arena on profound moral and spiritual grounds. Their stories produced in me a strong desire to contribute in some way myself to shaping the direction of society, especially in the realm of politics. Following that impulse, I completed my law studies and practiced for a few years as an environmental lawyer in Sydney, Australia. In my short career, I was involved in several legal battles against egregious development proposals (and succeeded with one of them). I also became more politically engaged. My earliest experiences in meditation of an underlying field of loving awareness had led me to embrace a much more inclusive political vision than the conservative perspective I had absorbed from my upper middle-class upbringing. I participated in numerous rallies for peace and environmental issues and helped out with a progressive national political campaign.

Yet amid these efforts, I sometimes wondered how much of our activism was truly effective in bringing about the world we desired. Many of the legal and political actions I was involved in, although well intended, seemed only to add to the cycle of reactivity and suffering we were attempting to resolve. For instance, many activists I encountered appeared to be clearly "acting out" their inner conflicts through their activism work, frequently discharging their anger reactively toward political opponents or people in positions of authority, and showing little empathy for the complex challenges those people might have faced. (Of course, I was also guilty of these tendencies at times.) And although many of us were motivated by our concern about global social and ecological trends, our passion was inevitably channeled into small regional clashes in which the big picture conversation was largely obscured by the details of the local conflict. Although these local battles seemed necessary, it felt dispiriting at times to be investing so much energy in trying to put out small fires here and there while the mighty engine of the industrial growth society continued to fan the flames of social and environmental injustice everywhere. Was it possible, I wondered, to engage in the work of social change in a way that targeted the underlying consciousness that kept reproducing these problems all over the planet? And what was the connection between the profound process of individual transformation and the nature of sociopolitical change? Could we somehow invite the healing balm of awakened consciousness into the public arena to support collective transformation?

Following these questions led me to study the ideas of many scientists, philosophers, and other visionary thinkers who have attempted to discern a deeper pattern of meaning amid the complex currents of our contemporary global situation. One of the most striking features of our age is the widespread sense of the precariousness of our condition, a narrowing of vision Wendell Berry (2003) once called "the loss of the future." Although millennial movements predicting the imminent demise of civilization have appeared quite regularly throughout Western history, in our times the threat of nuclear holocaust and evidence of catastrophic climate change, species extinction, and many other symptoms of a global ecological crisis provide considerable empirical support for the possibility of a cataclysmic breakdown of order absent a fundamental change in our present course. Anxiety about the viability of the human species has accordingly become in our age far more than the preoccupation of religious extremists but rather a broadly shared concern of the international scientific and political community.

Yet the deepest threat of all might be located in a subtler and much less frequently acknowledged dimension of the global situation: the crisis of meaning. Were we able to situate our present challenges in a context that gave them meaning and intelligibility, we might be able to summon the deep resources of the human moral and spiritual imagination to meet them. Yet so much of the modern and postmodern project (of the West) has involved the deconstruction of the great cultural stories and frameworks that previously provided humans with a meaningful orientation toward the cosmos.[1] The loss of this context is directly linked to the profound sense of alienation that so many writers have rightly seen to pervade and even characterize the modern mind. Social theorists from Emile Durkheim to Max Weber, novelists from Fyodor Dostoyevsky to Franz Kafka, and philosophers from Soren Kierkegaard to Jean-Paul Sartre have all relentlessly exposed the condition of estrangement as the dark underside accompanying the advances of modernity. As philosopher Richard Tarnas (2006) points out, at the very root of modern alienation lie the cosmological discoveries of modern science, starting with the Copernican revolution, which overturned the ancient presumption that human and Earth existed at the center of a divinely ordered cosmos and paved the way for a purely mechanistic conception of the universe. Freidrich Nietzsche dramatically caught the world-shattering implications of these developments in his famous passage from *The Gay Science*:

> What were we doing when we unchained this earth from its sun? Whither is it moving now? Whither are we moving? Away from all suns? Are we not plunging continually? Backward, sideward, forward, in all directions? Is there still any up or down? Are we not straying as through an infinite nothing? Do we not feel the breath of empty space? Has it not become colder? Is not night continually closing in on us? Do we not hear anything yet of the noise of the gravediggers who are burying God? . . . God is dead. God remains dead. And we have killed him. How shall we, murderers of all murderers, console ourselves? (Nietzsche 1974, 181–182)

As Tarnas (2006) notes, one of the most consequential effects of these early cosmological discoveries—an effect extended and amplified by the whole subsequent arc of modernity—was the deep impression these developments left in the modern mind that the more we learned about the cosmos, the more it was revealed to be random and meaningless. Indeed (to put things in very general terms for our introductory purposes here), a crucial outcome of modernity was to establish in the modern mind the presumption that the universe has no inherent purpose, consciousness, or interiority. Although we humans might experience ourselves to possess these qualities (e.g., we experience ourselves as having an inner world, as being conscious, soulful, meaning-seeking beings), from the dominant perspective we are seen to be unique in this regard in a cosmos that is utterly indifferent to our inner concerns. In this view, there is no intelligent principle in nature supporting the unfolding of the cosmos in any meaningful direction. Any human perception of meaning, consciousness, or purpose in the natural world is seen, from this dominant perspective, to be necessarily an anthropomorphic projection, a regression to a superstitious or sentimental stance that modernity is supposed to have outgrown. French biologist Jacques Monod (1970) spoke for many when he said: "Man knows at last that he is alone in the universe's unfeeling immensity, out of which he emerged only by chance" (180).

Although the dominant mechanistic perspective has brought forth unprecedented technical mastery of the natural world, its continued hold on the modern psyche has been recognized by a host of ecologically sensitive writers as now constituting one of the gravest obstacles to our capacity to overcome our current challenges. By dismissing as naïve any human perception of sentience or intelligence in the natural world, the dominant view is deeply implicated in the ecological crisis insofar as it has permitted and justified a profoundly irreverent attitude toward nature. With no part of the natural world regarded by the modern mind as sacred, nothing has inhibited humans from treating the Earth solely as a resource to be exploited for short-term economic gain. At the same time, by rejecting even the possibility that a larger sense of purpose may be involved in the evolution of the cosmos, the dominant perspective has profoundly diminished the capacity of humans to make sense of the crisis, thereby draining the collective imagination of the moral and spiritual depth that could inspire more deeply creative and courageous responses to our situation.

In the radically pluralistic milieu of contemporary academia and today's global marketplace of ideas, however, the dominant modern paradigm no longer possesses quite the same hold over the cultural imagination as it once did. Although the mechanistic perspective continues, of course, to be profoundly influential, postmodern arguments as to the historically and culturally mediated nature of all knowledge have radically undermined the notion that the modern scientific worldview represents a purely objective insight into reality.[2] The highly creative yet fragmented postmodern intellectual environment has allowed the assertion of a bewildering multiplicity of perspectives and paradigms, including the reemergence of many elements of the West's intellectual heritage that had previously been marginalized by the dominant view. In this context, a number of writers have returned with particular interest to sources within the Western tradition that have articulated holistic alternatives to the mechanistic perspective in the hope that these approaches might contribute to shaping a cultural vision better adapted to the realities of our contemporary global situation. Throughout modernity, we can observe the periodic flourishing of a significant strain of countercultural thought that, in creative and dynamic tension with the dominant rationalistic and mechanistic paradigm, has played a major role in constituting the Western sensibility. Esoteric scholar Wouter Hanegraaf (1998) identifies the modern origins of this countercultural tradition in esoteric elements of the Renaissance and traces subsequent expressions to the European Romantic and Idealist movements of the late eighteenth and early nineteenth centuries, American Transcendentalism, the 1960s counter-cultural movement, and contemporary New Age or New Paradigm thought.[3] Following much the same thread, philosopher Sean Kelly (2010) points out that although there is a substantial diversity of views within this lineage, common elements tend to include the adoption of the organism (as opposed to the machine) as the root metaphor for the cosmos as a whole, the associated intuition that all parts of the universe are interconnected in a living unity, and a (re-)enchanted worldview in which the cosmos is seen to be permeated and organized by soul or spirit.

From within this countercultural tradition, a number of thinkers have articulated a vision of evolution that posits a meaningful direction to the unfolding of both nature and human history. Beginning with the German Romantic/Idealist philosophers Fichte, Schelling, and Hegel,[4] this perspective is also associated with early to middle twentieth century figures Henri Bergson, Teilhard de Chardin, Owen Barfield, and Sri Aurobindo, and contemporary philosophers like Jean Gepser, Ken Wilber, Richard Tarnas, William Irwin Thompson, and Duane Elgin. Although the more sophisticated advocates of this approach acknowledge a substantial degree of contingency to the evolutionary process, they all nonetheless discern an overarching evolutionary purpose involving the production of ever higher, deeper, or more complex forms of consciousness. Although not widely recognized as an established school of thought, this view has been called "evolutionary panentheism,"[5] or simply "the evolution of consciousness."

The proposition that human civilization and consciousness might be developing in a purposeful direction is, of course, very much out of favor in today's academic circles. I have already mentioned the broad materialism of the mainstream scientific perspective, which interprets evolution in purely naturalistic terms and tends to regard metaphysical notions (like purpose or meaning) as unprovable hypotheses at best. Skepticism might also be expected from thinkers informed by the postmodern sensibility, who tend to suspect all "grand metanarratives" of obscuring—and thereby maintaining—the privileged position of a particular gender, culture, species, or other group within a supposedly universalist scheme. Others might be especially wary of the disastrous consequences that ensued from earlier misguided attempts to apply evolutionary ideas to human cultural development, as in the so-called Social Darwinism associated with figures like Thomas Malthus, Herbert Spencer, and Francis Galton (whose theories many regard as the foundation for the racist policies of Nazi Germany).

Nonetheless, I believe that an evolution of consciousness perspective, especially insofar as it takes into account certain postmodern intellectual developments, can offer a crucial unifying context that can help us to recognize a deeper meaning to our current precarious situation and thereby support us to face the coming challenges with more equanimity, faith, and resolve. Although postmodern concerns of totalitarian outcomes emerging from "totalizing" discourses are well founded, in a world that requires urgent, coordinated global action to respond to the multifaceted crises of our age, the extreme relativism and fragmentation that have frequently accompanied the postmodern mindset are not without their own pernicious real-world consequences. By developing a narrative about the evolution of consciousness that is transparent to its own potential biases, open to dialogue and continual revision, and committed to principles of diversity and inclusivity, I believe we can rescue the potential of this line of thought to provide shared, meaningful, yet nonexploitative cultural stories that can help to inspire heartfelt collaborative responses to the challenges of our times.

Let us now enter into this perspective on more intimate terms by examining the thought of three of its leading representatives.

THE PLANETIZATION OF HUMANKIND: TEILHARD DE CHARDIN

Our first example is the new vision of evolution advanced by French Jesuit priest and paleontologist Pierre Teilhard de Chardin. Teilhard recognized that the discovery of evolution enabled humanity to comprehend its place in the cosmos in a new and profound way. This new self-understanding, however, was not the deflating view that followed for many from Darwin, in which the human was seen as having been reduced from a noble creation of God to a mere intelligent animal. For Teilhard the story of evolution offered humanity a way to recognize its own journey as an expression of an immensely ancient unfolding drama charged from the outset with spiritual purpose.

Teilhard (1959a) identified a purpose to evolution through completely reappraising the role of consciousness in the evolutionary process. He argued that consciousness, or the "within" of things, far from being a mere epiphenomenon of biological processes that emerged late on the scene with the human, is a fundamental property of the universe present from the beginning. He claimed to be able to observe, amid the flux and complexity of evolutionary development, a continual rise in consciousness that corresponded with the development of increasingly complex physical forms. For example, when the vastly more complex living cell emerged from simple molecules, one could observe a "thrust forward in spontaneity," "the luxuriant unleashing of fanciful creations," and "the unbridled expansion and leap into the improbable"—circumstantial evidence, for Teilhard, that an internal change of "consciousness" had accompanied the external change of form (89). Or, claimed Teilhard, the development of ever larger and more complex brains in the evolution of primates paralleled an interior development of consciousness that eventually resulted in human self-awareness. The tendency of the universe to evolve toward ever-more conscious and complex modes of being was not, for Teilhard, simply an accident but revealed a clear evolutionary direction.

By elevating the role of consciousness in the story of evolution from negligible extra to central protagonist, Teilhard cast a new light on the place of the human in the cosmos. For him, the development of human self-reflexive consciousness was not a strange biological accident, but a crowning evolutionary achievement for which the universe had long prepared. After crossing the threshold of self-reflection, the evolutionary process continued to operate, claimed Teilhard, but now acted primarily in the realm of consciousness through advances in human thought and culture. Teilhard argued that the instincts of the animal world, as they crossed the threshold of reflection, underwent a metamorphosis and became "hominized" into cultural codes of behavior. For example, the sexual instinct became the evolution of human love, the need for nourishment (with its accompanying seizing and devouring behaviors) became the evolution of war, animal curiosity became human research, and so on. Thus Teilhard developed a vision of evolution (consistent with the ideas of German Idealist philosophers such as Schelling and Hegel) in which the unfolding drama of the cosmos, the Earth, life, and human civilization could be recognized as a single continuous process, governed by common evolutionary principles. As people came to recognize the essential unity of the evolutionary process, Teilhard believed they would realize that they are participating in larger evolutionary dynamics of immense grandeur and that this realization would infuse human life with tremendous dignity and meaning.

One key pattern Teilhard identified is that throughout the story of evolution, there are critical moments of transformation in which a quantum leap occurs to a fundamentally new level of organization. Teilhard noted that these evolutionary tipping points predictably take place when the elements of the existing level bunch progressively closer together to reach a critical degree of compression and complexity. Then a new "granule" emerges as the basic unit of the new level. For example, the granule of the living cell emerged from molecules binding together on the confined surface of the Earth; multicellular organisms from the grouping of cells; the human from the growth in brain size and complexity in primates.

Applying this axiom to humanity's contemporary situation, Teilhard observed several basic facts: Humans are exponentially increasing in population, living on a finite sphere, and growing ever-more complexly intertwined through an increasingly sophisticated global communications network. From these facts, Teilhard concluded that humanity is headed inexorably toward another evolutionary tipping point, a quantum leap comparable in magnitude to the great transitions from nonlife to life, or from life to human consciousness. This next historic step is the *planetization of humankind*: the gathering together of the human family into a single, balanced whole, a "harmonized collectivity of consciousness equivalent to a sort of super-consciousness" (Teilhard 1959a, 251). Teilhard also introduced the concept of the *noosphere* to describe a new "thinking membrane" or "living tissue of consciousness" that had enveloped the Earth, formed by the ever-increasing interconnectivity of human thought. The planetization of the human family would involve the "completion" of the noosphere so that the Earth would become "enclosed in a single thinking envelope so as to form, functionally, no more than a single vast grain of thought . . . the plurality of individual reflections grouping together and reinforcing one another in the act of a single unanimous reflection" (251).

Teilhard's work was an undeniably bold and brilliant attempt to synthesize the scientific account of evolution with a religious sensibility, and the hopeful context his vision provides continues to be a source of inspiration for many. Yet Teilhard also inherited certain problematic assumptions of the French Enlightenment that have limited the wider reception of his ideas in contemporary academic circles. For example, Teilhard's abundant (and very modern) faith in progress and human ingenuity led him to overemphasize scientific discoveries and technological achievements as signs of positive evolution, while overlooking their frequently negative social and ecological consequences. In his description of humans as the culmination of the entire evolutionary process, Teilhard tended toward an anthropocentric outlook inadequate to appreciate the intrinsic value of the diverse expressions of life on Earth. He also overstated the unique significance of Christianity compared with other religions as a central axis of the evolutionary process. Many of these criticisms were taken up by cultural historian Thomas Berry, who affirmed Teilhard's core insights while significantly adapting them in an ecological reworking of Teilhard's vision.

THE INTEGRAL EARTH COMMUNITY: THOMAS BERRY

Berry (2000, 2003) agreed with Teilhard that our era involves a transition of such enormous magnitude that it cannot be properly understood as just another historical period. But for Berry, the significance of the transition did not derive primarily from humanity's progress toward a collective superconsciousness. Although he acknowledged the extraordinary achievements of modern human civilization, Berry argued that our era is at least equally momentous for the unprecedented scale of the human's desecration of the

Earth: "The glory of the human has become the desolation of the Earth" (2003, 57). He maintained that, from the perspective of the Earth as a whole, the chief significance of our moment is that a 65-million-year period of unparalleled evolutionary inventiveness is coming to a close. Not since the extinction of the dinosaurs (which marked the beginning of this period) has the Earth experienced a contraction of biological creativity comparable to the one we are living through—and human activity is the cause of it. Berry argued that the imperative for the human is to appreciate that the Earth and all its living and nonliving components forms an integral community, that the human is a member of this community, and that we will find our greatest fulfillment by advancing the well-being of the total community. For Berry, the highest expression of the evolutionary process is not, as Teilhard believed, an integrated human community (reigning supreme over a degraded planet) but an integrated Earth community. Thus, the convergence of the human community predicted by Teilhard to form "a single, vast grain of thought" was extended by Berry to include the functional convergence of the entire Earth community, so that the Earth can operate "as a single cell" (2003, 65).

Berry pointed out that, for the first time in the Earth's history, one species is now extensively in control of the entire Earth process. Humans are no longer just one species among many but have acquired a macrophase power of a unique order of magnitude. The task of the human, for Berry, is to enter into a new mode of consciousness in which we become aware of this new planetary dimension. Along with the awesome capacities of our macrophase power comes a new responsibility to develop the corresponding macrophase wisdom. According to Berry, we must learn to evolve out of our competitive, territorial, microphase instincts and instead start to think and act from the perspective of the whole system. As Berry's colleague, mathematical cosmologist Brian Swimme (2003) puts it, in this new understanding we are not first and foremost Americans, or Westerners, or even members of the human family, but earthlings in interdependent relationship with all the human and nonhuman members of the Earth community. One way, therefore, to evaluate people, programs, and activities is "the extent to which they foster or obstruct the creative functioning of the larger Earth community" (Berry 2003, 64).

THE RE-ENCHANTMENT OF THE COSMOS:
RICHARD TARNAS

Philosopher and cultural historian Richard Tarnas (2001) interprets our present condition from a perspective that integrates Hegelian dialectics and philosophy of history with depth and transpersonal psychology. Just as countless individuals in recent decades have discovered the importance of bringing to consciousness, through psychological self-exploration, those unconscious forces from the past that shape our individual lives, Tarnas emphasizes the crucial need for our entire civilization to engage in a similar undertaking. In a Hegelian spirit, he asserts that self-reflection for a civilization involves an examination of its interior cultural history—its philosophy and science, its art, its cosmology, its myths. For Tarnas, these are the deep unconscious forces from our collective past that shape our contemporary global situation.

Focusing on the worldview of the modern West (principally because of the West's central role in determining our current global condition), Tarnas argues that the chief trait that distinguishes the modern mind from virtually all premodern perspectives is the sharp division it has created between the human self as subject and the world as object. In line with thinkers like Lucien Levy-Bruhl, Carl Jung, Mircea Eliade, and Joseph Campbell, Tarnas claims that most members of ancient and indigenous societies experienced themselves as living in an "ensouled" universe that communicated personally to them through meaningful signs and symbols. The features of the ancient or indigenous landscape were not simply physical objects; they were alive with spiritual or mythic significance. Thus, according to Tarnas, the ancients saw spirits in forests and perceived meaning in the flight of eagles across the horizon. The outer world of nature and the inner world of the human soul participated equally in the anima mundi, or world soul, which imbued both dimensions—inner and outer—with archetypal significance.

Tarnas notes that the modern worldview tends to regard such a perspective as a childish fantasy. For the modern mind, Tarnas points out, the universe possesses no intrinsic meaning or significance. All spiritual qualities and moral sensibilities reside solely within the human self. To see soulful qualities in nature or to interpret its signs as meaningful personal communication is, from the modern perspective, simply an error—a naïve projection of human attributes onto a soulless and indifferent universe.

Tarnas traces the evolution of this modern worldview through a series of intellectual developments beginning with the pivotal Copernican recognition that the Earth revolves around the Sun, thus displacing the Earth (and the human) from the center of the cosmos and setting the stage for a mechanistic interpretation of the universe. He argues that Galileo, Descartes, and Newton continued the process by building a model of the cosmos as a machine governed solely by physical laws of motion and force. Darwin extended the perspective by demoting humans from their unique spiritual status and representing them as just another animal species—not spiritual beings in special relationship with God but merely advanced products of biological evolution. Kant, notes Tarnas, is widely thought to have introduced a kind of Copernican revolution to philosophy by recognizing that human perception of the world is unconsciously determined by the ordering structures of the human mind, thus uprooting human knowledge from any certain foundation in the world at large. Finally, Tarnas lists numerous postmodern developments in a variety of intellectual disciplines that have extended Kant's insight into the relative and uncertain nature of human knowledge to complete the picture of the thoroughly alienated postmodern self.

At each stage of this journey of the Western mind, Tarnas identifies a dual development. On the one hand, the intellectual and moral autonomy of the human self was further differentiated out from the larger matrix of nature and community and radically empowered to act on the world according to its own will. On the other hand, each step forward in autonomy was simultaneously a step away from the primordial cosmic unity. The outcome, for Tarnas, is the fundamental condition of the modern human: the supremely individuated and empowered self who at the same time experiences himself to be profoundly alone in a spiritually barren and meaningless cosmos.

With the development of depth psychology, however, Tarnas claims that the Western mind took a pivotal turn. Although Freud's discovery of the unconscious at first further relativized the status of the human being (by revealing that even the human's own conscious ego was unconsciously influenced by powerful instinctual drives), the finding (especially by Jung) that the psyche is informed at deeper levels by archetypal structures opened up the possibility for a new interpretation of even the modern worldview itself. For if, as Kant proposed, the deep structural principles of the human mind decisively shaped our reality and if, as Jung argued, the archetypes were those very structural principles, then, notes Tarnas, even the disenchanted character of the modern worldview could itself be interpreted as an expression of a particular archetypal constellation and not an absolute reality. And indeed, for Tarnas, the alienated condition of the modern psyche bears a remarkable similarity to a crucial phase in the archetype of the death–birth initiation process that was initially explored by Jung and later investigated in detail by psychologist Stanislav Grof and mythologist Joseph Campbell.

Initiation processes in indigenous and ancient cultures throughout history typically put initiates through a trial involving their physical removal from the community and an intense confrontation with suffering and death before allowing them to return to start a new phase of life as initiated adults. Tarnas contends that the estrangement of the modern human from the community of being—in an intellectual and spiritual sense through the epistemological "prison" of modernity, but also in a pragmatic sense through the threat of nuclear annihilation and the global ecological crisis—can be seen as a kind of collective dark night of the soul analogous to that experienced by the initiate during his or her removal from the community. For Tarnas, this suggests that the whole trajectory of the Western mind—in which it has forged the intellectual and moral autonomy of the self while growing increasingly alienated from the ground of being—can be understood as having been meaningfully informed all along by archetypal dynamics, which are now drawing things forward to a critical phase of the process. Tarnas maintains that human civilization is passing through its own evolutionary rite of passage, a collective initiation through the death–rebirth process into a new way of understanding and relating to the cosmos. What is on the other side cannot be predicted with any precision but, claims Tarnas, seems likely to involve a new vision of our relationship to the universe, one in which we will recover our sense of participating in a larger matrix of meaning and purpose but from a new position of mutuality. In this vision, we will understand ourselves to be neither separate subjects imposing our will on a soulless cosmos, nor simply puppets acting out the predetermined intentions of the world soul, but creative co-participants in a dialogical dance with an intelligent universe.

SUMMING UP

These frameworks suggest ways for us to perceive more clearly a coherent thread of meaning running through the particular events of our contemporary world. For Teilhard, the deep significance of our times lies in the process he called the "planetization of humankind"—the progression toward an increasingly integrated human consciousness spanning the Earth. For Berry, it is the awakening of humans to our planetary dimension but also to our role as benign stewards for the entire Earth community. For Tarnas, our moment is best understood as a collective rite of passage, one that may require humanity to pass through some form of collective death, but which offers the promise of a rebirth into a re-enchanted cosmos.

What these perspectives share, firstly, is the fundamental notion that we are living through an historical period of momentous transition, rather than one of relative stasis. For Teilhard, Berry, and Tarnas, our moment is one of those highly unstable yet vitally creative periods between eras, when the decisions we make have disproportionate consequences down the ages. Our times are not like those of, say, an average Roman citizen living in the middle of two hundred years of *Pax Romana*, or a north European living in medieval feudal society in the twelfth century CE when the social structures and rituals of life followed a relatively well-established and predictable groove. These authors suggest that our times are more analogous to critical historical turning points when the old order was running out of steam and sweeping changes to all facets of society were imminent (such as the periods just before the fall of Rome or the Industrial or French Revolutions).

Moreover, Teilhard, Berry, and Tarnas share a conviction that the cultural shift we are called to make is one of a distinct order of magnitude. Teilhard believed the process of humans becoming "planetized" would be an evolutionary leap equal in magnitude to the great transitions from matter to life and from life to human self-reflexive consciousness. For Berry, the significance of the shift could be appreciated only by seeing it from the perspective of geological time. Due to the current extinction spasm caused by the impact of human industrial civilization, he claimed that we are effectively ending the Cenozoic Era, a 65-million-year period of unparalleled biological creativity that began after the age of dinosaurs.[6] For Tarnas, the rite of passage facing humanity represents a critical fulcrum point in the evolution of the Western psyche, containing the potential to fulfill the "passion" of the Western mind by reuniting it with the ground of being, thereby bringing to a certain completion the whole trajectory of Western thought. These authors clearly view our times as more than just another transition, but the stage for a potentially rare and profound historical drama.

Teilhard, Berry, and Tarnas maintain that the cultural transition we are called to make is most fundamentally a shift in consciousness or worldview. Although we will, of course, require many specific new laws, policies, scientific discoveries, technological breakthroughs, and so on, to meet the collective challenges we face, these authors stress the underlying shift that must take place at the level of the collective human imagination: We are called to revise our entire cultural story about what it means to be human and what our relationship ought to be with each other, the planet, and the cosmos. As Tarnas points out, such a shift will need to involve all the dimensions of the human imagination: not just intellectual, but also psychological, ethical, and spiritual. Teilhard, for example, emphasized love as a crucial ingredient in the transition (specifically, the love of humanity for the emerging planetary "being"). Berry urged the development of a wider sense of ethical responsibility for the well-being of the Earth community to correspond with our planetary-sized power. Tarnas suggests the need for us to develop the "epistemologies of the heart" (such as the capacity to listen more empathetically to the voices of the "other") and the importance of our being willing to undergo a sustained process of grieving for all that has been left behind and damaged in the lopsided advance of Western civilization. For all of these authors, it is only through such an integral act of imagination—entailing a great collective turn of heart, of soul—that we will be able to navigate our way successfully through the current crisis.

THE PATH OF SUBTLE ACTIVISM

In light of these frameworks, let us now return to the questions posed at the start of this chapter. How might we engage in the work of social change in a way that targets the underlying consciousness that keeps reproducing our problems all over the planet? What is the connection between the processes of personal and collective transformation? Can we invite the transformative power of awakened consciousness into the public arena to support social change and, if so, how? This book is about a path that has emerged for me as an answer to these questions. I call it the path of *subtle activism*.[7]

What Is Subtle Activism?

I define *subtle activism* as "spiritual or consciousness-based practices intended to support collective transformation." Examples include a global meditation intended to help promote a peaceful solution to an international political crisis or a prayer vigil to bring healing to a region after a major natural disaster.

The first point to highlight in the definition is that subtle activism involves various forms of practices, where the practices themselves are seen to constitute a subtle form of social or political action. The practices are thus regarded not merely as a means to prepare for social activism out in the world, but are themselves seen as a subtle form of activism. These practices are not a substitute for physical action, but they may offer a crucial form of support that complements more concrete initiatives in the context of a more integrative approach to social change.

The practices can take a variety of forms: meditation, prayer, ritual, chanting, ecstatic dance, mindful movement, shamanic journeying—any spiritual or consciousness-based practice, really, from any tradition. I am deliberating adopting an inclusive view of spirituality and do not seek to associate subtle activism with any particular spiritual perspective. Many spiritual traditions have developed elaborate maps of the inner terrain involving various types of subtle beings and realms. Others have been more concerned with transcending intermediate forms to realize total emptiness or nonduality. And still others emphasize the cultivation of the direct presence of God, rather than total identification with the Absolute or divine. My intention is to create a broad framework where a variety of perspectives and practices can be welcomed, united in shared commitment to collective healing and transformation. For this purpose, the field of subtle activism is best served by a participatory and pluralistic vision of human spirituality that affirms the possibility of many valid spiritual realizations and goals.[8]

The second point to notice in the definition is that the practices are intended to support collective, rather than individual, transformation. Thus, meditating for the purpose of one's own liberation should not, in my view, be considered subtle activism, but meditating for peace in the Middle East should be. Praying for the health of one's personal friend or family member is not subtle activism, but praying for a community struck by natural disaster is. There is a deep connection, of course, between the processes of individual and collective transformation, and it would be artificial to draw a rigid boundary between them. Whether the purpose of a practice is to heal oneself, a personal friend or relative, or a community or nation, the same fundamental principles are involved. Nonetheless, it is specifically the extension of these principles to the collective domain that constitutes what I mean by subtle activism.[9]

A third aspect of the definition is that the practices are spiritual or consciousness-based. These words are notoriously difficult to define and there are no widely accepted meanings associated with them. I consider a practice to be "spiritual" if it helps to facilitate a transformation of the individual and/or community toward fuller alignment with that which is "sacred" and expresses such universal values as love, compassion, and peace.[10] A practice need not be explicitly spiritual to be included in this definition. For example, a practice that evokes a sense of awe and reverence for the natural world would be "spiritual" by this definition.

The term *consciousness* has been used to mean so many different things that some thinkers have recommended abandoning the concept altogether. Hundreds of scholarly books on consciousness have been written in the last few decades, without any consensus being reached on a precise definition. We can, however, develop a sufficient, if rudimentary, understanding of the term for our purposes by pointing out that it is often used synonymously with words like "awareness," "experience," and "subjectivity." A distinction is frequently made between the content of experience and experience itself, with the latter being equated with consciousness. For example, Kurt Johnson and David Ord (2012) assert that a mind is conscious when it is aware of another state of mind, such as thought. A practice could thus be said to be "consciousness-based" if it facilitates a heightened or deepened awareness of subjective experience.

The fourth and final point to note in the definition is that the practices are *intended* to support collective transformation. A broad interpretation of intentionality is called for here. Some spiritual practices explicitly incorporate an intentional statement or thoughtform as part of the practice, but others specifically exclude intentional elements. A number of Eastern meditative traditions, for example, emphasize letting go of all mental content, including intentions, in order to rest in a state of total emptiness, or pure consciousness. However, even these methods can be applied in a way that includes a meta-level intention for the practice to support collective transformation. For example, although focusing on mental intentions is discouraged during the practice of TM, large TM group meditations have often been located near war zones and other trouble spots in the belief that these events would help bring peace to those regions. The organizers of these events clearly design them with an intention to benefit the communities in question, even though this intention is not incorporated into the practice per se.

Let us consider some real-world examples of what I am calling subtle activism. In 2002, an estimated 650,000 Sri Lankans participated in the world's largest ever peace meditation, hosted by the Sarvodaya organization to support the ceasefire that had recently been negotiated between the Sinhalese-identified government and the Tamil Tiger secessionist party. For more than an hour, in excess of half a million people, all dressed in white, sat together in deep meditation in the public parks of the sacred city of Anuradhapura. The event was clearly intended to have a political impact, yet there were no placards or speeches—simply silence. During World War II, as many as 5 million people throughout the British Commonwealth united daily for a minute of silence during the chiming of Big Ben on BBC radio at 9 p.m. (just before the evening news). The practice was intended to strengthen the moral and spiritual resolve of the allied forces during the ordeal of war. In recent years, the expansion of the global interfaith movement and the emergence of the Internet have given rise to countless global meditation and prayer events that link individuals and communities around the world in shared silence and prayers for peace. For example, in early 2003 during the buildup to the Iraq war, the Global Interfaith Prayer Vigil united more than 100,000 monks, nuns, and other practitioners from a variety of faiths for a fifteen-week vigil to support a peaceful solution to the crisis. My own organization, the Gaiafield Project, organized the WiseUSA 2008 and WiseUSA 2012 subtle activism initiatives. These programs brought together dozens of socially engaged spiritual leaders and thousands of participants for a series of online meditation and prayer events intended to call forth wise and compassionate leadership in America from the 2008 and 2012 US electoral processes. Instances involving smaller groups include the "Magical Battle of Britain," in which a small group led by esotericist Dion Fortune met weekly in a house in London during World War II to engage in magical practices designed to protect Britain from the Nazi threat. For subtle activism by individuals, there is the example of Indian philosopher-sage Sri Aurobindo, who claimed to have played a role in affecting the outcome of World War II through applying a kind of spiritual force from his bedroom in Pondicherry. In all of these cases, the focused mental and/or spiritual attention of the individual or group is seen as having the potential in and of itself to positively influence events in the sociopolitical realm.

"Weak" and "Strong" Versions of the Hypothesis

Needless to say, the hypothesis of subtle activism goes beyond currently orthodox scientific theories. An understanding of consciousness as a nonlocal phenomenon is highly controversial within science because it transgresses the materialist paradigm and carries historical associations with religion and magic, modes of thought that science is supposed to have left behind in its emergence from premodern superstition. But before we examine the plausibility of nonlocality as an explanatory principle let us consider the more modest proposal that subtle activism could support social change through influencing the subsequent (overt) actions of the practitioners involved.

Take the case of a meditation or prayer circle that dedicates its practice to supporting a peaceful resolution to an impending international conflict. Regardless of any perceived or actual impact on the worldly situation, the practice will typically have a transformative effect on the participants themselves. For example, participants in the hundreds of subtle activism processes I have helped facilitate since 2004 often report experiencing a sense of empowerment from having meaningfully engaged with a sociopolitical situation they would otherwise feel powerless to influence. These effects inevitably carry over into the participants' lives, influencing their subsequent actions and interactions in mostly subtle, but occasionally striking, ways. One person might re-engage with her work for social justice from a place of restored hope. Another might be inspired to implement an idea for a creative social action that came to him during the meditation. And another might simply radiate a little more joy toward her friends and family. Although these effects may seem minor, a regular practice can significantly shape the nature of a person's contribution to society. If the practitioner happens to be a person of significant social or political standing, the effect may be especially consequential. Probably the most famous example in this regard is that of Mahatma Gandhi, who received the inspiration for his massively successful Salt March in an intuitive flash while meditating on the direction of the movement at his ashram. Here, the social benefits of the practice are seen to be mediated through conventional channels of action and communication. Such a principle represents the common view of socially engaged spirituality, where the role of spirituality in the work of social change is understood primarily to be one of inspiring wise (outer) action in the social sphere. For our purposes, the notion that subtle activism practice leads to social change through the subsequent overt actions of the actual practitioners involved can be seen as the "weak" version of the subtle activism hypothesis, to be contrasted with the "strong" version, which maintains that the social effect is immediate and nonlocal.

As for the strong version, a healthy place to start, in my view, is with the recognition that any nonlocal social effects of spiritual practice are highly and irreducibly mysterious. While acknowledging that we have much more to understand about these effects, I would like to offer some speculative comments as to their nature. First, I do not believe that the practice of subtle activism directly produces obvious, macro-scale effects on the physical plane or necessarily results in instant, radical changes to the social sphere. As powerful as our focused collective intention might be, we can't use it to pick up the Empire State Building and move it to China. I am more inclined to regard the effect as a kind of quantum event, whereby the consciousness of the practitioners involved participates at very subtle dimensions of reality in energizing or co-creating certain forms of awareness and thought, thus making them more accessible to collective levels of human consciousness. These thought forms or awareness states are so subtle that their effects on complex modern social systems might appear to be negligible. Yet the action is occurring at very fundamental (and causal) levels of reality, and may create a ripple effect that amplifies in magnitude to an unknown extent as it translates from subtler to more manifest dimensions. I propose that the act of intending a practice to benefit a particular social unit (city, state, nation, world, etc.) creates a bridge that connects the subtle phenomena elicited by the practice with the layer of collective consciousness associated with the targeted social unit. For example, in our WiseUSA initiatives in 2008 and 2012, our intention was to call forth "the deepest wisdom and the highest compassion" from "the heart and soul of America." According to the hypothesis of subtle activism, this intention would have created a channel that facilitated the transmission of the qualities of wisdom and compassion into the collective consciousness of the United States. Once transmitted, these subtle phenomena may then begin to activate corresponding forms of thought and awareness in the consciousness of individual members of the targeted social unit, causing those thought forms or spiritual qualities to rise more prominently into their conscious awareness. Individuals who resonate with these ideals may be inspired to enact them in the outer world. Men and women of great social, economic, or political influence, in particular, could give expression to these principles in ways that lead to significant social change.

It is important to bear in mind that, like any force, this subtle power is likely to be more or less effective depending on a number of factors. Some of these factors are quantitative, such as the number of practitioners involved and the duration and consistency of the practice. But qualitative elements, like the degree of coherence, depth, or love generated by the practice, could also be expected to affect the outcome. Indeed a certain quantitative and qualitative threshold undoubtedly needs to be surpassed in order for effects to manifest in the sociopolitical sphere. Although it might strain credulity to suppose, for example, that a handful of people engaged in half-hearted prayers for humanity will make any difference to the world, the effect starts to become more believable if we imagine the involvement of very large numbers of participants, and/or teams of highly experienced practitioners with advanced knowledge of how to work with the dynamics of the collective psyche. With the exponential rate of development of the global telecommunications infrastructure, the rising planetary awareness, and the proliferation of groups dedicated to convening global meditation and prayer events, increasingly sophisticated technologies and initiatives for harnessing the power of collective consciousness are emerging all the time. As higher-quality programs develop and more people become involved, the social effects of subtle activism practice are likely to become stronger and more evident.

BROADENING THE SCOPE OF ACTIVISM

For many who feel that there is an urgent need for humanity to make a fundamental course correction to avoid social and ecological catastrophe, participation in some form of activism represents a natural calling. The conventional understanding of activism is usually limited, however, to direct, frequently confrontational, forms of engagement with the overt structures of the economic or political establishment, as in a street demonstration or a worker's strike. For example, *Merriam-Webster's Dictionary* defines *activism* as "a doctrine or practice that emphasizes direct vigorous action especially in support of or opposition to one side of a controversial issue." Similarly, the *Cambridge Advanced Learner's Dictionary* defines it as "the use of direct and noticeable action to achieve a result, usually a political or social one."

A broader definition of activism, however, can be found on Wikipedia: "[any] intentional action to bring about social and political change." If we adopt this expanded view, traditional methods of frontline activism involving marches, demonstrations, putting one's body in front of bulldozers, etc., can be seen as only the most immediate and direct expressions of actions taken for social change. As philosopher Sean Kelly (nd) points out, we can identify a spectrum of social action that ranges from the more concrete or overt forms down a graded scale of increasing subtlety (as in Figure 1.1).

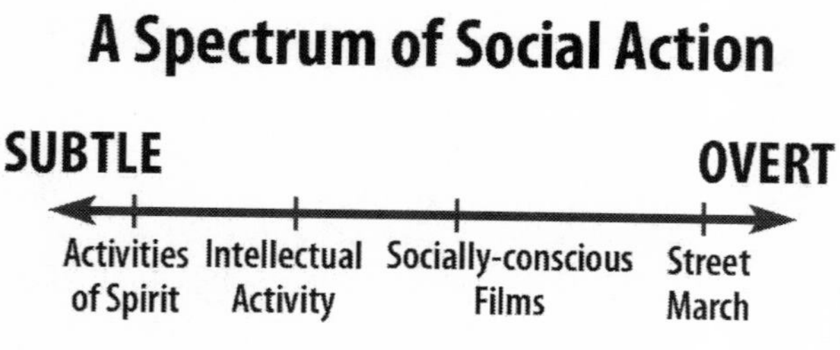

A Spectrum of Social Action

SUBTLE   **OVERT**

Activities   Intellectual   Socially-conscious   Street
of Spirit   Activity   Films   March

Figure 1.1. A spectrum of social action.

As Figure 1.1 illustrates, certain kinds of intellectual activity (e.g., paradigm-shifting breakthroughs) and artistic expressions (e.g., socially conscious films, music, and literature) are examples of actions that influence social and political change more indirectly and subtly than overt forms of political action like marching in the streets. These activities do not place direct political pressure on decision makers but they shape the wider intellectual or cultural context in which social and political decisions are made. Although more indirect, interventions that transform the core unstated assumptions of society can lead to massive changes throughout the system. Here is Ralph Waldo Emerson (1887) on the power of ideas to affect systemic change:

> Every nation and every man instantly surround themselves with a material apparatus which exactly corresponds to . . . their state of thought. Observe how every truth and every error, each a thought of some man's mind, clothes itself with societies, houses, cities, language, ceremonies, newspapers. Observe the ideas of the present day . . . see how timber, brick, lime, and stone have flown into convenient shape, obedient to the master idea reigning in the minds of many persons. . . . It follows, of course, that the least enlargement of ideas . . . would cause the most striking changes of external things. (177)

At even subtler levels, certain activities of consciousness (which from the outside might appear to involve no obvious action at all) can also be recognized as potentially potent forms of social action.[11] These activities can be seen as forms of social action because they transform (or so I will claim) what we might call the collective psychical context out of which ideas themselves, and, therefore, decisions and actions, arise. If a shift in ideas would result in "the most striking changes of external things," it follows that a change at even subtler levels of consciousness could produce even more consequential results. As Gandhi famously said, "the more efficient a force is, the more silent and the more subtle it is."

Strictly speaking, what I am calling subtle activism might more precisely be called "spiritual or consciousness-based subtle activism" to distinguish it from other subtle forms of social action. Although it is not necessary to try to draw a definitive line on the spectrum of action for social change (Figure 1.1) that would distinguish "subtle" from "not-subtle" approaches, we might reasonably view actions such as eating a vegetarian diet, making green consumer choices, or engaging in certain local community projects as forms of subtle activism, along with the examples already given of paradigm-shifting intellectual work and socially conscious forms of the arts. I have chosen to define subtle activism in terms of spiritual or consciousness-based approaches simply because I want to emphasize the potential of these usually overlooked methods to contribute to positive social change.

An Integrated Approach to Activism

In recent decades, many who have begun to articulate creative spiritual responses to the challenges of our times have recognized the need to integrate the paths of inner and outer transformation. Often inspired by the legacy of leaders like Mahatma Gandhi, Martin Luther King, and Thich Nhat Hanh, figures such as Joanna Macy, Starhawk, Julia Butterfly-Hill, Donald Rothberg, Cornel West, and Michael Lerner have called for more "socially engaged" forms of spirituality. These approaches seek, on the one hand, to return meaning and depth to the public sphere through the principles and practices of mature, nondogmatic forms of spirituality. On the other, they aim to overcome the tendencies in many spiritual circles to regard involvement in the process of outer social change as secondary to (or even a distraction from) the "real" work of inner transformation. Subtle activism, which also attempts to build a bridge between the inner world of spiritual practice and the outer world of social and political affairs, is clearly consistent with these approaches and can be seen as a specialized component of a more socially engaged spirituality. Like other kinds of socially engaged spirituality, subtle activism encourages spiritual practitioners to direct their attention to contemporary social and political issues and to engage in the process of social transformation (albeit primarily on subtle planes of consciousness).

However, the perspective of subtle activism is arguably an even deeper affirmation of the socially transformative potential of spirituality than at least some expressions of engaged spirituality, which tend to view spirituality primarily as a resource to help inform or nourish those involved in the outer work of social change. For example, S. Kelly (nd) cites a major study on Engaged Spirituality sponsored by the Ford Foundation in 2002 that contains the following statement:

> Spirituality, while sometimes viewed as being a strictly inward, even narcissistic activity, has the potential to propel people into lives of social service and public engagement. Spirituality in this sense is a vital resource, sustaining people in the hard work of social change and, on regular occasions, inspiring them to imagine possibilities that exceed realistic expectations. (Stanczak and Miller 2002, 18, cited in S. Kelly nd)

As S. Kelly points out, by regarding spirituality as a "vital resource" that can sustain people in the "hard work of social change," the authors imply that spirituality is not, therefore, itself a form of work, or action, in the social realm, a view that tacitly accepts the modern Cartesian split between the domain of spirit or consciousness, on the one hand, and the ("real") world of action, on the other. Although the authors presumably intend to counter the view commonly held by activists that spirituality is escapist, they actually reinforce the modern marginalization of consciousness, to some extent, by implicitly denying its more active potential. Subtle activism provides an expanded view of social engagement in which the inherent power of spirituality is recognized in and of itself as a legitimate component of an integral approach to social change.

It is important to acknowledge, however, that a potential pitfall of subtle activism is that it could be used by some as a spiritual rationalization for remaining disengaged from social or political affairs—a kind of social spiritual bypassing. Such an attitude, however, would represent a narcissistic distortion of my proposal, which seeks to ground subtle activism in the world by linking it with more conventional forms of activism as part of an integral approach to social change. I am not suggesting, for example, that subtle activism on its own is sufficient to solve the world's problems (any more than a meditation practice on its own is sufficient to solve all our personal problems). Direct action will always be needed and can itself be seen as a sacred calling. However, for many people with a certain temperament, or who possess certain spiritual or psychic gifts, subtle activism could represent the most effective means at their disposal to make a meaningful contribution toward social change.

BROADENING THE SCOPE OF SPIRITUALITY

As noted earlier, a number of transpersonal scholars (e.g., Buddhist scholar Donald Rothberg, and transpersonal theorists Jorge Ferrer and Ken Wilber) have pointed out that most people drawn to explore a spiritual path in the contemporary West have been deeply conditioned to approach spirituality primarily as an individual quest for self-actualization through profound inner experiences. One of the consequences of this interpretation of spirituality has been that certain dimensions of human experience, such as participation in social, ecological, and political realities, have usually not been seen as valid arenas for our spiritual presence and attention. Rothberg's (1993, 2008) analysis of the historical relationship between the social and the spiritual dimensions of life is especially helpful for understanding the modern situation. Rothberg traces the recent roots of the focus of contemporary Western spirituality on individual inner experience to the often unacknowledged influence of psychedelics—which supported an association of spirituality with breakthrough individual experiences and nonordinary states of consciousness—as well as to the selective reception of mainly those components of contemplative traditions (Asian and Western) that involve subjective experience (e.g., incorporating meditation while deemphasizing elements that relate to intersubjective relationships and study, such as ethics training and community). Going further back, Rothberg notes that this selectivity was itself profoundly influenced by the root assumptions of modernity, in which spirituality had long been relegated to the private and subjective arena.

Rothberg (1993) argues that although a tension between the spiritual and social realms has permeated Western thought since at least the ancient Greek separation of the spiritual (or "contemplative") from the political or practical (based on the distinction between the supposedly timeless and transcendent quality of spirituality and the supposedly this-worldly quality of social and political action), with modernity, the split became acute because of the "antireligious" origins of the era. The modern temperament, Rothberg notes, was centrally shaped by a fundamental and wide-ranging critique of all religion and spirituality, a critique that was instrumental in creating a space in which the scientific study of the "objective" world of nature and the political revolutions concerning democracy and human rights could proceed without the constraints of religious authorities and dogma. Although he lists many significant modern critics of religion (including Voltaire, Freud, and Nietzsche), Rothberg highlights the influence of Karl Marx, whose famous denunciation of religion as the "opium of the people" set the course for many modern social justice traditions. The outcome of these sustained attacks was the virtual exclusion of religion and spirituality from the modern public domains of science, democracy, and social justice, which became increasingly dominated by rational norms and procedures.[12] With the retreat of spirituality from public life, Rothberg notes, it was forced to find a home primarily in the private lives and subjective experiences of individuals and small communities.

Rothberg lists many recent modern critics (e.g., Berman, Habermas, Taylor) who point out that, despite modernity's impressive achievements, the increasing domination of the "instrumental rationality" of empirical science in all domains of life has led to a severe decline of meaning in the public sphere, as well as to a fragmentation of human experience (e.g., the gulf between private and public worlds or the separation of ethical and social considerations from much of science and technology). In this context, Rothberg suggests that new forms of spirituality might attempt to address the central systemic problems of modernity by facilitating a greater integration of the three modern worlds (the natural, the social, and the subjective), while seeking to preserve the positive achievements of modernity (e.g., respect for diversity and human rights, individual creativity and uniqueness, and the positive dimensions of science and technology). He also proposes that new spiritual forms would help us to respond meaning-fully to the main global practical concerns of our times—including the ecological crisis, the increasing gap between rich and poor exacerbated by globalization, the high level of violent conflict, and the weak state of global governance—and would enable us to make sense of the diversity of spiritual and religious approaches and support interfaith dialogue. As one response, Rothberg proposes a "postmodern" socially engaged spirituality that encourages an extension of spiritual awareness and practice into all the different domains of practical life, including personal relationships and participation in social and political systems. Based on his many years of experience in guiding trainings in socially engaged Buddhism, Rothberg offers a "Matrix of Nine Modes of Spiritual Practice" that suggests how spiritual practice might be expanded to encompass all dimensions of our lives (Figure 1.2).

The top row of the matrix represents three basic domains in which spiritual work can occur: the individual, the relational, and the collective. These domains can be seen as the object, or focal point, of spiritual practice. Thus, we can bring our spiritual attention to the individual, by focusing on the personal, psychological, and behavioral responses of an individual to any given situation. We can focus on the relational domain by considering our interactions in intimate relationships, families, groups, or communities. And we can focus on the collective domain by bringing awareness to our participation in larger social, cultural, economic, and political systems.

The left-hand column of the matrix represents three basic categories of practitioners who engage in spiritual practice. For example, we can engage

Rothberg's Nine Modes of Spiritual Practice

		DOMAIN		
		Individual	Relational	Collective
PRACTITIONER	Individual			
	Relational			
	Collective			

Figure 1.2. Matrix of Nine Modes of Spiritual Practice. Reprinted with permission from Donald Rothberg (2008).

each of the three domains as individual practitioners. An individual can focus on his or her own basic nature, as in meditation or in some other contemplative practice. We can work individually on the relational domain by reflecting, for example, on our patterns of relating in intimate relationships. And we can work individually on the collective domain by examining, for instance, how we personally may have internalized collective social patterns, such as racism, sexism, or homophobia.

We can also understand the spiritual practitioner as a relational unit that can focus on each of the domains. For example, we can work relationally while focusing on an individual, as in psychotherapy or in individual work with a spiritual teacher or small group. We can work relationally on the relational domain, such as when a couple mutually inquires into the dynamics of their relationship. And we can work relationally while focusing on the collective domain, such as when a group considers how cultural prejudices such as racism or sexism manifests in the relationships between group members. Finally, Rothberg notes that we can even conceive of the collective as practitioner, as in the case of South Africa's Truth and Reconciliation Commission, or, possibly, the social movements associated with Gandhi, King, and other such leaders.

Rothberg points out that because most spiritual approaches have been limited to the upper-left block (the individual practitioner working "internally" on what appears in his or her own inner experience), most of the possible modes of spiritual practice associated with the other eight blocks are relatively undeveloped. In this context, we can understand subtle activism to constitute a creative exploration and development of spiritual practices originating at the individual, relational, or collective level and focused on the collective domain (Figure 1.3).

Examples of subtle activism practices engaged in by individuals include Sri Aurobindo's supposed spiritual intervention in World War II from his bedroom in Pondicherry, David Spangler's (2008) subtle activism or "World Work" (see later), and Christopher Bache's (2000) account of his experiences engaging previously unresolved trauma in the collective "species' mind" through deep inner work catalyzed by entheogens. Examples of subtle activism practiced in a relational context include John Heron's (2006) description of the "extraordinary forms of subtle activism" that arise spontaneously in his long-term inquiry group, involving the co-creative participation of humans and presences from subtle realms, Will Keepin's (2007) "gender reconciliation" work, in which the gender healing effected by the group is seen as contributing to healing gender divisions in the collective psyche, and Marianne Williamson's "citizen circles," (or "peace circles"), in which small groups engage in mindful dialogue about current social and political issues and then hold these issues in meditation and prayer. Finally, we can

Rothberg's Nine Modes of Spiritual Practice

		DOMAIN	Subtle activism
		Individual	Relational	Collective
PRACTITIONER	Individual			
	Relational			
	Collective			

Figure 1.3. Rothberg's Nine Modes of Spiritual Practice. Adapted with permission from Donald Rothberg (2008).

consider mass global meditation and prayer events, such as the Harmonic Convergence in 1987 or the Sarvodaya peace meditation described earlier in this chapter, as examples of subtle activism as practiced by the collective. In all of these cases, whether the subject engaging in the practice is an individual, a relational unit, or the collective, the object of the practice is to transform the collective domain.

Thus, although subtle activism is not itself a complete spiritual path, it can be understood as a creative component of an integrative spirituality that seeks to encompass the full range of human experience. Previous proposals for integrative spiritual approaches include various kinds of "Integral Transformative Practices" which attempt to integrate all human dimensions (body, instincts, heart, mind, and consciousness) into a more fully embodied spiritual life (e.g., Leonard and Murphy 1995; Wilber 2000; Ferrer 2003). As we have seen, Rothberg's expanded view of spirituality meets the challenge of integration from a different angle, aiming to encourage an approach to spiritual practice that spans the intrapersonal, relational, and sociopolitical contexts of our lives. Subtle activism can take its place within such a framework as one way to work with the collective, sociopolitical realm.

Two contemporary proposals that do incorporate subtle activism as part of their version of integral spiritual practice are David Spangler's "Incarnational Spirituality" and John Heron's participatory or relational spirituality. Spangler (2008) describes three levels of change explored by Incarnational Spirituality: (a) inner change—the change to our personal self; (b) individual life change—the change we bring to the shape of our lives and our immediate relationships and environment; and (c) change in the world (or "World Work")—engagement with the world using subtle energies and spirit (i.e., subtle activism). Heron (2006) outlines three aspects of spiritual inquiry that constitute his approach to integral spiritual practice: (a) engagement with situational spirit—practices related to the presence "in-between" persons and entities of all kinds; (b) enlivenment with immanent spirit—practices related to the spiritual potential embedded within creation; and (c) enlightenment with transcendent spirit—practices related to transcendent consciousness.

Heron writes that his long-term inquiry group, working with these three aspects over many years, regularly report the spontaneous emergence of presences in subtle realms "who interact with us and together with us engage in extraordinary forms of subtle activism" (54). Heron proposes that such practices have a transformative impact on the "psychosomatic field of the human race" through "instant morphic resonance between us and the rest of embodied humanity through specific patterns of genetic, psychological, cultural, historic, and subtle affinity" (54). We can recognize in both of these approaches an emerging integral spirituality that allows the attention of practitioners to flow organically between personal, interpersonal, and collective dimensions.

GLOBAL MEDITATION AND THE EVOLUTION OF CONSCIOUSNESS

Global meditation and prayer events may be a subtle activism practice with special significance for our times. These events can potentially involve many thousands of people from different countries, cultures, and religions engaging simultaneously in spiritual practice like meditation or prayer dedicated to a common intention. With the increasing sophistication of teleconferencing and Internet communication technologies, the sense of interrelatedness between participants can be enhanced by audio and video connections. Such events represent two degrees of innovation in terms of Rothberg's "Matrix of Nine Modes of Spiritual Practice": they involve both the collective as practitioner and the collective as domain, or object, of the practice.

The collective as practitioner deserves consideration as a spiritual innovation in its own right. Collective spiritual practice brings to mind Buddhist monk Thich Nhat Hanh's famous statement that the next Buddha may not be an individual but a loving community (sangha), a vision echoed by Belgian integral theorist Michel Bauwens (nd), who claims that "The Next Buddha will be a Collective." Noting the emergence of Internet phenomena like wikis and blogging, Bauwens argues that contemporary society is evolving toward a dominance of "distributed networks" involving "peer-to-peer" social relations, as distinct from hierarchical systems, in which resources are produced and shared in communities of peer producers, with no pre-established hierarchies controlling the process. Bauwens claims that these peer-to-peer dynamics both reflect and further impel a shift in the evolution of consciousness toward "a conscious return to collectivism where individuated, or self-actualized, individuals voluntarily—and temporarily—pool their consciousness in a search for the elusive collective intelligence which can help us to overcome the stupendous challenges now facing us as a species" (para. 28). For Bauwens, emerging forms of spirituality are bound to reflect this shift in consciousness and will likely exhibit peer-to-peer relational dynamics in which spiritual knowledge and practice will be co-created by a community of equals rather than being passed down by a pre-established spiritual hierarchy.

The practice of global meditation clearly has the potential to be an expression of this trend. If framed in a pluralistic and nondogmatic way, a global meditation event can involve a diverse range of practitioners who participate according to their own tradition or creative inspiration, in a manner not prescribed by any single spiritual authority. Such events would seem to be an obvious component of a contemporary planetary spirituality, one that might emerge from the creative encounters of cultures and religions across the globe and the growing recognition of our shared destiny as members of what Berry has called the Earth Community. While Spangler (2008) rightly cautions against idealizing the power of large spiritual gatherings—arguing that the more precise attention of an individual or small group may often accomplish more than the sheer volume of energy generated by very large numbers—I believe that the public nature and global scope of these events enables them to play a potentially unique role in the evolution of consciousness.[13]

It is perhaps obvious that the practice of global meditation could help to catalyze the process of planetization anticipated by Teilhard de Chardin. A global meditation event provides a singular opportunity for the emerging global consciousness to reflect back on itself in a sustained act of contemplation. Participants commonly report experiencing a sense of joy from feeling united at a deep level with others from different cultures, religions, and regions of the world. In this way, global meditation events may help to inspire the kind of "quasi-adoration" for the emerging global being that Teilhard saw as essential to the planetization process. Similarly, these events can easily be framed in a way to enhance our awareness of our relationship with the wider Earth community, as emphasized by Thomas Berry. For example, participants could be invited to include in their meditation an awareness of the connection between their breath and the oxygen producing plants on the planet.

Finally, these events may hold significance as a source of support for humanity's journey through what Richard Tarnas has described as our collective rite of passage. To recall, Tarnas conceives of our moment as potentially representing a collective initiation for humanity through a death–rebirth process into a fundamentally new way of understanding and relating to the cosmos. The challenge, for Tarnas, is compounded by the fact that we are navigating this initiatory crisis with virtually no guidance from wise elders. The global scale of the initiation is too unprecedented; we are all in it together. Nonetheless, Tarnas claims that we can draw from the experience of those mystics and shamans who have passed through death–rebirth initiations and from our own psychospiritual journeys into and through darkness. Here I want to suggest a particularly crucial role that the practice of global meditation may play in this transition. Although there may be no initiated individuals who possess the necessary wisdom to guide us through the crisis, might the support we need be found in the emerging capacities of our collective spiritual intelligence? One of the more critical roles played by an elder in an initiatory rite of passage is simply to "hold the space" for the initiate, providing a calm and reassuring presence that allows the initiate to gather the courage to endure the dismemberment phase and emerge, reborn, on the other side. I propose that the practice of global meditation and prayer could provide a similar function for the collective modern psyche. The consistent practice of global meditation by a sufficient number of spiritually grounded people could lead to the emergence of a planetary field of presence that will contain the precise wisdom and support humanity will need to successfully navigate the collective initiation. Since this *Gaiafield*[14] would emerge from the shared experience of planetary consciousness by many thousands of people, it would make sense that it might possess a spiritual intelligence uniquely suited to the task of guiding humanity to the next evolutionary level. In particular, the Gaiafield could support humanity to gather the courage to face the crisis and to willingly and consciously undergo the necessary journey of descent.

CHAPTER TWO

SUBTLE ACTIVISM AND SPIRITUALITY

In this chapter, I expand our understanding of subtle activism by presenting examples from a variety of the world's spiritual and religious traditions. My purpose for doing so is threefold. First, I want to show that nearly all the world's major religious traditions have used spiritual practices for collective as well as individual benefit. Second, I want to identify some of the historical roots of contemporary subtle activism. Third, I want to stir up the imagination of would-be subtle activists by telling several remarkable tales of our forefathers and foremothers in this field.

All the stories I am going to cite take place in the modern era. In many respects, the concept of subtle activism only really makes sense in a modern context. Following the work of social theorists Max Weber and Jurgen Habermas, modernity can be understood as a differentiation of the relatively integrated medieval religio-political framework into three "worlds":

1. The "natural" or "objective" world (connected to the empirical sciences and technology).

2. The "intersubjective" world of political, social, and ethical relations (connected to democracy and community).

3. The "inner" or "subjective" world (connected to the autonomous self and modern forms of creative artistic expression and self-inquiry).

As noted in chapter 1, Buddhist scholar Donald Rothberg (1993) makes clear that the fate of spirituality in the modern project was to be banished, almost exclusively, to the private or subjective world. That is, a modern person has been free to seek meaning and transcendence through a variety of private avenues (e.g., creative experiences of art, music, and literature, self-inquiry through psychotherapy and psychoanalysis, intense private relationships, personal spiritual explorations) but has generally been discouraged from extending that ground of meaning into the public domain—whether in the objective world of science or the intersubjective world of democracy and social justice (with some notable exceptions, e.g., the social movements led by Gandhi and King as well as the lip service that must be paid to religion by candidates for higher political office). Subtle activism, as we saw, can be understood as part of an emerging, multifaceted cultural impulse to reintegrate these now fragmented worlds into a more coherent whole. In particular, like other varieties of socially engaged spirituality, subtle activism aims to reestablish a connection between certain nondogmatic forms of spirituality and the intersubjective realm of democracy and social justice, while preserving the positive attributes of modernity (e.g., the positive dimensions of empirical science and technology, respect for individual differences on the basis of human rights and democratic standards of self-determination, and support for the creative expression of individual uniqueness).

In premodern cultures, the three realms (subjective, intersubjective, objective) were generally undifferentiated. As seen in chapter 1, thinkers like Lucien Levy-Bruhl, Carl Jung, Mircea Eliade, Joseph Campbell, and Richard Tarnas point out that, in the indigenous or primal worldview, both the inner world of the human soul and the outer world of nature were seen to be permeable to archetypal influences, with no sharp boundaries being drawn between the two. In such cultures, the divinations of the shaman or medicine man were enormously influential in shaping the collective destiny of the group, to the extent that the functions of shaman and tribal ruler were occasionally even combined in one person or family. Ancient civilizations as far back as Sumer used seers to interpret the messages of the gods and to advise the monarchs who enacted laws that were felt to be in harmony with the divine edicts. In medieval Europe, the line between church and state—religion and politics—also was often imperceptible. Thus, it makes little sense to talk about subtle activism as a distinct phenomenon in premodern cultures, when those societies widely assumed spirituality and politics to be closely intertwined or even inseparable. All of the stories that follow are therefore from modern times.

Nonetheless, I briefly survey a variety of basic tenets and practices from premodern traditions that are precursors to modern forms of subtle activism. Although it is important not to embrace uncritically premodern religious perspectives (which many modern people might be tempted to do on the basis that these approaches present a welcome contrast to our current disenchanted worldview), the quest for a more integrated perspective will inevitably involve a recovery of certain modes of wisdom that have been marginalized and repressed by the single-minded modern pursuit of objective, sensory-based knowledge. As Rothberg noted, most modern critics of religion (e.g., Voltaire, Hume, Marx, Freud, Nietschze) did not distinguish the spiritual/contemplative dimension from other more conventional aspects of religious traditions. Rather, such critics tended to use institutional Western Christianity as the model by which they determined all religious expressions to be antithetical to the spirit of modernity. By acquainting ourselves with a variety of premodern religious beliefs and practices consistent with subtle activism, then, we may be able to recover important dimensions of our spiritual heritage that can guide our efforts to extend the transformative power of spirituality into the public domain of social justice and democracy.

Two more brief points before we begin our survey. My presentation is by no means intended to be an exhaustive account of the field. My aim is simply to whet the appetite of the reader by providing a selection of the most fascinating stories of subtle activism I could find. Also, I do not attempt to assess the validity of the claims made in the stories. The issue of how to evaluate the claims of subtle activism is a complex one that I address in chapters 3 and 4. For now, let us simply enjoy the accounts on their own terms.

SHAMANISM

We begin our survey with shamanism, humanity's original and oldest religious tradition. The word *shaman* comes from the language of the Tungus people of Siberia meaning "one who is excited, moved, raised" (Walsh 2007). It has been widely adopted by anthropologists as a catchall term to describe people in diverse indigenous cultures previously known as medicine men, witch doctors, sorcerers, wizards, magicians, or seers. Although shamanism is notoriously difficult to define, a central practice involves the voluntary entrance by shamans into altered states of consciousness where they experience themselves traveling to other realms and contacting nonhuman entities to acquire knowledge and serve their community. Anthropologists have extensively documented the remarkable similarity in shamanic beliefs and practices in indigenous cultures throughout the world, notwithstanding the radical differences between those societies in language and other social practices. The cosmology of shamanism is usually comprised of three worlds: upper, middle, and lower, with the middle world representing the Earth. The shaman is able "to transcend the human condition and pass freely back and forth through the different cosmological planes" (Furst 1972, ix). During these "journeys," the shaman may meet various animals or spirits for knowledge and power in relation to a patient's illness or an important issue to the community (e.g., where to find game); or he or she may intercede with demonic entities on the community's behalf.

In many ways, the path of shamanism can be seen as the original template for what I call subtle activism. Although shamans were regularly consulted to heal individuals of their illnesses, their primary function appears to have been to serve as guardians of the psychic and ecological equilibrium of the tribe as a whole. The ecologist and philosopher David Abram (1997) writes:

> For the magician's intelligence is not encompassed *within* the society; its place is at the edge of the community, mediating *between* the human community and the larger community of beings upon which the village depends for its nourishment and sustenance . . . by his constant rituals, trances, ecstasies, and "journeys," [the shaman] ensures that the relation between human society and the larger society of beings is balanced and reciprocal, and that the village never takes more from the living land than it returns to it—not just materially but with prayers, propitiations, and praise . . . hence, the traditional magician or medicine person functions primarily as an intermediary between human and nonhuman worlds, and only secondarily as a healer. (6–8)

Thus, as Abram concludes, humanity's original religious practitioners extended their spiritual attention not, primarily, "up" toward a transcendent God nor, exactly, "in" toward a private, individual experience but "out" into the world where they used their spiritual power and knowledge to mediate between the tribal unit and the wider community of being. Matthews and Matthews (2003) similarly claim that the shaman's principal responsibility was to the spiritual balance of the tribe (not its individual members) and argue that the shaman affected the quality of the group mind on subtle levels not immediately perceptible to normal consciousness. Shamans informed and shaped the tribal unit not only by directly communicating their visions with tribal members but also indirectly by engaging and animating the particular spiritual forces most related to the group, such as the tribal totem, the tribal ancestors, and the genius loci, or spirit of the local place. In other words, shamans acted on subtle planes of consciousness primarily for the benefit of the community as a whole—a spiritual orientation that clearly foreshadows the approach of subtle activism.

Let us consider some concrete examples of shamanic practices and traditions that can be seen as precursors to modern day subtle activism. The rain dance ceremony practiced by the Pueblo Indians in the Southwest region of the United States contains elements that are similar to what I call subtle activism. The rain dance is a "spiritual" practice that involves the invocation of dimensions of reality sacred to the Pueblo tribe. The practice is intended to support the health of the entire community (not just individuals) by bringing rain during dry summer months. And the dancers believe that their ceremony has a nonlocal influence on the weather.

The shamanic practice of recognizing and revering certain spaces as sacred is also relevant for subtle activism. That the life force of the Earth's energy is especially focused in certain places and that these sites contain potent healing energies appears to have been a virtually universal intuition among indigenous cultures throughout the world. These holy places were marked in such a way that they would be clearly defined and recognized, in many places with circles of stone monoliths decorated with symbols that indicated their sacred function (e.g., Stonehenge). These structures have been found at sites as far apart as America, China, Egypt, Norway, and Britain, all with remarkably similar siting arrangements and even with similar sacred patterns and symbols carved into them (Matthews and Matthews, 2003).

Related to the phenomenon of sacred sites is the theory that a network of energy paths connects the sites to each other. The study of this phenomenon is known as *geomancy*. Chatwin (1987) describes the Australian Aboriginal concept of *songlines*. Songlines are subtle energy currents in the Earth that guided the nomadic movements of the Aboriginal people. The people, in turn, maintained the songlines by singing dreamtime stories about the land as they traveled through it. In Britain, a number of writers have proposed the existence of a network of "ley lines" connecting sacred sites throughout the British Isles (see, e.g., Watkins 1970; Michell 1982; Devereux and Thompson 1979).

Some thinkers argue that the remarkable similarity in the arrangement and decoration of sacred site structures around the world, along with the phenomenon of ley or songlines, points to the existence of an ancient global energy grid, sustained by the practice of indigenous rituals and ceremonies. Such a notion, if true, would underscore an uncanny parallel between shamanic wisdom and modern subtle activism, as a common goal of many contemporary global meditation projects (including the well-known Harmonic Convergence in 1987) has been to activate this "global grid" by consciously connecting the sacred sites with each other through ritual and meditation.

The story I want to share about the modern use of shamanic practices as a form of subtle activism comes from my own experience. From 2003 to 2006, I was involved with a team of colleagues from the California Institute of Integral Studies in an action research project to investigate holistic approaches to community development. We conducted a pilot project in a small community in the Santa Cruz Mountains in Northern California.

Shortly after we began the project, a major political issue erupted in the community. The San Jose Water Board (SJWB) owned a large piece of land in the area. In summer 2005, the SJWB granted a license to a timber company to harvest a significant section of a redwood forest that was part of the land. The SJWB and the timber company lodged a development proposal containing the details of their logging plan with the California Department of Fire and Forestry containing the details of its logging plan. Potentially affected community members were duly notified. The response from the community was immediate and vigorous. The magnificent redwood forests in the region are the defining feature of the landscape and were cherished by most residents. An action group formed to oppose the development and a highly organized political campaign ensued. One of the leaders of the action group (I will call her Susan) had attended our meetings and was intrigued by the possibility of using subtler approaches to community activism to complement the legal and political actions of her team. She had heard about a female shaman named Arwyn Dreamwalker, a Jungian-trained psychologist of Irish and American Indian ancestry who taught in the ceremonial tradition of a Navajo holy man. Susan worked with Arwyn's people to create a workshop for community members to bring together environmental activism and "shamanic dreaming" to support the resolution of the logging issue. I attended the workshop.

The workshop was a fascinating blend of inner and outer activism. On a Saturday afternoon, we received an excellent presentation from Susan and her team about the details of the logging proposal, the status of the legal campaign, and the practical ways we could help. Susan is a software engineer who works for Google. She had pioneered the use of Google Earth maps to help citizen groups like ours become better informed about contentious development proposals. She led us in an animated three-dimensional Google Earth "fly-by" of the proposed logging terrain, with notable community landmarks highlighted to provide an easy way to understand the extent of the proposal. By the end of the afternoon, we were fully informed about the issue from the conventional "outer" perspectives of science, law, and politics.

In the evening, Arwyn led us into ritual space for a powerful 3-hour long ceremony to investigate the "inner" dimensions of the situation. Arwyn carefully constructed a human mandala out of the thirty or so participants. She selected people one at a time to occupy positions on the mandala that corresponded to particular duties. For example, the person in the position of North was responsible for grounding the energies in the Earth, the person in the East held a space for mental clarity, the person in the West held space for deep feeling, and so on. When the mandala was complete, the ritual proper began. We invoked the four directions, Mother Earth, Father Sky, and other benevolent spiritual forces. We were then guided to make inner contact with the redwood trees and the human energies that were swirling around them. Arwyn asked her experienced practitioners to tune into the nature of the forces that threatened the trees and to speak their visions into the circle. Bold words and clear voices rang out into the circle. I was struck by the tremendous power and strength in the room. Arwyn then directed us to listen inwardly to the wisdom of the redwood trees. We spent a long time communing psychically with the trees. I remember connecting inwardly with one particular tree—it was indescribably majestic and magnificent. Eventually, the ritual came to a close. There was a palpable feeling of weary satisfaction in the room as though we knew we had earned a good night's sleep.

The next morning we visited a redwood forest in a state park near the proposed logging site. We slowly meandered through the trail, greeting these mighty giants one by one. I found it striking to notice how much more intimate I felt with the trees than usual, something I attributed to our deep inner communion with them the night before.

When local community members first began to organize around the logging issue, government officials told them that the regulatory agencies almost always approved these kinds of requests. However, in September 2007, the California Department of Forestry and Fire Protection denied the SJWB's logging plan. Ultimately, the reason for the denial was a technical issue. The SJWB owned too much land to qualify for the kind of permit it was seeking. However, this issue came to light only after sustained legal and political pressure from the local community action group. The extent to which our ceremony contributed to the outcome by strengthening the morale of that group, or in other, more mysterious ways, is impossible to know in any objective sense. In my opinion, one can only really make an intuitive assessment, based on one's perceptions of the subtle energetic fields with which one is working. In this case, my sense of the power and integrity of the field we created during the ceremony leads me to believe that we did make a real contribution to the final result.

YOGA, HINDUISM, AND THE VEDIC TRADITION

The *Vedas* are the oldest sacred texts of Hinduism, thought by most mainstream historians to have been compiled in India between, approximately, 1500 BCE and the sixth century BCE. The *Vedas* contain the source texts for Vedanta, the philosophical and spiritual system that forms the basis of Hinduism. Yoga is an intrinsic component of the Vedic (and later Hindu) tradition, both as a school of Indian philosophy and as a system of mental and physical disciplines designed to result in the practitioner's liberation from the limitations of worldly existence. Although Indian philosophy has frequently characterized the world as ephemeral and illusory, leading to an emphasis on withdrawal from worldly affairs in order to attain the bliss of spiritual emancipation, there are, nonetheless, several aspects of the Vedic tradition that refer to the positive influence of spiritual practices on society at large and thus could be seen to be in alignment with the concept of subtle activism.

First, the Vedic tradition believes that certain sounds or mantras in the Vedic literature represent the most basic vibrations in nature and effectively constitute something like a blueprint for the functioning of the universe. A traditional role of the Vedic "pandits" (Brahmins who are learned in Sanskrit and Hindu philosophy and religion) is to recite the Vedic sounds in their proper sequence. This practice is believed to maintain order both in the individual and in the society as a whole. Sometimes these recitals occur in the context of a Vedic ritual known as a *Yajna* (anglicized as *yagya*), a central element of which involves a ceremonial fire into which oblations (in the form of different types of food and drink) are offered as sacrifices to the divine. According to Vedic scholar Robert Wallace (2005), one kind of yagya, known as *Ati Rudrabhishek Maha Yagya*, is traditionally performed for the well-being of all humanity and to ensure universal peace and prosperity.

Second, the so-called "siddhis" or miraculous powers attributed to advanced Yogic practitioners include many extraordinary capacities of subtle perception and influence across space and time that reflect the principle of nonlocality that underlies the concept of subtle activism. The following siddhis are especially pertinent: *Paracitta-jnanas*, telepathic knowledge of the minds of other people; *Vasitva*, control and mastery over nature, both internal and external, including the ability to control the mind and behavior patterns of other people by projecting powerful suggestions into the bioenergetic existence field; and *Saktipata*, the ability to transmit spiritual energy to others who are sufficiently receptive.

Third, the Yoga Sutras of Patanjali—widely regarded as the foundational text of the Yogic tradition—contain two "aphorisms" especially relevant for subtle activism. These sutras have been used by Maharishi Mahesh Yogi to support his "Super Radiance Assemblies" (or "Peace Assemblies"), which involve the practice of TM and other Vedic techniques by large groups for the benefit of society.

The first aphorism is *Tat sannidhau vairatyagah* (Yoga-Sutra 2.35) [In the vicinity of Yogic influence, conflicting tendencies do not arise]. In ancient Hindu mythology, in reference to this sutra, it was said that in the forests where the saints and sages lived—practicing Yoga and the way of nonviolence—even the animals would only kill when they were hungry. This principle suggests that a kind of peace-inducing field emanates out from the Yogic practitioner, eliminating negative tendencies in his or her environment before they have a chance to emerge.

The second aphorism is *Heyam duhkham anagatam* (Yoga-Sutra 2.16) [Avert the danger before it arises]. This sutra advocates the wisdom of a preventative approach to peace, which Maharishi maintains is most effectively achieved by the establishment of "prevention groups" of people practicing TM meditation and other Vedic practices.

This brings us to a closer look at Maharishi's system of "Vedic defense," probably the largest sustained subtle activism program of modern times. Building on the principle of Yogic influence set out in Yoga Sutra 2.35, Maharishi predicted, in the early 1960s, that if as little as 1 percent of any given population regularly practiced TM in their own homes, they would create a measurable influence of harmony throughout that population. The prediction appeared to be confirmed by two early studies conducted by TM researchers in the late 1970s and early 1980s that found statistically significant decreases in crime rates in twenty-four US cities in which the number of people practicing TM had surpassed 1 percent of the total city population, compared with crime rates in control cities (Borland and Landrith 1976; Dillbeck, Landrith, and Orme-Johnson 1981). After these studies, the phenomenon came to be known as the "Maharishi Effect" because the results seemed to confirm Maharishi's earlier prediction. In the late 1970s, with the introduction by Maharishi of more advanced Vedic practices known as the TM-Sidhi technique and Yogic Flying, and the discovery of the much greater potency of group meditations,[1] a new prediction was made: If just the *square root* of 1 percent of any given population practiced TM and the more advanced techniques in a large group setting, they would create a measurable positive influence throughout the whole population. The new hypothesis was called the "Extended Maharishi Effect" and it has since been tested in more than forty published studies, including twenty-eight in academic journals, many of which maintain stringent peer-review procedures and are considered highly prestigious in their field (e.g., *Journal of Conflict Resolution, Journal of Mind and Behavior, Journal of Crime and Justice, Social Indicators Research*).[2] The results of the research have consistently shown highly statistically significant correlations between the practice of TM and the more advanced techniques in large-group settings and improvements in a broad range of indicators of social harmony in nearby populations, including crime rates, auto accidents, fires, war deaths, and other measures.[3]

Because this research represents one of the most directly relevant lines of scientific inquiry into subtle activism, I examine it in detail in the next chapter. Here it may be helpful to present the basic method and philosophy of the approach, along with one leading case study.

A typical Maharishi Effect program brings together the requisite number of TM-trained practitioners in a central location relatively near the "target" area (i.e., the city or country the group aims to influence) for, essentially, a meditation retreat for the duration of the program. The requisite number of participants is the number sufficient to exceed the square root of 1 percent threshold for any given population. The group meditates together in a large hall or room at least twice per day, for at least twenty minutes per session. Some people practice TM, others the more advanced techniques like the TM-Siddhi program and Yogic Flying. Some participants attend additional meditation sessions throughout the day. Other activities include watching videotaped discourses from Maharishi and helping with the maintenance of the gathering itself (e.g., cooking or administration). The TM approach does not encourage the formation by practitioners of any particular thought forms or intentions. Rather, the method relies on the attainment by the practitioners of a state of pure consciousness or pure existence. The assumption is that the energy or consciousness generated by the group meditations automatically radiates out to everyone within the vicinity of the group field (whose boundaries are roughly defined by the square root of 1 percent formula) and infuses the collective consciousness of that population with the qualities of pure, transcendent consciousness (e.g., peacefulness, invincibility), resulting in a collective atmosphere in which hostile or negative tendencies are diminished.

One of the flagship studies in this series was called the "International Peace Project." The project brought approximately two hundred TM practitioners together in a hotel in Jerusalem in August and September 1983 during the height of the Israel-Lebanon war. This number was considered sufficient to surpass the square root of 1 percent threshold theoretically required to produce an influence on the populations of Israel and Lebanon. The formula also took into account the effect of the approximately 30,000 Israelis who practiced TM daily in their own homes. Based on the results of previous studies on the Maharishi Effect, predictions about the effect of the meditation group on the war and other social indicators were made in advance and lodged with independent scientists in the US and Israel. As it turned out, although the goal of the study was to have two hundred practitioners present for the entire program, practical considerations made this impossible, and the number of meditators rose and fell irregularly throughout the experimental period. This unexpected inconsistency in participation, however, proved to make for a compelling experiment, because changes in the social indicators being measured could now be tracked for correlations with the size of the meditation group on multiple occasions.

The results confirmed the predictions. Statistically significant correlations were found between the size of the meditation group and positive changes in a variety of social indicators, including war deaths, war intensity, car accidents, reported fires, and the performance of the stock market. When the data from all the social indicators was combined into a single quality-of-life index, the correlation between the numbers of people meditating and the sum of these variables was especially striking, as illustrated in Figure 2.1.

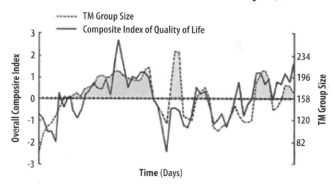

Figure 2.1. Changes in TM group size compared with changes in a composite index of quality of life. Reprinted with permission from Orme-Johnson et al. (1988). Reprinted by Permission of Sage Publications.

Other significant results included the following:

- During the 25 percent of days when there was highest attendance at the assembly, war deaths in Lebanon dropped by an average of 76 percent, compared with the 25 percent of days when attendance was lowest.

- During a 13-day period in which group size was raised to a high level (average of 197.1) according to a preassigned schedule independent of the level of fighting, the average number of daily war deaths was 1.5 compared with 33.7 for the 13-day periods immediately before and after the experimental period.

- When the assembly attendance figures rose, lower variability was observed between the various social indicators. In other words, when assembly attendance was high, social phenomena that are typically unrelated to each other, such as car accidents, the stock market index, and crime rates, became correlated to a statistically significant degree.

Remarkably—given the unconventional premise of the Maharishi Effect—the study was accepted for publication by Yale University's *Journal of Conflict Resolution*, one of the most prestigious publications in the field of peace studies (Orme-Johnson et al., 1988).

The philosophy underlying the Maharishi Effect starts with the concept of the transcendental field of consciousness, which was understood
by Maharishi to both underlie and permeate all phenomena. According
to Maharishi, it is eternal and indestructible because anything that might
disturb it is an expression of its own "self-interacting" dynamics. When,
through the practice of TM or other Vedic techniques, a person experiences
this state of transcendental consciousness, he or she is said to "enliven the
field," automatically mediating an influence of peacefulness to everyone in
the vicinity. To illustrate this principle, Maharishi used an analogy with a
central broadcasting station that sends electronic waves through the electromagnetic field, allowing anyone with a television to receive the signals. In
physics, a fundamental attribute of fields is the phenomenon of "action at
a distance," whereby an event at one location can exert an influence that
carries information throughout the field. Similarly, argued Maharishi, when
an individual meditator or group experiences the state of transcendental
consciousness, they radiate a calming effect toward society at large because
consciousness also displays fieldlike attributes and can therefore generate
fieldlike effects such as action at a distance. Maharishi claimed that if the
square root of 1 percent of the population of any nation were to practice the
TM-Sidhi program and Yogic Flying in a large-group setting, the properties
of invincibility and indestructibility inherent to the field of pure consciousness would begin to characterize the nation as a whole. Similarly, he argued
that if the square root of 1 percent of the world's population were to engage
in these practices, the entire world consciousness would become significantly
more coherent and world peace would be assured (Varma, 1996).

The TM movement is currently focused on an ambitious plan to
implement this vision. The centerpiece of the proposed program involves
the establishment of a permanent group of eight thousand Yogic Flyers at
the Maharishi University of Management in Fairfield, Iowa, including a
core group of five hundred Vedic pandits, and a group of forty thousand
Vedic pandits in India. (Eight thousand represents approximately the square
root of 1 percent of the current world population.) The Vedic pandits will
spend each day practicing TM and Yogic Flying, and will also perform the
Ati Rudrabhishek Maha Yagya—a ritual intended to prevent war and international conflict—several times each day. Among the forty thousand Vedic
pandits in India, subgroups will be assigned to each nation on Earth and
will perform certain rituals (yagyas) intended to avert any potential danger
that may threaten the nation for which they are responsible. Finally, the
TM movement intends to establish "Peace Palaces" in the world's largest
three thousand cities, with each Peace Palace housing one to two hundred
practitioners of TM and the more advanced Vedic techniques (Wallace,

2005). The scope of the vision is certainly impressive. If implemented, it would represent the largest ongoing program of what I am calling subtle activism in modern times.

Let us now consider, by way of contrast with the vast numbers involved in the TM program, an instance of subtle activism by a solo practitioner. This example also comes from the Vedic tradition, in the person of the renowned Indian philosopher/sage Sri Aurobindo. Born in 1872, as a young man Sri Aurobindo was actively involved as a leader of India's Nationalist movement and spent a year in jail in 1908 awaiting trial for conspiracy. During his time in jail, he experienced a profound spiritual awakening that changed the direction of his life. In 1910 he moved to the French-controlled province of Pondicherry, where he devoted himself to a disciplined practice of Yoga. For the rest of his life (he died in 1950), Sri Aurobindo lived in Pondicherry, writing voluminously on spiritual and philosophical topics and directing (with his partner "the Mother") the ashram that developed around his teachings. As S. Kelly (nd) notes, a conventional interpretation of Sri Aurobindo's life would likely characterize his early years as ones during which he was actively engaged in political affairs, followed by a long contemplative phase during which he dedicated himself primarily to spiritual matters and was no longer directly active in the political arena. However, as S. Kelly points out, Sri Aurobindo himself believed that his most effective influence on worldly affairs occurred later in life solely through a form of "spiritual action" he conducted from his bedroom in Pondicherry. An especially fascinating claim involves Aurobindo's spiritual interventions to support the Allied cause in World War II. Here is Aurobindo (referring to himself in the third person) on this topic:

> But this (Aurobindo's retirement from conventional political activity in 1910) did not mean, as most people supposed, that he had retired into some height of spiritual experience devoid of any further interest in the world or in the fate of India. . . . In his retirement, Sri Aurobindo kept a close watch on all that was happening in the world and in India and actively intervened whenever necessary, but solely with a spiritual force and silent spiritual action; for it is part of the experience of those who have advanced far in Yoga that besides the ordinary forces and activities of the mind and life and body in Matter, there are other forces and powers that can act and do act from behind and from above; there is also a spiritual dynamic power that can be possessed by those who are advanced in the spiritual consciousness, although all do not care to possess or, possessing, to use

it, and this power is greater than any other and more effective. It was this force that, as soon as he had attained to it, he used, at first only in a limited field of personal work, but afterward in a constant action on the world forces. He had no reason to be dissatisfied with the results or to feel the necessity of any other kind of action . . . when it appeared as if Hitler would crush all the forces opposed to him and Nazism dominate the world, he began to intervene. He declared himself publicly on the side of the Allies, made some financial contributions in answer to the appeal for funds and encouraged those who sought his advice to enter the army or share in the war effort. Inwardly, he put his spiritual force behind the Allies from the moment of Dunkirk when everybody was expecting the immediate fall of England and the definite triumph of Hitler, and he had the satisfaction of seeing the rush of German victory almost immediately arrested and the tide of war begin to turn in the opposite direction. This he did, because he saw that behind Hitler and Nazism were dark Asuric forces and that their success would mean the enslavement of mankind to the tyranny of evil, and a setback to the course of evolution and especially to the spiritual evolution of mankind. . . . He had not, for various reasons, intervened with his spiritual force against the Japanese aggression until it became evident that Japan intended to attack and even invade and conquer India. . . . *When negotiations failed, Sri Aurobindo returned to his reliance on the use of his spiritual force alone against the aggressor and had the satisfaction of seeing the tide of Japanese victory, which had till then swept everything before it, change immediately into a tide of rapid, crushing and finally immense and overwhelming defeat.* (Aurobindo 1953, 68–71, my emphasis)

Without any further details of the specific method used by Sri Aurobindo, we can only speculate about the nature of the "spiritual dynamic power" he claimed to possess and how a solitary individual might use such a power to shape the destiny of nations. Again, I am not attempting here to assess the validity of these (admittedly extraordinary) claims but rather to demonstrate that the concept of using spiritual methods for collective benefit has been embraced by a wide number of religious and spiritual traditions and has been practiced in a variety of forms. Aurobindo's case represents a unique example of a single, exceptionally advanced Yogic practitioner directing his spiritual force toward the resolution of an historic global conflict. It demonstrates his conviction that this kind of intervention is not only possible but, indeed, is the most efficient form of action available to one who has the capacity to use it.

BUDDHISM

Buddhism appears to have been divided, since its inception, between the value of responsible social engagement and the need for withdrawal from society to achieve individual liberation. On the one hand, the Buddha did advise serious practitioners to leave behind the "dusty, crowded" world of family and society to become monks or nuns and to dedicate their lives to individual awakening. On the other hand, the Buddha also spoke in terms of cultivating the conditions for social harmony, and his five ethical precepts (to refrain from killing, stealing, lying, sexual misconduct, and the harmful use of intoxicants) have frequently been interpreted as guidelines for society. For example, the famous Indian emperor Ashoka, in the third century BCE made Buddhism the state religion and issued edicts based on the precepts.

Moreover, the nature of Buddhist liberation—usually expressed both as freedom from identification with the separate individual self (and the suffering such identification entails) and as an awakening to the truth of "dependent co-arising" (meaning, in simple terms, that everything depends on everything else)—is typically understood to lead spontaneously to a condition of compassion for all beings and a desire to help alleviate their suffering. Such an orientation is most fully expressed in the Mahayana Buddhist ideal of the *bodhisattva*, the person who commits her life to the enlightenment of all sentient beings.

In modern times, an explicitly socially engaged approach to Buddhism has emerged through the leadership of such figures as Vietnamese Zen monk Thich Nhat Hanh and Dr. A. T. Ariyaratne, founder of the Sri Lankan Sarvodaya movement. Thich Nhat Hanh is well known for encouraging mindful social engagement by Buddhist monks and nuns during the Vietnam War and beyond. Dr. Ariyaratne applied Buddhist mindfulness principles to his organization's village development and peace-building work in the context of the Sri Lankan civil war. American activist and Buddhist scholar Joanna Macy (1991, 1998) also pioneered the application of traditional Buddhist methods to social issues by creating practices in which participants bring attention to their unacknowledged pain and grief for the suffering of the world. Jones and Kraft (2003), Loy (2003), and Rothberg (1993, 2006, 2008) have each articulated comprehensive intellectual frameworks for socially engaged approaches to Buddhism. Their books suggest, among other things, ways for practitioners to extend their mindfulness and equanimity training into sociopolitical contexts, and how Buddhist principles can be applied to institutions and societies to alleviate collective suffering and encourage a "culture of awakening."

These elements reveal a significant strain within Buddhism in alignment with the social or collective orientation of subtle activism. As for aspects of Buddhism that demonstrate a belief in the possibility of the nonlocal influence of spiritual practice, there are numerous references in the Buddhist scriptures (as in the Vedic tradition) to various extraordinary powers ("Abhinna" or "iddhis"[4]) accessible to advanced practitioners, including the capacity to hear distant sounds and communicate telepathically across great distances. Tibetan Buddhists tend to regard the capacity for telepathic communication (which they describe as "messages sent on the wind") as natural for those who, because of enlightenment, have ceased to consider themselves and "others" as entirely distinct entities. Of even greater relevance for subtle activism, the practice of *metta* (loving-kindness) meditation—in which the practitioner radiates loving-kindness to an ever-expanding circle of relationships that eventually encompasses all sentient beings—is traditionally thought to contribute not only to the well-being of the practitioner but also to the well-being of the world. For example, Buddhist scholar Buddharakkhita (1989) notes, "what is even more wonderful [than the impact of metta on the individual practitioner] is the impact which metta has on the environment and on other beings . . . as the Pali scriptures and commentaries illustrate with a number of memorable stories" (Section 8, para. 1). These stories include one in which the impact of the Buddha's loving thoughts caused a charging elephant to become entirely pacified—"as though a drunken wretch had suddenly become sober"—and others that tell of ordinary people overcoming various dangers, including weapons and poison, through the power of *metta*.

As for the use of Buddhist practices for sociopolitical benefit, Japanese religious scholar Ryuichi Abe (1999) describes how, in eighth-century Japan, the primary duty of the Buddhist clergy was seen to be the protection of the nation through the magico-religious effects of their services. The religious mindset of the times can be observed in the following edict issued by Emperor Konin in 774 following the outbreak of an epidemic of pox:

> I have heard that all the regions under heaven are now filled with the sick, and there is no medicine that has proven effective against the illness. . . . It is said that the *Prajna-paramita* (Perfection of Wisdom) is the mother of all the Buddhas. When I, the Son of Heaven, recite it, the nation is safe from invasions and rebellions; when my people invoke it, their households are protected from the demons of illness. Let us rely on its compassionate power to save us from our present misfortune. I therefore

encourage all those in every province under heaven, both men and women, both young and old, constantly to recite the *Prajna-paramita*. Those of you who serve my court, in both civilian and military ranks, recite the sutra on your way to work and at any interval between your duties. (Abe 1999 20)

A similar belief in the worldly efficacy of prayer was clearly still operating in thirteenth-century Japan when, following the successful defense of the nation from the Mongol invasion of 1281, religious institutions pressed claims for reward every bit as insistently as warriors. The basis for the claims was that the prayers of the temples had contributed to the victory, primarily through the blowing of a typhoon that had wrecked the Mongol invasion fleet. That the state believed these claims is shown by the fact that at least two temples, and possibly more, received rewards before any samurai warrior did (Turnbull 2006).

In modern times, Dr. A.T. Ariyaratne has arguably done more than anyone else to promote the use of Buddhist meditation practices as part of a comprehensive approach to social change. As founder of the Sarvodaya Shramadana movement in the late 1950s, Ariyaratne has guided the development of a grassroots network that today involves more than fifteen thousand Sri Lankan villages in civil war relief efforts and long-term community development projects. Said to be organized around Buddhist principles and Gandhian methods, the Sarvodaya organization embraces an integral approach to development and peace that encompasses three interdependent spheres: consciousness, economics, and power.

Since the early 1980s, Sarvodaya has convened a wide array of peacebuilding programs to help bring an end to the country's decades-long civil war. These activities have included peace dialogues between religious and ethnic groups, exchange programs (in which young people from communities in the North are taken to live with communities in the South and vice versa), youth peace camps, conflict resolution training, and many other programs. In the late 1990s, Sarvodaya launched a series of massive peace meditations designed to shift what Ariyaratne called the "psychosphere" of the nation toward unity and peace. On August 29, 1999, about 170,000 individuals participated in a peace meditation in Colombo, the nation's capital. On March 15, 2002, an estimated 650,000 individuals took part in a peace meditation in the sacred city of Anuradhapura. An additional 200,000 participated in a peace meditation in Colombo on September 21, 2004 (the UN-designated International Day of Peace). Numerous other smaller meditations involving tens of thousands of participants also have been held.

The 2002 event in Anuradhapura drew international attention. Participants represented the full range of Sri Lankan ethnic and religious diversity:

Sinhalese, Tamils, and Moors; Buddhists, Hindus, Muslims, Bahais, and Christians. Sri Lankan President Chadrika Kumaratunga issued a statement of encouragement to the participants, saying, "It is essential that we first purify our minds to achieve peace" (Sri Lankan Government, 2002, para. 10). The event was carried live throughout the nation on television and radio. At 1 p.m. on the day of the meditation, bells were rung simultane-ously at temples, mosques, and churches throughout Sri Lanka. At 3 p.m., members of the clergy of all the religions of Sri Lanka each said a brief prayer to bless the gathering. Then Dr. Ariyaratne guided the audience in a short breathing meditation, followed by a metta meditation, and then a practice of "adhistana," or "settling into firm resolve" to establish peace.

Several prominent participants have attempted to convey the profun-dity of these events. American activist and Buddhist scholar Joanna Macy, one of the participants at Anuradhapura, describes her experience after the meditation began:

> The silence was the most exquisite sound I've ever heard. It was the sound of a half million people—actually it turned out to be 650,000 people—being quiet together, in the biggest meditation ever held on planet Earth. I said to myself, "This is the sound of bombs not exploding, of land mines not going off, of machine guns not firing. . . ." That is what I went to Sri Lanka to hear. (Macy 2002b, para. 9)

Former director of Sarvodaya USA, Richard Brooks, reports his experi-ence of a smaller peace meditation involving about ten thousand individuals on the grounds of a Buddhist temple in Kegalle. Soon after the meditation started, it began to rain:

> Not a soul moved. As far as one could discern behind closed eyes and open ears, not one person rose to run for shelter. We just . . . sat . . . and listened . . . and imagined that somehow the beauty of the moment might have meaning beyond our individual selves and the collective consciousness of the thou-sands. We breathed in minutes and minutes of complete silence except for the sound of birds, barking dogs, faraway traffic and rustling coconut palms in the wind and quiet rain. One could not imagine a more peaceful time or place. . . . There are many more of these peace meditations to go, each one with . . . the highest of expectations and prayers that somehow these brief moments will awaken this beautiful country to the serenity it has long missed. (Brooks nd, para. 9)

The Sarvodaya movement believes that its massive peace mobilization campaign, in which the peace meditations played a leading role, was a primary factor in the shift in public consciousness that led to the formal ceasefire in 2002 between the Government and the Tamil Tigers. Ariyaratne himself is clearly of the view that the contribution of the meditations to the peace process was more than symbolic. After the huge peace meditation in Colombo in 1999, a reporter asked Ariyaratne whether a meditation, even as large as that one, could really affect a Tamil Tiger rebel hiding in the jungles of northern Sri Lanka. Ariyaratne replied, "Spiritual energy is powerful. A meditation like this could affect people in Iceland!" (Mitchell 2000, para. 18).

JUDEO-CHRISTIAN TRADITION

A concern for social justice and the moral integrity of society has been a central theme of the Judeo-Christian tradition since the time of the Old Testament prophets. The moral force with which the ancient Jewish prophets spoke out against the injustices and corrupting influences of their day established a tradition that came to regard the intention to "repair the world" (*tikkun olam*) as a spiritual imperative. Jesus continued in that lineage by championing the poor and the oppressed, fearlessly challenging religious hypocrisy, and throwing the money changers out of the temple. Furthermore, the Christian interpretation of Jesus's life as the incarnation of divine love, with his suffering and death offering redemption to all of humanity, led to a conception of the divine as intimately involved in the world and concerned with the outcome of human history. Such a theology has supported a widespread Christian impulse to work toward alleviating social problems, as a way both to follow the example of Jesus and to help bring God's "Kingdom" to Earth. Biblical scholar Walter Wink (1992) makes the point as follows: "The gospel is not a message of personal salvation *from* the world, but a message of *a world transfigured, right down to its basic structures*" (83).

In modern times, a socially engaged orientation has been advanced in the Christian tradition by figures such as Trappist monk Thomas Merton, Catholic social activist Dorothy Day, African-American intellectuals James Baldwin and Cornell West, and, most famously, civil rights leader Martin Luther King, all of whom advocated a path of social transformation based on love. Such an approach has also been championed (especially in South America) by the liberation theology movement, which emphasizes the Christian mission to bring justice to the poor and the oppressed, particularly through social and political activism. Leading figures who have called for a socially engaged approach to modern Judaism include Rabbi Michael Lerner, whose books have argued passionately for a more prominent role of progressive spirituality and ethics in American public life, and Rabbi Zalman Schachter-Salomi, founder of the "Jewish Renewal" movement. The Jewish Renewal movement aims to reinvigorate Judaism with mystical, Hasidic, meditative, and musical practices drawn from a variety of sources, including some outside of Judaism. *Tikkun olam* ("the healing of the world") is a central principle of the Renewal movement, and, because of the movement's mystical emphasis, is expressed in novel forms, such as infusing prayer and other spiritual practices with an orientation toward social healing. For example, in 2004, Rabbi Zalman Schacter-Salomi initiated a "Rishi" project that explored the use of subtle energies by groups to support the healing of trouble spots on the planet.

In terms of the use of spiritual practice as the means for achieving social change, in the Judeo-Christian tradition we are talking primarily about "intercessory" prayer, or prayer for the benefit of others. In the Hebrew Scriptures, numerous stories describe the Israelites crying out to Yahweh for help during periods of foreign oppression, and Yahweh responding by sending a deliverer to restore their freedom (most famously, Moses in Egypt). The possibility of God's intervention in worldly affairs in response to the prayers of the people is explicitly endorsed in the book of Chronicles, where God is recorded as saying, "If my people, who are called by My name, *will humble themselves and pray* and seek My face and turn from their wicked ways, then will I hear from heaven and will forgive their sin *and will heal their land*" (2 Chron. 7:14 King James Version, emphasis added).

In the New Testament, many of Christ's teachings emphasize the virtually unlimited power of prayer to bring about God's reign on Earth. For example, as noted by Robb and Wilson (2000) in support of their idea that "prayer is social action," Jesus said in Matthew 18, "I tell you the truth, whatever you bind on earth will be bound in heaven and whatever you loose on earth will be loosed in heaven. Again, I tell you that if two of you on Earth agree *about anything you ask for*, it will be done for you by my Father in heaven." The early Christians joined together constantly in prayer as the principal method to support and implement their world-transforming mission. Numerous Christian churches and monasteries adopted the practice of continuous prayer (*laus perennis* in Latin) to serve as a blessing on their communities and nations, such as St. Maurice in Switzerland (where the *laus perennis* was practiced continuously for 1500 years), Bangor Abbey, St Patrick's monastery in Ireland (which practiced continuous prayer for more than two hundred years), and the eighteenth-century Moravian community near Dresden, Germany (which began a continual prayer meeting in 1727 that lasted more than one hundred years). In addition to these, and many other, examples of specific monasteries or communities using prayer as a means to support collective well-being, one could cite the very common

Christian practice of praying for the sick, the poor, and the suffering as an example from the Christian tradition of the use of spiritual practices for wider social benefit.

Walter Wink (1992) has developed a sophisticated theological frame-work that argues for the crucial role of intercessory prayer in helping to shape human history. Wink emphasizes a passage in the Book of Revelation to highlight this point. Jesus Christ is opening one by one the seals on the Scroll of Destiny. As he breaks open the seventh and final seal,

> there was silence in heaven for about half an hour. I saw the seven angels who stand in the presence of God: they were given seven trumpets.
>
> Another Angel came and stood at the altar, holding a golden censer. He was given much incense to offer *with the prayers of all God's people* on the golden altar in front of the throne, and the smoke of the incense from the angel's hand went up before God *with his people's prayers*. The angel took the censer, filled it with fire from the altar, and threw it down on the earth; and there came peals of thunder, lightning-flashes, and an earthquake. (Rev. 8:1–5, quoted in Wink 1992, 299, emphasis added)

Wink (1992) comments: "This scene reverses the usual unrolling of fate, where heavenly decisions are acted out on earth. Human beings have intervened in the heavenly liturgy. . . . What happens next happens because people prayed" (299). For Wink, the message is clear: "*history belongs to the intercessors, who believe the future into being*" (299). Even a small number of people, claims Wink, faithfully committed to the irresistibility of their shared vision, can decisively affect the shape the future takes.

Wink contrasts the Biblical God—with whom leading figures of the Scriptures are constantly "haggling" in a "spirited give-and-take" that helps shape God's actions and thus the future—with the "unchanging, immu-table God of Stoic metaphysics," whose will was fixed from all eternity. For example, Wink points to the story in Genesis of Abraham talking God out of his intention to destroy the city of Sodom, or Moses persuading Yahweh to "repent" of "the evil which he thought to do to his people" (when God declared that he was ready to "consume" the Israelites for their idolatry). What the God of the Bible does, claims Wink, "depends on the interces-sions of those who care enough to try to shape a future more humane than the present" (301–302).

As for the question of why human prayers do not appear to be always, or immediately, answered, Wink has a straightforward response: the "Principalities and Powers" that preside over so much of human reality are able to assert their will against the will of God and can, temporarily, prevail. The Principalities and Powers are, for Wink, those "socio-spiritual" forces that constitute the "Domination System" that has prevailed on Earth for millenia. Wink distinguishes the Domination System from the physical creation in general: The Domination System is the "human sociological realm that exists in estrangement from God"; the creation is affirmed as inherently good. Although the Powers are not, in Wink's theology, intrinsically evil and can themselves be redeemed, they can and do exercise their freedom by actively resisting and blocking the will of God. Thus, for Wink, a kind of invisible spiritual warfare between God and the Powers frequently occurs and this slows the turning of the wheels of justice. In such a context, prayers are not "magic" that immediately result in the desired outcome, but they are "the necessary opening that allows God to act without violating our freedom" (312). Recognizing the role of the Powers in opposing prayer can, paradoxically, liberate our faith, claims Wink. For prayer that fails to acknowledge the Powers tends to blame God for evils committed by the Powers. However, prayer that recognizes the role of the Powers is a form of social action that lifts the Powers to God for transformation. In this sense, claims Wink, intercessory prayer, far from being an escape from action, changes what God can do in the world and thus is a means for focusing and creating action.[5]

In the modern era, the Christian faith has been one of the most active of all traditions in promoting the use of spiritual practices for collective benefit and has inspired numerous large-scale prayer initiatives. For example, Father Patrick Peyton of Los Angeles founded a post-World War II prayer movement called the "Family Rosary Crusade" that convened many massive rallies in large cities around the world involving tens of thousands of people coming together to recite the rosary. One of the main objectives of the "rosary rallies" was to support world peace. Indeed, Peyton coined the phrase, "a world at prayer is a world at peace" as the slogan for these events. Peyton firmly believed that his work had important political implications, arguing that "[t]he rosary is the offensive weapon that will destroy Communism—the great evil that seeks to destroy faith" (Wilford 2008, 187). In 2007, the tradition was revived by Holy Cross Family Ministries, which convened a "Rosary Bowl" that brought tens of thousands of people together at the Rose Bowl football stadium in Pasadena, California for a collective recital of the rosary, specifically intended to support "world peace and the strength and unity of families, especially in war-torn areas" (Rosary Bowl).

The International Prayer Council (IPC) is an organization that formed shortly after September 11, 2001 to connect Christian prayer networks worldwide to focus prayer on global concerns. The IPC employs the power of prayer "for the blessing, healing, and transforming of the nations" and regularly supports special prayer initiatives that focus on matters of regional or global concern. For example, in 2007, the IPC sponsored a "Prayer Initiative for the United Nations" to focus collective prayer on the UN and its officials and on world economic and political concerns that are affected by decisions made by the UN. A central event on the IPC calendar is the annual "Global Day of Prayer" (GDP) held every year on Pentecost Sunday (i.e., seven weeks after Easter Sunday). The origin of the GDP was a vision that came to South African businessman Graham Power in 2000 for a "Day of Repentance and Prayer" to unite Christians in South Africa. In March 2001, more than 45,000 Christians filled Newlands Rugby Stadium in Cape Town to pray for the healing and transformation of South Africa. By 2004, the initiative had spread throughout the African continent, and, on May 2 of that year, Christians from all fifty-six African nations participated in a continental "Day of Repentance and Blessing" for Africa. The IPC became involved in 2005 and decided to make the project the centerpiece of its strategy to better connect prayer networks worldwide. The GDP has since become the largest annual Christian prayer event. In 2008, according to the GDP website, millions of Christians from 214 nations participated in a global prayer vigil "for the blessing and healing of the Nations." The IPC intends to support the GDP for many years to come and aims to help connect participants by satellite, Internet, and other means "to enable believers in every nation to pray together for the transformation of our world" (International Prayer Council, 2010).

WESTERN MYSTERY TRADITIONS

Alongside the official, monotheistic religions of the West, there has always existed an assortment of lesser-known (and usually highly marginalized) spiritual traditions that can be identified, on the basis of certain characteristics they share, as branches of a single tree, known to many as the *Western Mysteries*. Some scholars identify two principal strands to the Western Mysteries: the "native" tradition, comprised of individuals and groups who carried forward the indigenous wisdom of early European cultures (e.g., the so-called "Druidic Mysteries" of Britain), and the "Hermetic" tradition, consisting of a variety of esoteric schools whose lineage traces back to the legendary Hermes Trismegistos and the mystery schools of Egypt, Greece, and Rome.[6] Although the native and Hermetic traditions have fed into each other and cannot be entirely separated, the native path has been described as centered on the archetypal figure of the *shaman* or *witch* and primarily focused on ancestral, indigenous wisdom, with its innate respect and concern for the Earth, whereas the Hermetic tradition can be represented symbolically by the *magus* and emphasizes the pursuit of knowledge and self-realization. As we have already considered the path of shamanism and its relevance for subtle activism, I focus my discussion here on the Hermetic strand of the Western Mysteries.

The Hermetic tradition is a coat of many colors, its lineage a complex tapestry of dozens of mystery schools and wisdom traditions that have often been woven together to produce creative hybrids or entirely novel spiritual forms.[7] For our purposes, it is sufficient to familiarize ourselves with just the main currents.[8] The tradition is generally seen to consist of three main "rivers": the so-called "traditional sciences" of alchemy, astrology, and magic. Esoteric scholar Antoine Faivre (1992) identifies four main "streams" that feed into these rivers and together comprise the main components of modern Western esoteric thought. The first stream is Christian Kabbalah, regarded as an adaptation of Jewish Kabbalah. The second is neo-Alexandrian Hermeticism, a tradition centered on a body of literature called the *Hermetica*, containing many works, including the renowned *Corpus Hermeticum*, that are attributed to the legendary Hermes Trimegistus. (The tradition was revived in Renaissance Europe after the translation by Marsilio Ficino of the *Corpus Hermeticum* in 1463.) The third is a "Paracelsian" type of spiritual philosophy of Nature, named after the sixteenth-century Swiss physician/alchemist/ philosopher Paracelsus. Faivre considers this philosophy a strand of German *Naturphilosophie*. The fourth stream is theosophy and Rosicrucianism.

Despite the wide variety of approaches represented by these sources, Faivre (1992) claims that Western esotericism (or Hermeticism) can be identified as a distinct form of spirituality because of the presence in each of its schools of four intrinsic characteristics: correspondences, living nature, imagination and mediation, and the experience of transmutation.[9] Correspondences refers to the belief that there are symbolic and/or real correspondences between all parts of the visible and invisible universe, as in the ancient saying, "that which is above is like that which is below." Here we see the basis for the astrological hypothesis that the movements of the planets correspond meaningfully to events in the human world and the ancient idea that the human body is a holographic expression of the cosmos, a microcosm of the macrocosm. Living nature is the notion that Nature is seen and felt to be essentially alive in all its parts and occupies an essential place in the cosmos.[10] Imagination and mediation refers to the belief that the imagination can be used as an "organ of the soul" to establish visionary contact with those entities that mediate between the divine world and Nature (e.g., angels).[11] The experience of transmutation is a concept originating from alchemy that describes the kind of transformation that is the goal of the esotericist's work. Although it has become quite widely recognized that the focus of the alchemist was not solely to turn base metals into gold but also to transmute the psychic condition of the practitioner, the use of the term *transmutation* nonetheless often implied a belief that a change did in fact take place in nature just as much as in the experimenters themselves.

We can recognize in these characteristics a philosophical worldview highly amenable to the concept and practice of subtle activism. Permeating each principle is a decidedly "this-worldly" spiritual orientation, a path less about transcending the world so much as manifesting the divine within it. As Matthews and Matthews (2003) write, "the magician of any time seeks to bring the inner impulse to the outer world" (263). And psychologist Ralph Metzner (2008) notes that one of the traditional definitions of alchemy was that it involved "a marriage of the subtle and the dense" (10). Here we can see an obvious parallel with the approach of subtle activism, which aims to infuse "dense" outer social and political realities with subtle energies and thought forms derived from contact with inner realms.

The actual practices of the Hermetic path, however, have historically been cloaked in secrecy, in part due to the very real danger of persecution from dominant religious authorities (e.g., as in the Inquisition), but also to protect against misuse of esoteric knowledge by those motivated by greed or power. Thus, it is difficult to uncover the precise extent to which Western esoteric groups applied their methods to support collective, as well as individual, transformation. Certainly, there is considerable evidence to suggest that esoteric groups and individuals have often been interested and involved in shaping political affairs. For example, Lachmann (2008) argues that the Rosicrucian message (which combined elements of alchemy, astrology, and other esoteric disciplines) was not limited to the transformation of the individual but aimed to transform European society as a whole. Indeed, Lachmann makes a convincing case that the ill-fated Protestant campaign to install Frederick V, *Elector Palatine* of the Rhine, onto the Bohemian throne in defiance of the Catholic Hapsburgs—one of the main events that triggered the Thirty Years' War—may have been significantly inspired by the Rosicrucian vision of a reformed Europe.

The prominence of Freemasons in the founding of America is another, better known, example. George Washington and Benjamin Franklin are widely acknowledged to have been Masons, as are many other signatories of the Declaration of Independence.[12] Many authors have pointed out that the great seal of the United States is permeated with Masonic symbols, especially the reverse side combining the "all-seeing" eye with the pyramid—both images being highly suggestive of Egyptian esoteric symbols commonly used in Freemasonry.

In addition to these instances where esoteric ideals and philosophies appear to have been embraced by leaders of actual political movements, it is a common esoteric belief, at least since the emergence in the late nineteenth century of Madame Blavatsky and her brand of theosophy, that behind the everyday world there exists an elite group of (disembodied) adepts—variously known as the Great White Brotherhood, the Ascended Masters, the Elder Brethren, and other names—who are guiding the collective evolution of humanity. Although these may all be fascinating claims, none of them tells us anything about whether esoteric groups actually engaged in spiritual practices intended to nonlocally influence events in the collective realm (a.k.a. subtle activism).

However, there is the case of Dion Fortune (1993) who, in *The Magical Battle of Britain*, unveils a detailed account of an esoteric method designed specifically to open a channel for spiritual influences to uplift the "group mind" of the British nation during the darkest hours of World War II. Fortune was a leading member of the renowned Hermetic Order of the Golden Dawn, a British-based magical order founded in the late nineteenth century that greatly influenced nearly all twentieth-century esoteric developments. At the beginning of October 1939, one month after the outbreak of World War II, Fortune sent a letter to all the members of her "Fraternity of the Inner Light" announcing the start of a magical project to support the national war effort by opening a channel "whereby spiritual influences can contact the Group-mind of the race." The letter contained instructions for a specific meditation practice that all members were asked to perform each Sunday from 12:15 to 12:30 p.m. and then again daily at any regular time of their choosing. Every Wednesday, a new letter containing the instructions for the next week's meditation was sent out to arrive in time for the following Sunday. Participants were asked to face London, to sit in an upright posture, and to rest their hands on the weekly letter in their laps while they meditated. Meanwhile, each Sunday, also from 12:15 to 12:30 p.m., a small group of experienced fraternity members sat in meditation circle under Fortune's guidance at the network's "Sanctuary" (located in a private home in London) to form the focusing point for the meditation work.

The meditations by the group in the Sanctuary were based on a common esoteric method of using the imagination to visualize certain symbols and thought forms that were believed to attract and focus spiritual forces that acted through them. (The wider network did a more general form of meditation to support the "active" work of the core circle.) The starting point for the work was the Rosicrucian symbol of the Rose upon the Cross. Although the formulation of this and other symbols initially required the use of the imagination, Fortune describes that, early on in the work, the symbols "came alive," indicating that they had been contacted by an inner spiritual reality, and took on "astral forms" that then maintained themselves of their own accord. Thereafter, the symbols developed organically, "like a growing plant throwing up a shoot," with the shoot forming the basis of the meditation work for the following week.

For example, after starting with the symbol of the Rose on the Cross, the group immediately found it surrounded by "golden light of great brilliance," and soon thereafter the golden light and the Cross were perceived to be inside a cavern. In this way, week by week, an elaborate symbolic system gradually developed. Each new symbol was recognized by Fortune, an experienced adept, as a known feature of an inner terrain well mapped out by esoteric tradition, enabling definite meanings to be assigned to the growing symbolic metastructure.

An especially significant symbol that emerged over time was a three-sided pyramid structure consisting of an oval of white light at the apex and three rays of different colors that formed the sides and base. Specific figures were seen in association with the pyramid: "Master Jesus" at the apex, King Arthur, seated on a horse and bearing Excalibur, the "Sword of Chivalry," in connection with the red ray, Merlin, seated on a throne and holding a scepter, the "Rod of Power," in connection with the blue ray, and the Virgin Mary standing in the purple ray holding the Cup of the Holy Grail. Fortune interpreted the appearance of these figures to mean that that the group was working to inoculate the "group mind" of the British nation with the archetypal ideals of chivalry and bravery associated both with Christianity and, especially, with the myth of King Arthur and the quest for the Holy Grail—a myth derived from and in harmony with the national tradition. (In contrast, Fortune believed that the primordial forces fueling Nazi Germany were the thunderous, "blood-stained" gods of Norse mythology.[13]) The goal of this stage of the work was to let "the primordial energies of [their] ancient race be loosed on a Quest" (Fortune 1993, 63). Another component of the work called for the visualization of angelic presences, "red-robed and armed," patrolling the British coastline, keeping watch so that nothing alien could trespass without being noticed.

The general theory informing the work can be described as follows. Fortune maintained that the primary task of the work was to form a channel for spiritual forces to transmit certain archetypal ideals into the collective consciousness of the nation. In particular, Fortune saw the main target for the transmission of the thought forms as the "group mind" of the nation, which she distinguished from the "group soul." The group soul, in Fortune's conception, is the older, relatively stable layer of the collective psyche that contains all the accumulated experiences of the past, and includes the archetypal ideas that give rise to national myths, symbols, dreams, and art. Fortune likened this level to the unconscious in an individual. The group mind, on the other hand, is, for Fortune, the more superficial and changeable aspect of the collective psyche—something like the current state of the national mood or opinion—and was compared to the conscious mind of an individual. As in psychotherapy for an individual, a major aim of the work was to bring about a harmonization between the conscious and unconscious elements of the psyche that is (in the context of the collective psyche), between the group mind and group soul of the nation.

This harmonization was primarily accomplished through the creation of symbolic thought forms believed to be expressive of the archetypal ideals of the national tradition. Fortune understood the work of building the thought forms to have been performed in collaboration with presences from the inner planes known as the "Masters" or "Elder Brethren." These presences were regarded as former human initiates of the mystery traditions that choose, after they die, to remain connected to the Earth plane. Fortune claimed that when her circle members used their imagination to form the Rose-Cross set of symbols, the "Elder Brethren," being accustomed to using the same symbolism, were "called up." The Elder Brethren then built the thought forms downward from the higher levels while the human practitioners built upward from the Earth plane. Fortune also understood the gradual evolution of the symbolic meta-structure to have been guided by the Elder Brethren, who, in turn, were informed by the "racial Archangels." These angelic presences were regarded as the source for the archetypal ideas that underlie the group soul of a nation. These "inner-plane" sources, Fortune believed, psychically communicated the archetypal principles to the human practitioners in the form of spontaneous changes to the symbols during the meditations. By coming together as a group and meditating with the imagination, Fortune claimed that the group created a "miniature collective subconscious," which enabled access to the corresponding level of the national mind. Because the myth the group created was in deep harmony with the national tradition, it was believed to have been easily accessible to the group mind. Individual minds, Fortune argued, picked up the ideas unconsciously, brought them through to consciousness and started to contemplate them. Finally, experts in various arenas of society gave concrete expression to the ideals through action in the world.

Fortune's network maintained their weekly meditation circle for three years, during the most challenging period of the war when the national morale most needed support. In October 1942, Fortune announced the conclusion of the project, on the basis that it had more or less achieved its purpose. Although Fortune (1993) wrote, "[w]e are not so foolish or fantastic as to claim that our work as a meditation group is controlling the fate of nations," she nonetheless believed that their activities exercised a clear influence in world affairs (15). Indeed, she maintained that the ideals that were formulated on the inner planes could consistently be seen to manifest in the national consciousness approximately six months later, often in a form that corresponded so closely to the esoteric principles as to be almost humorous. For example, she claimed that the leading articles of

The Times—which Fortune noted was then widely regarded as the mirror of the national mind—came to give expression to the ideals of the work in a way that was "not only adequate but often verbatim" (Fortune 1993, 84). Well before events in the outer world might have suggested it, Fortune wrote that "[t]he war need cause us no anxiety; it is already won on the Inner Planes" (58), reflecting a remarkable confidence on her part in the external results of their "inner" work.[14] I put "inner" in quotation marks here because, if there is any validity to these claims, it makes no sense to think of this work as occurring only within the subjective interior experience of the individual practitioners.

ECLECTIC/INTERFAITH

To conclude our review of subtle activism practices among the world's spiritual traditions, let us consider a few examples of projects that have been intentionally framed to welcome the participation of practitioners from a wide range of religious and philosophical backgrounds. First is the remarkable story of the "Big Ben Minute," yet another initiative developed to counter the Nazi threat in World War II. On November 10, 1940, BBC radio reintroduced the chiming of Big Ben at the beginning of their broadcast of the nine o' clock news. The practice was introduced at the urging of Major Wellesley Tudor Pole to encourage the universal observance of one minute of silence by people everywhere as a way to rededicate themselves each day to the war effort. Tudor Pole, an officer in the British army in World War I and a follower of various esoteric and mystical traditions, claimed to have been inspired by a conversation he had in 1917. The conversation was with a fellow British officer while they were in a cave in the mountains around Jerusalem on the eve of a battle. The officer is said to have had an intuition that he would not survive the upcoming battle and to have told Tudor Pole that he (Tudor Pole) would live to see another, greater conflict to be staged on every continent. Tudor Pole claimed that the officer then asked him to create, during that later conflict, a period of silence each day to allow those "who have gone on ahead" to help in unseen ways. The officer did indeed die in the battle near Jerusalem and the "Big Ben Minute" was Tudor Pole's response to the man's request. Tudor Pole engaged in a vast marketing campaign to promote his idea, sending out, in 1940, more than twenty thousand leaflets and letters to all Members of Parliament in both houses, Church leaders, and the heads of religious and social organizations, heads of schools and universities, representatives of leading newspapers, intellectual and spiritual leaders throughout the Commonwealth and in the United States, and influential members of the British aristocracy. He secured public endorsements of the project from King George VI,

Prime Minister Winston Churchill, the Foreign Secretary, the Archbishop of Canterbury, the Archbishop of Westminster, the Chief Rabbi of England, and dozens of other distinguished leaders of society. The project was also announced daily in all the leading English newspapers. On April 23, 1943, the BBC included the "Big Ben Minute" in its official daily program and made a formal announcement explaining the significance of this "deliberate pause" in the day's broadcasting. It has been estimated that as many as five million people observed the Big Ben Minute on a daily basis at the height of the program (Dakers nd).

Although the program was conceived and implemented in the predominantly Christian context of World War II Britain, it was framed in very inclusive terms to encourage participation by the widest number of people. The practice itself—a minute of pure silence—could not be associated exclusively with any one religion or philosophy and was thus accessible to people of all faiths (or even agnostics and atheists). The "Minute" was promoted as, simply, "an occasion for everyone to give expression to the highest ideals to which their consciousness has attained" (Dakers nd, 24). For the spiritually minded, this typically meant prayer or meditation, but the invitation was also extended to those who rejected spiritual concepts and practices, but who had reached the intellectual conclusion that "thoughts of good-will and kindliness are more intelligent than their antitheses" (24). Such people were encouraged to contribute their kind and positive thoughts to the endeavor.

The deepest significance of the Big Ben Minute, according to Dakers, was the opportunity it provided for a "regular, unified shining of millions of individual lights" that radiated good will into the world and thus helped to dispel its darkness. Dakers especially stressed the importance of the synchronized timing of the practice:

> Perhaps this [the importance of observing silence at the same time] can be made clear if we imagine humanity as living most of the time in a dark world, a world which is filled with windows which are shuttered, keeping out the light behind them. At each window—imagine millions of them—is one of us human beings, aware that the shutters can be opened and knowing that they can be opened by an act of will on our part. The idea behind the Silent Minute Observance is not just to let the Light of God into our own window; that is a private matter for all times. The idea is that all—or as many as possible—of the windows should be simultaneously unshuttered so that the Divine Light may pour in and illuminate the mind of mankind in one great revealing flood of radiance. Prayer, thought, and silence provide the power that opens the shutters and keeps them open. . . . This is the

supreme value of the Silent Minute Observance, that, instead of
the light streaming in through isolated windows at all sorts of
odd times, lighting up only little pools in the prevailing darkness,
the light flows in through all the windows at once, brightening
the whole and, because of that which it reveals, encouraging us
to keep the shutters thrown back, not for a minute a day, but
always. (44–45)

Several contemporary initiatives intended to provide support for transformation at the planetary level are noteworthy as pluralistic approaches to
subtle activism. On August 16, 1987, the "Harmonic Convergence" brought
large numbers of people together worldwide—especially at locations believed
to be sacred sites—for meditation, prayer, song, and ritual to support a
global awakening to unity. As is common for New Age spirituality, the
event invited an eclectic approach to participation, encompassing practices
as diverse as African drumming, Native American sweat lodges, and Buddhist meditation.

The "Gaiamind" Global Meditation and Prayer on January 23, 1997
involved hundreds of thousands of participants. It was intended to "help
catalyze the evolution of consciousness and potentiate global healing" (Gaiamind 2009). Participants were invited to meditate, pray, or "do whatever
brings you into closer contact with the Divine" for five minutes after the des-
ignated starting time. The event was monitored by psychologist Roger Nelson's global network of random number generators (RNG), which detected
a significant trend toward nonrandom behavior during the five-minute peak
period of the program (Nelson 1997).

The International Day of Peace Vigil (IDP Vigil) is the largest annual global meditation and prayer event, held since 2001 on September 21,
the UN-designated IDP. According to the IDP Vigil website, the event
is intended "to demonstrate the power of prayer and other spiritual practices in promoting peace and preventing violent conflict." The invitation
to participate in the vigil is extended to "every house of worship and place
of spiritual practice" and to "all religious and spiritually based groups and
individuals, and . . . all men, women and children who seek peace in the
world." Be The Peace is an annual event on the IDP that links hundreds
of meditation gatherings worldwide in shared intention to support a shift
to a planetary culture of peace. The program features guided meditations by
teleconference and audio web cast and hundreds of live meditation events
in public locations.

WiseUSA 2008 and WiseUSA 2012 are examples of recent subtle
activism initiatives that aimed to provide support for a national electoral
process. WiseUSA 2008 was a five-week program that invited people from

around the United States and the world to unite in meditation and prayer in the lead up to the 2008 US elections. It was the first public program of the Gaiafield Project, a nonprofit project I helped establish in 2005. The program involved a series of teleconferences and audio web casts featuring more than a dozen socially engaged spiritual teachers from different traditions, who guided participants in a variety of practices intended to support the highest and best outcome of the political process. The peak event of the program was a "Global Ceremony" on Sunday November 2 (two days before the election) that linked by videoconference live gatherings at All Soul's Church in Washington, DC and the Center for Spiritual Enlightenment in San Jose, California, and streamed a live audio broadcast to a national online audience. The intention of the program was expressed in the following prayer:

"We, the people,
The ancestors of our great, great grandchildren,
Call forth the deepest wisdom
And the highest compassion
From the heart and soul of America,
For the benefit of the entire Earth community,
And the next seven generations.
May Wisdom prevail in the USA.
May Peace prevail on Earth."

Although these programs represent some of the larger and better-organized initiatives in the category of pluralistic approaches to subtle activism, many others could be listed.

CAVEATS

Before concluding this chapter, it is important to mention some examples that illustrate the potential dangers and limitations of subtle activism. First, there are many accounts of the use of spiritual or magical practices for nefarious purposes—so-called "black magic." In the shamanic tradition it is not uncommon to find stories of battles between rival shamans involving the use of magical "darts" intended to cause illness or even death in the victim. Many have claimed that the Nazis had occult connections and used black magic practices to undermine the morale of foreign nations (e.g., Fortune 1993; Levenda 2002). By all accounts, the ultimate consequences are disastrous for those who succumb to the temptation of using these powers for personal gain. The common view is that the malicious intentions directed outward ultimately rebound on the practitioner involved with many times the force with which they were sent. Some authors also warn of the risk for exposure to occult attack that can come with certain kinds of subtle work. I have limited personal experience in this realm, but I want to acknowledge that dealing with darker forces is potentially an important dimension of subtle activism practice.

Another variant on this theme involves the use of spiritual practices by religious fundamentalists to support social change in alignment with their agenda. For example, various evangelical Christian organizations have launched extensive prayer campaigns to end abortion in America. Such a phenomenon raises intriguing questions about how subtle activism might work. For example, is it essentially a neutral force that can be made to serve a range of purposes, from black magic to religious fundamentalism to peace? Or are practices that express universal spiritual ideals (such as love, peace, and truth) ultimately more effective than those motivated by negative emotions (fear, envy, lust for power)? In any event, if we assume that all human endeavors tend to involve a mixture of conscious and unconscious motivations, how can we determine the "purity" of any particular practice? Can we articulate ethical criteria that could help us to distinguish more from less desirable forms of subtle activism? These questions raise important but complicated philosophical and theological issues that are beyond the scope of this book to explore, so I simply flag them here for future consideration.

Finally, although most of the programs I have presented in this chapter correlate with events in the world that suggest a "successful" outcome, we can undoubtedly find many cases where no such positive correlations can be made. For example, the 2003 Global Interfaith Prayer Vigil brought together an estimated one hundred thousand monks, nuns, and other practitioners from multiple traditions for a forty-day prayer vigil in the lead-up to the US invasion of Iraq. But it did not result in the hoped-for outcome of a peaceful resolution to the situation.[15] Similarly, no miracles at the ballot box occurred following a series of global meditations I helped organize in 2004 to support the presidential campaign of Democratic candidate Dennis Kucinich. We can presume, too, that many indigenous cultures would have attempted to use their traditional rituals and ceremonies to help in their cataclysmic encounters with European powers, to no apparent avail. One might be tempted to conclude in such cases that the practices did not "work." However, just as it is very difficult to quantify the extent to which subtle activism programs may have contributed to successful worldly outcomes, so is it impossible to say with certainty that these activities had no effect when the goal was not reached. The outcomes might have been worse, for instance, had the spiritual interventions not taken place. Or, as Wink suggests, in these situations the worldly "Powers" may have been capable of resisting, at least temporarily, the will of the heavens. The spiritual work, although not producing immediate results, may nonetheless have helped to mobilize a divine response that, in the end, may still prevail. In any case, these examples remind us that the practice of subtle activism is not so magical that one should expect immediate or miraculous results as a rule. In relation to short-term outcomes, subtle activism might, at most, tip the probabilities toward a more positive result in any given situation. However, in a world that seems so delicately poised between possibilities of collective breakdown or breakthrough, who would want to argue that such a shift in probabilities is not eminently welcome?

CHAPTER THREE

SUBTLE ACTIVISM AND SCIENCE

Ever since physicists turned the scientific world upside down with their strange discoveries about quantum reality—discoveries such as the phenomenon of "nonlocality" and the apparent role of human consciousness in affecting quantum events—many scientists and philosophers have wondered about the implications of these findings for our everyday world. Although numerous New Age writers have been willing to see in the new physics evidence for the capacity of humans to influence reality through our thoughts and intentions, what scientific data is there to support this view? And is there any evidence to suggest that the power of consciousness can affect not just our personal lives but also levels of social harmony?

This chapter reviews the scientific evidence of the phenomenon of *nonlocality*, defined as the direct interaction between two objects or entities separated in space (or time), with no intermediate agency or mechanism. Our journey begins with the discovery in physics of quantum nonlocality. I then present a summary of the evidence from parapsychology and distant healing studies regarding alleged nonlocal phenomena at the macro level. I also examine evidence from three lines of investigation of particular relevance for subtle activism: research into the so-called Maharishi Effect by investigators associated with the TM organization, the Global Consciousness Project, a parapsychological study that assesses the effect of collective attention during global events on a worldwide network of RNGs, and the Global Coherence Initiative, which studies the connection between humanity and Earth's energetic systems through a global network of ultra-sensitive magnetic field detectors. I discuss some of the philosophical and epistemological issues involved in evaluating this kind of research as well as its implications for the topic of subtle activism.

LESSONS AND METAPHORS FROM QUANTUM PHYSICS

The claim of subtle activism, to reiterate, is that the use of spiritual or consciousness-based practices intended to support collective transformation can have a subtle, positive, nonlocal effect on worldly events. Obviously, this notion runs counter to both the assumptions of classical physics and to our every day perception of things appearing to be affected only by local actions. However, as is now widely known, quantum physics has revealed a much different and weirder universe than the one that appears to our senses. Of particular relevance is the discovery by physicists that reality is fundamentally nonlocal in nature.

The discovery of quantum nonlocality can be traced to a thought experiment that Albert Einstein and two of his junior colleagues devised in the context of an ongoing debate between Einstein and Niels Bohr about the completeness of quantum theory. The "Einstein–Podolsky–Rosen" (EPR) thought experiment asks us to imagine a pair of photons emitted by a common light source that move apart in opposite directions and do not interact with anything else until we decide to measure or observe one of them. Because Einstein knew that quantum theory dictates that the momentum of two such particles should be correlated regardless of the distance between them, he argued that we could calculate the momentum of one particle by measuring the momentum of the other. Since we can calculate the momentum of the "unobserved" particle and know the position of the measured particle, Einstein argued that we should be able to deduce both the momentum and position of the particle that was not measured. And this, Einstein claimed, would violate Bohr's "Copenhagen interpretation" of quantum theory, which holds that particles do not have definite attributes like position or momentum until measured. If the Copenhagen interpretation were to be valid, Einstein argued, the position and momentum of the second, "unobserved" particle must depend on the process of measurement carried out on the "observed" particle—a process that, Einstein thought, could not disturb the second particle in any way. Assuming that all causation was local causation (which was an unquestionable truth among physicists at the time), Einstein argued that only a signal traveling faster than the speed of light could cause such an influence to occur, and this would violate the theory of relativity and undermine much of the basis of modern physics. Thus, Einstein concluded, orthodox quantum theory must be incomplete.

However, in 1964, John Bell developed a mathematical proof known as "Bell's theorem," which demonstrated that no local model of reality could account for the facts of the EPR experiment. Subsequent experiments testing Bell's theorem by French physicist Alain Aspect and his colleagues in 1982 and Swiss physicist Nicolas Gisin in 1998 and 2004 have categorically proven that the correlations between particles in situations like the

EPR experiment are, in fact, instant and immediate, regardless of distance. These findings have provided experimental validation for Bell's contention that beneath the phenomenal world lies an invisible nonlocal reality that is immediately and instantly interconnected. As a result of these experiments, physicists now generally accept nonlocality as proven fact.

Many scientists and philosophers have recognized the revolutionary implications of the discovery of nonlocality for the scientific worldview. Berkeley physicist Henry Stapp (1988), for example, describes nonlocality as possibly "the most profound discovery in all of science" (40). Physicist Robert Nadeau and historian of science Menas Kafatos (1999) point out that, with the Aspect and Gisin experimental results, nonlocality has transcended quantum theory to become a general property of nature. That is, even if quantum theory should someday fail, Bell's theorem and nonlocality, being based on empirical facts, will remain. Furthermore, it is crucial to recognize that nonlocality is not confined to the interactions of discrete pairs of photons as in EPR-type experiments. All particles in the history of the cosmos have interacted with all the other particles in the manner revealed by the Aspect and Gisen experiments. Particles in our bodies and those that can be found in the most distant star, for example, were once essentially conjoined as part of the original cosmic fireball. The discovery of nonlocality thus suggests that the entire universe could be a vast web of particles that remain immediately and instantly interconnected at a fundamental level. Although such a finding does not lend support to conceptions of a divine purpose or plan associated with any particular religious tradition, Nadeau and Kafatos point out that it does make it "no longer possible to argue that a profound sense of unity with the whole, which has long been understood as the foundation of religious experience, can be dismissed, undermined, or invalidated with appeals to scientific knowledge" (198).

The discovery of nonlocality at the quantum level has inspired a natural curiosity in many scientists about its implications for our everyday world. Science has been forced to acknowledge that the physical universe is a considerably stranger place than was previously assumed. This finding has opened the door for many scientists to reexamine certain phenomena from our everyday world that had previously been considered absurd or irrational. For example, scientists interested in psychic phenomena such as telepathy could now point to quantum nonlocality as providing at least a conceptual analogy on which to base their investigations (if two electrons can be connected nonlocally, why not two minds?). Of course, the very idea of nonlocal connections at the level of everyday life is highly controversial, as it involves phenomena like spiritual healing, intercessory prayer, and psychic experiences that are virtually taboo areas in science due to their historical associations with religion, magic, and superstition. Nonetheless, many adventurous scientists have taken up the challenge of attempting systematically to gather evidence for occurrences of nonlocal phenomena in our everyday world. The two disciplines that have compiled the largest body of research in this regard are parapsychology and distant healing.

PARAPSYCHOLOGY

Parapsychology is the scientific study of *psi* phenomena. *Psi* is a term introduced in the 1940s by parapsychologists Robert Thouless and B.P. Wiesner to describe various kinds of psychic phenomena that fall into two general categories: psychokinesis (mind–matter interaction, such as mentally causing coins to flip heads more often than tails) and extrasensory perception (ESP). ESP includes telepathy (information exchanged between two or more minds without the use of the ordinary senses), clairvoyance or remote viewing (information received from a distance, without using the ordinary senses), and precognition (information received about future events, where the information could not be inferred by ordinary means).

The Controversial Science

Few topics incite greater polarization of views than that of the validity of psi phenomena. Arguments for and against the existence of the paranormal have been recorded since at least the 1600s. The scientific study of psi phenomena is generally thought to have begun with the establishment of the Society for Psychical Research (SPR) in London in 1882. At the time, there was an explosion of interest throughout the Western world in paranormal phenomena associated with the emerging religion of Spiritualism. Séances involving alleged communication by mediums with spirits of the dead had become widespread. Much of the SPR's early work involved the investigation and exposure of fake spiritualist claims. But a number of mediums seemed consistently to produce convincing phenomena under what could be called experimental conditions.[1] The SPR also focused on the collection of carefully analyzed case studies of spontaneous experiences of the paranormal, such as telepathic communication in life-threatening situations. Psychologist J.B. Rhine is usually considered the father of modern experimental parapsychology, pioneering laboratory investigations of psi phenomena at Duke University in the 1930s. Rhine developed the now famous ESP card experiments and tested the effect of human intention on dice tossing. In both cases, Rhine found evidence in support of the psi hypothesis at levels well beyond chance expectations. New and increasingly sophisticated experimental designs, masses of empirical data, and a vast literature analyzing the results have since emerged. Several lines of research have demonstrated relatively consistent, statistically significant results in favor of the hypothesis.

Yet decisive progress toward a resolution of the debate has not occurred. Proponents tend to believe that the existence of psi phenomena has already been convincingly established. They argue that experimental parapsychology should now turn its attention to the task of better understanding the conditions that support or inhibit the expression of psi rather than attempt to accumulate more evidence that such phenomena exist. Skeptics, including a majority of the orthodox scientific community, maintain that the entire body of experimental evidence for psi can be explained away as methodological and statistical flaws or outright fraud. Why has it been so difficult to settle the question after more than 130 years of research and debate?

One of the most significant reasons is surely ideology. The psi hypothesis appears to contravene the materialistic and mechanistic assumptions of modern science. Many scientists view parapsychology as providing pseudo-scientific support for religion. They therefore routinely dismiss evidence in favor of the hypothesis a priori. French philosopher Edgar Morin (1991, cited in S. Kelly, nd) argued that intellectual paradigms are functionally equivalent to living organisms, being self-reproducing and self-maintaining. Like biological organisms, paradigms possess something like an immunological response that rejects ideas that threaten the core identity. The knee-jerk hostility toward parapsychology exhibited by many scientists indeed often seems more irrational prejudice than informed opinion. Consider the following statement about telepathy by Hermann von Helmholtz, a prominent German physicist and physician in the nineteenth century:

> I cannot believe it. Neither the testimony of all the Fellows of the Royal Society, nor even the evidence of my own senses would lead me to believe in the transmission of thought from one person to another independently of the recognized channels of sensation. It is clearly impossible. (cited in Griffin 1997, 26)

At the other end of the spectrum are extreme believers who seem to rush to embrace the reality of any number of exotic paranormal phenomena as a way to vindicate their personal religious or spiritual beliefs. Scientists are rightfully wary of the credulous attitude of many elements of the public toward such phenomena. Many extreme believers tend to stretch the implications of parapsychological research far beyond the limits of the actual empirical evidence. Professional parapsychologists occupy a sometimes-tenuous middle ground between these extremes.

It is doubtful, however, whether anyone approaches the topic from a purely neutral position. The question of psi phenomena touches on the most profound beliefs we hold about the nature of reality. Evidence that contradicts these beliefs can produce the distinctly uncomfortable experience of cognitive dissonance. According to social psychologist Leon Festinger's (1957) theory of cognitive dissonance, people will try to reduce dissonance by avoiding situations and information likely to increase it, seeking support from those with similar beliefs, or attempting to persuade others. Festinger's theory accounts well for why respectful, productive exchanges between proponents and skeptics of psi phenomena have been rare. It may be more difficult to maintain an open mind on the subject than most researchers and critics in the field care to admit. Furthermore, as psychologist Douglas Stokes (1997) points out, the tendency of people to conform to group opinion and to obey authority figures is well established by psychological experiments. Within the present academic community, as Stokes observes, these pressures are likely to strongly favor skepticism toward psi phenomena.

Apart from ideological and psychological factors, however, a major reason that parapsychological research remains controversial is that psi phenomena are not easily replicable on demand. It has therefore not been possible for parapsychologists to provide definitive laboratory or public demonstrations of psychic phenomena in a way that would satisfy critics. The debate has thus become centered on the question of statistical replication, which in essence means that studies show outcomes consistently above chance expectations. In recent decades, a technique known as meta-analysis has been used broadly in psychology and other sciences to more accurately review the combined data from multiple sets of similar experiments. As we will soon see, meta-analyses of several types of parapsychological experiments reveal statistically significant effects that seem quite reliable. Yet even the most robust lines of research show considerable variation across individual study outcomes. One of the reasons proposed for this variation is the "experimenter effect." For years it has been well known that certain experimenters manage to be consistently more successful than others at obtaining evidence in favor of psi. Not surprisingly, "successful" experimenters tend to have more positive attitudes toward psi phenomena than "unsuccessful" experimenters. Although there are several interpretations of the experimenter effect, of most interest for our purposes is the possibility that the experimenter is a source of unintentional psi that directly affects the experimental outcome. If "experimenter psi" is indeed a reality, it entails the radical epistemological implication that the successful replication of parapsychological experiments may *require* an experimenter with a psi-positive (or at least neutral) attitude.

Such an approach is obviously at odds with the traditional objectivist epistemology associated with science, in which results are usually seen as reliable only when they can be replicated by a researcher who is skeptical toward the hypothesis. Yet, in the context of parapsychological research, to apply an objectivist epistemology that assumes a fundamental separation between the mind of the researcher and the minds of the subjects is to prejudge exactly what is at issue. On the other hand, to adopt a participatory epistemology that acknowledges the possible role of the observer in influencing experimental outcomes can appear to critics to undermine the usual scientific basis for determining replicability. On this point, the debate seems to have reached an epistemological impasse. It cannot be resolved by an appeal to the normal evaluative procedures of science, for these are based on a particular paradigm, and that paradigm is now itself in question. As Thomas Kuhn pointed out, arguments across paradigms are inevitably circular, their authority ultimately only that of persuasion. Although arguments are still necessary and relevant, Kuhn noted that shifts in allegiance from one paradigm to another tend to be conversion experiences that cannot be forced. At the present time, the scientific evidence for parapsychology seems neither strong nor weak enough to inspire large-scale conversions by either skeptics or proponents respectively.

Before turning to the evidence itself, it will be helpful to address a common but misguided stereotype of parapsychology frequently accepted by orthodox scientists as conventional wisdom on the topic. That is the assumption that the only people who believe in the reality of psi phenomena are those who are poorly educated, highly gullible, or deficient in critical intelligence or integrity.[2] This view stems from the notion that belief in psi phenomena is a remnant of prescientific superstition and that, like other irrational ideas discarded by science, is now preserved only in the lower stratas of culture. However, as parapsychologist Dean Radin (2006) pointed out, numerous surveys demonstrate that although higher education is known to reduce belief in traditional religious concepts (such as heaven, hell, the devil, and creationism), it correlates with increased levels of belief in psi. In line with these findings, many well-known proponents of the psi hypothesis over the past 130 years have been public intellectuals of impeccable credentials and standing. Philosopher David Ray Griffin (1997) compiled a list of renowned psi proponents that includes: (among philosophers) Henri Bergson, Curt Ducasse, C.D. Broad, and Henry Sidgwick; (among psychologists) William James, Sigmund Freud, Carl Jung, William McDougall, and Pierre Janet; (among physicists) David Bohm, Sir William Crookes, Thomas Edison, Helmut Schmidt, Nobel Prize winner Lord Rayleigh, and Nobel Prize winner Brian Josephson; (among biologists) A.R. Wallace, Nobel Prize winner Claude Richet, and Nobel Prize winner Alexis Carrel; (among astronomers) Sir Arthur Eddington and Camile Flammarion (founder of the *Societe Astronomique de France*); (among writers) William Blake, Aldous Huxley, Thomas Mann, Mark Twain, and Upton Sinclair. This is clearly not a list of people lacking in education, social status, or critical reasoning abilities.

Evidence for Spontaneous Psi

Many people have had an odd experience or two that seem inexplicable within a conventional mechanistic understanding of reality. These experiences might take the form of a strikingly meaningful synchronicity, thinking of a friend just before he or she calls, having a strong intuition that a loved one is in danger, or other such phenomena. An example from my own life is a particularly vivid dream I had several months before my father was diagnosed with stage 4 melanoma cancer. In the dream my father looked directly at me with a troubled look on his face, as if to communicate that something was seriously wrong. He opened his mouth and blood trickled out. At the time of the dream my father showed no sign of illness. The fact that these kinds of experiences are so common is undoubtedly a major reason why nearly three-fourths of Americans polled by the Gallup organization in 2005 reported believing in some form of psi phenomena (Musella 2005).

Some incidents are especially compelling, such as the following one involving the nineteenth-century landscape painter Arthur Severn and his wife Joan:

> I [Joan] woke up with a start, feeling I had had a hard blow on my mouth, and with a distinct sense that I had been cut and was bleeding under my upper lip, and seized my pocket-handkerchief and held it to the part, as I sat up in bed, and after a few seconds when I removed it, I was astonished not to see any blood and only then realized it was impossible anything could have struck me there, as I lay fast asleep in bed and so I thought it was only a dream! But I looked at my watch, and saw it was seven, and finding Arthur was not in the room, I concluded (rightly) that he must have gone out on the lake for an early sail, as it was so fine. . . . At breakfast Arthur came in rather late and I noticed he rather purposely sat farther away from me than usual, and every now and then put his pocket-handkerchief furtively up to his lip, in the very way I had done. I said, "Arthur, why are you doing that?". . . .
>
> He said, "Well when I was sailing a sudden squall came, throwing the tiller suddenly around, and it struck me a bad blow in the mouth under the upper lip . . ." I said then, "Have you any idea what o'clock it was when it happened?" and he answered, "It must have been about seven." I then told what had happened to me, much to his surprise and all who were with us at breakfast. (Radin 1997, 23–24)

A number of researchers believe that spontaneous cases of psi phenomena are the natural subject matter of parapsychology. Certainly, the origin of psychical research stemmed from a desire to understand these anomalous experiences, and they continue to sustain interest in the discipline. It has often been pointed out that it is very difficult to reproduce in the laboratory the conditions involved in the spontaneous occurrence of psychic phenomena. For example, most of the reported cases of spontaneous telepathy involve crisis states in which a person is dying or in physical distress, scenarios that obviously cannot be duplicated in a laboratory. Geologist and parapsychology commentator Robert Schoch (Schoch and Yonavjak 2008) notes that many aspects of nature are not reducible to laboratory settings, including volcanoes, meteorites, quasars, and planetary nebulae. Although some components of these phenomena can be studied in a laboratory, to understand them more completely requires that someone be in the right place when the event occurs in nature. Similarly, although psi phenomena may be glimpsed in the laboratory, we must look to spontaneous cases for a more holistic view of the subject.

One of the main projects of the early researchers associated with the SPR was the collection and analysis of spontaneous cases, summarized in the classic *Phantasms of the Living*. The original volume of *Phantasms* includes 702 case reports. The heart of this volume is a collection of "crisis apparitions"—putative telepathic visions and intuitions experienced by a "receiver" or "percipient" in conjunction with a crisis situation, often death or distress, experienced by a "sender." Critics often object that spontaneous cases can be explained away as instances of faulty memory, psychosis, imagination, coincidence, or simple fabrication. To counter these criticisms, the authors of *Phantasms* invested great effort in examining and verifying the authenticity of each case reported in the work. Psychiatrist Ian Stevenson (1970) took a similar rigorous approach in his *Telepathic Impressions*, an analysis of 195 spontaneous cases of telepathy. Stevenson developed the following criteria for inclusion:

1. The percipient has a strong feeling about a distant person that closely corresponds to that person's situation at that time, without any normal way of knowing about it.

2. The percipient reports this feeling to someone else or takes some appropriate action, and this fact is independently corroborated.

3. The percipient's statement or action was unusual, thereby not interpretable as simply one of many that happened this time to correspond to reality.

The following report from *Telepathic Impressions* provides an example of a case that met these criteria:

> Around the middle of June 1964, Linda and I decided to visit the Travis' [sic] to congratulate them on their new child. After supper we put the children to bed and we asked Linda's grand-mother to babysit for a while.
>
> We arrived there and Paul Travis fixed our drinks. As he was showing me the blueprints of his new house I stopped and had a feeling as if something bad had happened at home, the nature of which I was not aware.
>
> I asked Linda to call home. She said: "I will in a few minutes." I said: "You'd better call now. Something is wrong."
>
> Linda went into the bedroom where the phone was and I followed and my feelings were then of distress. Our . . . neigh-bor answered the phone. Both children were screaming in the background. She informed us that Linda's grandmother had hurt her back just a few minutes earlier and [that] the children were so frightened. . . .
>
> We arrived home and the neighbor met us at the door, saying that Linda's grandmother had called upon her after she hurt her back. Scott, my son, was frantic and refused to go to Linda and clutched me for comfort. What is surprising about this incident is the sudden feeling of distress and my insistence on Linda to call home and my premonition that something bad [had] happened. (Stevenson 1970, 49–50)

The percipient's wife corroborated the report. She said that her hus-band had never previously shown strong anxiety about something being wrong at home and had never previously asked her to telephone a babysitter while they were away.

It is frequently argued that although any given case of spontaneous psi phenomena, such as the one just described, can be countered by skeptical explanations, these explanations become less plausible in relation to the entire body of spontaneous case material. Louisa Rhine, wife and colleague of J.B. Rhine (the "father" of experimental parapsychology), contributed more than anyone else to amassing evidence of spontaneous psi and her case collection remains the largest in history. L. Rhine (1961) adopted a strategy of accepting cases more or less on face value and then analyzing them for common patterns. Her assumption was that patterns emerging from a large number of cases were likely to reflect the genuine nature of psi phenom-ena because spurious cases based on individual fantasies or untruths would fall outside the patterns and become eliminated from further study. Over a thirty-five-year period, Rhine gathered more than thirty thousand spontaneous cases from individuals around the world from diverse backgrounds in age, sex, culture, religion, and socioeconomic status. She categorized telepathic experiences into three major modes: hallucinatory experiences, intuitive experiences, and dreams. Hallucinatory experiences are telepathic visions of remote people or events that occur while the individual is awake. Intuitive experiences also occur in the waking state and usually involve a feeling that something is wrong at a distant location. Dreams were subdivided into "realistic" dreams that involve a mostly literal account of the confirming event and "unrealistic" dreams in which events are represented symbolically.

Dutch parapsychologist Sybo Schouten (1979, 1981, 1982) compared Rhine's collection with that of the British Society for Psychical Research, and with a German collection compiled by a group associated with the University of Freiburg. Despite the broad range of populations involved, Schouten found a remarkable degree of consistency in the case reports. Some of the more notable patterns revealed by his and other analyses include the following:

- Dreams are the most commonly occurring type, with one analysis showing them responsible for about 65 percent of the experiences. About one-fourth of the cases were intuitive experiences, and the remaining 10 percent were hallucinations.

- Dreams tend to be precognitive, whereas waking experiences (hallucinatory and intuitive experiences) more often relate to contemporaneous events.

- Dreams typically contain more detail about the event than do intuitive experiences, but intuitive experiences tend to involve a greater sense of conviction that the experience refers to a real event and are more likely to lead to the percipient taking some sort of action related to the event.

- Cases of all types usually relate to events occurring to members of the percipient's immediate family rather than events occurring to strangers or casual acquaintances.

- Events perceived telepathically are mostly negative ones involving death or serious injury to a close family member.

- Many more women than men report having telepathic experiences (see Stokes 1997, 78).

The existence of these consistent, cross-cultural patterns across several large case collections supports the reliability of the overall data set. This conclusion is bolstered by analyses that demonstrate correlations between spontaneous cases of psi and certain natural phenomena, connections one would not expect if the reports were simply fabrications. For example, in analyzing several case collections, neuroscience researcher Michael Persinger found global geomagnetic activity to be lower than usual on days of reported telepathic experiences but higher than usual on days of reported poltergeist activity (see Persinger and Gearhart, 1986; Persinger, 1987). One of Persinger's hypotheses is that geomagnetic activity may enhance the receptivity of the brain to extrasensory signals, noting that sudden decreases in geomagnetic activity may decrease the likelihood of certain kinds of electrical seizures in the brain. As Schoch and Yonavjack (2008) point out, these findings support the view that the overall body of evidence for spontaneous psi is genuine, "unless one wants to suggest that hoaxes of telepathy are more likely to take place on days of low levels of geomagnetic activity, whereas days of high geomagnetic activity tend to inspire poltergeist hoaxes" (64–65).

Nonetheless, most parapsychologists today believe that the anecdotal evidence of spontaneous psi by itself cannot conclusively establish the existence of psi phenomena. A resolute skeptic is usually able to reject all such reports on the basis of coincidence, unreliable memory, delusion, or fraud. Yet a summary dismissal of the entire body of spontaneous evidence seems unjustified. Many of the skeptical counter-explanations proposed for spontaneous reports themselves appear highly improbable. For example, as Broughton (1991) points out, the argument that spontaneous cases can be explained as chance coincidences is highly implausible in relation to experiences involving hallucinations or remote psychosomatic pain, as in the case of Arthur and Joan Severn described earlier. As Stokes (1997) argues in relation to a similar case, it is surely unreasonable to maintain that people are experiencing invisible blows to the mouth all the time and that one of these occasions is bound to coincide with an actual blow to the mouth of a member of one's immediate family! A number of commentators have indicated that they are ultimately more convinced of the authenticity of psi phenomena by spontaneous cases than by experimental studies (e.g., White 1992; Alvarado 1996; Stokes 1997; Schoch and Yonavjak 2008). Spontaneous cases should thus be seen as a significant strand of evidence in their own right that supplements the experimental evidence from laboratory studies.

Experimental Evidence of Psi Phenomena

Parapsychologists turned to experimental studies largely as a way to address skeptical explanations of spontaneous phenomena, especially the objection that such cases are simply chance occurrences. Readers familiar with the field will be aware that there is a vast literature concerning attempts to establish the reality of psi phenomena through laboratory studies. Informed commentators generally accept that compelling evidence has been demonstrated in several lines of psi research that cannot be ascribed to chance alone. Debate continues about the interpretation and replicability of these results, but not, for the most part, about whether anomalous effects have been found. The following discussion features several of the more prominent studies in the field.

J.B. RHINE'S PEARCE-PRATT SERIES

Although John Coover conducted experimental investigations of ESP at Stanford University in 1917, Duke University psychology professor J.B. Rhine is generally credited with launching modern parapsychology. In the late 1920s, Rhine developed a simple card-guessing procedure to test the ESP hypothesis. The experiments involved a special deck of twenty-five cards consisting of five groups of five symbols (square, circle, wavy lines, star, and triangle). A "sender" selected a card and attempted to mentally "send" that symbol to a receiver in a remote location who tried to guess which type of card had been selected. This procedure was repeated twenty-five times, resulting in twenty-five guesses whose accuracy was compared with chance expectation of five correct guesses. The participants were shielded from the target cards to rule out the possibility of sensory access to the symbols. By August 1933, Rhine had conducted 85,724 trials with an average score of 7.1 correct guesses per 25 guesses. Although this might not appear to be a large effect, the odds that such a result could occur by chance are statistically minute (J. Rhine 1964).

The Pearce-Pratt series is one of the most frequently cited individual experiments from the Rhine era. It represents the methodological culmination of Rhine's early attempts to obtain laboratory evidence for ESP. To exclude all possibilities of error, the series implemented special precautions that included two experimenter controls, randomization of the card-selection procedure, independent records, and the receiver being in a different building several hundred yards from the handler of the target cards. The results from 1,850 individual trials showed 558 hits, amounting to 188 hits above chance expectation, for an average hit rate of 7.54 per 25 guesses, where 5 would be expected by chance. The odds of this result occurring by chance were astronomically small (Rhine and Pratt 1954).

Skeptical psychologist Mark Hansel (1966, 1980) published a critique of the series in which he argued that, although he accepted the outcome could not be explained by chance, it was conceivable that the participant could have cheated. Hansel described several imaginary scenarios, including

one where the participant drills a hole in the trap door in the ceiling, and
then later fills in the hole without being seen, to enable access to sensory
information of the target cards. Yet there was never any evidence of cheating
by the participant. As psychologist K. Ramakrishna Rao (2002) points out,
the implausible scenarios made up by Hansel demonstrate that a determined
skeptic "can always draw attention to certain features of an experiment to
make it look less than definitive" (76).

HELMUT SCHMIDT'S PRECOGNITION REG EXPERIMENTS

In the 1960s, physicist Helmut Schmidt developed a special machine to test
precognition in a way that controlled against all known experimental arti-
facts, such as recording errors, sensory cues, subject cheating, and improper
analysis of data. The "Schmidt machine" featured a panel of four differently
colored light bulbs. The bulbs were randomly lit by a random event gen-
erator (REG) that used the radioactive decay of strontium 90, a quantum
process that is in principle unpredictable under modern theories of physics.
Participants were asked to select which of the four lamps would light and
to press the corresponding button in front of the chosen bulb. After the
individual had made the selection, the REG would cause one of the bulbs to
light. The individual's guesses and the bulbs actually lit were automatically
recorded, eliminating the possibility of human recording errors. All three
of Schmidt's experiments gave highly significant results suggesting ESP on
the part of the participants. In the first experiment, the three participants
performed 63,066 trials and scored 691.5 more hits than would be expected
by chance (or 26.1 percent, where chance expectation was 25 percent). The
probability that such a result could occur by chance was calculated as less
than two in a billion (Rao 2002, 78).

MAIMONEDES DREAM TELEPATHY STUDIES

As noted earlier, dreams account for 65 percent of spontaneous psi experiences, according to some analyses. In the 1960s, psychiatrist Montague Ull-
man and other researchers used the Maimonedes Dream Research Laboratory
in Brooklyn, New York to test whether thoughts and images could be transmitted telepathically to someone while they were asleep and dreaming. In a
typical "dream telepathy" experiment, a receiver slept overnight in a dream
laboratory, while a remote sender attempted to telepathically send images
of a randomly assigned target picture to the receiver with the aim of influencing the receiver's dream. Toward the end of each rapid eye movement
period (the receiver was monitored for brain waves and eye movements), a
third person would awaken the receiver and ask him or her to describe any

dreams he or she could remember. The receiver's descriptions were recorded and later analyzed by a group of independent judges. The judges compared the receiver's description of his or her dream with a number of pictures including the target image (the judges were blind as to which picture was the target). The judges would rank the pictures, say from one to eight, with the picture that most fit the description of the dream being ranked No. 1. If the judges ranked the actual target picture in the top half of the list (one through four) the result was considered a hit. The hit rate was then compared with the expected chance hit rate of 50 percent.

Independent analysis of the overall results of the Maimonedes group over a ten-year testing period concluded that the dream reports were clearly more similar to the target pictures than the controls to a statistically significant degree (Child 1985). A meta-analysis of 450 Maimonedes ESP trials revealed an average overall hit rate of 63 percent, with odds against chance of 75 million to 1 (see Radin 1997, 71–72).

GANZFELD STUDIES

Evidence from spontaneous case collections suggests that if telepathy occurs, it occurs most often when the receiver is in an altered or relaxed state and the sender is experiencing an emotional crisis (Parker 2003, 116). In the 1970s, researchers attempted to replicate these conditions by placing the receiver in a hypnotic-like state while the sender viewed emotionally engaging video clips. The procedure they developed involved the use of a sensory-reduction method called the *ganzfeld technique* that had been developed by psychologists early in the twentieth century.[3] The ganzfeld condition is created by placing ping poll ball halves over each eye of the subject, while simultaneously shining a soft red light on his or her face and playing white noise (like the static between radio stations) on headphones. Most participants report experiencing mild visual and auditory hallucinations within a few minutes. Once a receiver is placed in the ganzfeld condition, a typical test involves a remote sender viewing a randomly selected video clip and attempting mentally to send the image to the receiver. The receiver speaks aloud his or her mental impressions, which are recorded. The receiver is then presented with a selection of pictures containing the target image and three decoys. The hit rate expected by chance is thus 25 percent.

In 1985, parapsychologist Charles Honorton and skeptical psychologist Ray Hyman independently published meta-analyses of twenty-eight published ganzfeld studies from ten different laboratories. They both found a combined hit rate of 37 percent (compared with the 25 percent that would be expected by chance) with enormous odds against chance. Hyman conceded that there was an overall significant effect that could not reasonably be explained by "selective reporting,"[4] but claimed that the effect might be due to certain flaws in the experimental design. So Hyman and Honorton (1986) published a joint communiqué in which they specified the standards that future ganzfeld experiments should follow. Honorton then conducted a six-year ganzfeld research program that implemented the new design protocol. The results from more than 354 sessions found a combined hit rate of 34 percent, with odds against chance of 45,000 to 1 (Bem and Honorton 1994). However, psychologists Julie Milton and Richard Wiseman (1999) performed a meta-analysis of thirty additional ganzfeld studies published after Honorton's study and found the combined hit rate did not differ significantly from chance, thus throwing into doubt whether the ganzfeld method was replicable. Subsequently Daryl Bem, John Palmer, and Richard Broughton (2001) analyzed ten additional experiments published after Milton and Wiseman's review. With the addition of the ten extra studies, the meta-analysis again revealed a statistically significant effect, although smaller than the one found in the earlier studies. The authors noted, however, that a number of studies included in the updated database (comprising the experiments analyzed by Milton and Wiseman and the ten additional studies considered by the authors) appeared to differ significantly from the Hyman-Honorton standard protocol. So they recruited independent researchers to carry out blind ratings of the degree to which studies since the Honorton-Hyman joint communiqué deviated from the new standard ganzfeld procedure. They then compared the statistical significance of standard versus nonstandard studies. The results showed that studies that followed the standard protocol demonstrated statistically significant effect sizes comparable with the earlier studies. A subsequent meta-analysis by Radin of all eighty-eight ganzfeld experiments conducted from 1974 to 2004 supported these findings, revealing a combined hit rate of 32 percent (compared with the chance-expected 25 percent), and very large odds against chance (Radin 2006, 120).

REMOTE-VIEWING STUDIES

Remote-viewing experiments are similar to ganzfeld experiments except that receivers are not placed in the ganzfeld condition of sensory isolation and the description is predominantly drawn instead of spoken. In a typical experiment, a receiver is isolated in a sensory-shielded room in a laboratory. At a prearranged time, an assistant at a distant location randomly selects a photograph from a large predefined set of possible target images. The receiver spends the next fifteen to twenty minutes trying to describe the target, using sketches and narratives. After the receiver has finished the description, he or she is shown the target photograph for feedback. After a series of sessions has been completed, an independent judge compares the receiver's sketch and narrative description with a set of five photographs including the target and five decoys. The judge ranks each of the photographs according to how closely they match the receiver's description, with a ranking of one denoting the closest match. The results are compared with what would be expected by chance.

The largest series of remote-viewing experiments was conducted by a program initiated in the early 1970s by various US government agencies interested in the potential use of psi capacities for intelligence and defense purposes. From 1973 to 1988 the program was based at the Stanford Research Institute (SRI). In 1990, the program moved to a think-tank called Science Applications International Corporation (SAIC). A meta-analysis conducted by May and others (1988) reviewed the results of 154 experiments at SRI from 1973 to 1988 involving more than 26,000 separate trials (these included both forced-choice experiments like ESP card tests as well as free-response tests like the remote-viewing experiment as just described). The statistical results were overwhelmingly significant. The overall effect size for novice remote viewers was small at 0.164, although for experienced remote viewers effect size was significantly higher at 0.385. Interestingly, the analysis showed that psi performance among a small group of selected individuals far exceeded the performance of unselected volunteers, with 1 percent of remote viewers found to be consistently successful. This latter result is important evidence against the charge that design flaws could be responsible for the positive results, for if design flaws were the only cause of the outcome, one would expect the performance of all participants to be relatively consistent.

In 1995, the US government commissioned statistician Jessica Utts and psychologist Ray Hyman to review the remote viewing research at SAIC. Utts concluded:

> It is clear to this author that anomalous cognition is possible and has been demonstrated. . . . No one who has examined all of the data across laboratories, taken as a collective whole, has been able to suggest methodological or statistical problems to explain the ever-increasing and consistent results to date. (1995, 310)

Hyman, a long-term skeptic of parapsychology research, agreed with Utts:

> the effect sizes reported in the SAIC experiments and in the recent ganzfeld studies probably cannot be dismissed due to chance. Nor do they appear to be accounted for by multiple testing, file drawer distortions, inappropriate statistical testing or

other misuse of statistical inference. . . . So I accept Professor
Utts' assertion that the statistical results of the SAIC and other
parapsychologists' experiments "are far beyond what is expected
by chance." (1996, 39)

Discussion of Experimental Psi Research

As can be seen from this brief review, several lines of experimental research
have demonstrated results consistent with the psi hypothesis to a degree
well beyond what would be expected by chance alone. Informed skeptics
generally do not contest this conclusion.[5] Although it is beyond the scope
of this book to survey the detailed debate about alleged design flaws in psi
experiments, it should be pointed out that several meta-analyses of the principal lines of investigation have shown that, contrary to the expectations
of skeptics, improvements in methodological controls have not resulted in
lower scores (Radin 1997).

Arguably the main (rational) obstacle to scientific acceptance of parapsychological evidence has been the difficulty encountered by researchers in
consistently replicating successful results. Yet a number of parapsychological
experiments have clearly been replicated to a certain degree. The strongest
candidate for a reliable psi experiment is the ganzfeld procedure, especially
where it follows the standard protocol as outlined by Hyman and Honorton.
There has been a broad range of replications of the ganzfeld experiment
over thirty-five years involving almost ninety studies at some dozen different laboratories, showing a relatively robust and consistent effect among
studies that follow the standard protocol. Various investigators have also
successfully replicated dream telepathy (Sherwood and Roe 2003), REG
(Jahn 1982; Nelson, Dunne, and Jahn 1984), and remote-viewing (Jahn
and Dunne 1987) experiments. Yet no psi experiment has achieved universal replicability, where successful results can be reliably reproduced by
anyone, anywhere. It is apparent that psi effects, if real, are delicate and
complex phenomena that require very particular conditions to manifest in
the laboratory.

It should be noted that the difficulty in achieving strong replicability
is not unique to parapsychology, but is becoming an increasingly widespread
issue in cutting-edge scientific research in general. The problem is especially
acute in the behavioral sciences, where precise duplication of conditions
in two different experiments is almost impossible to attain. Psychologist
Seymour Epstein (1980) described the dilemma of conventional psychology
in *American Psychologist*, the leading journal of the American Psychological
Association:

Psychological research is rapidly approaching a crisis as the result
of extremely inefficient procedures for establishing replicable
generalizations. The traditional solution of attempting to obtain
a high degree of control in the laboratory is often ineffective
because much human behavior is so sensitive to incidental sources
of information that adequate control cannot be achieved. . . . Not
only are experimental findings often difficult to replicate when
there are the slightest alterations in conditions, but even attempts
at exact replication frequently fail. (790)

Recently, scientists have begun to express significant concern about
the unreliability of experimental results in the *physical* sciences. A 2014
article in *The New York Times* by science writer George Johnson begins:

Replication, the ability of another lab to reproduce a finding, is
the gold standard of science, reassurance that you have discovered
something true. But that is getting harder all the time. With the
most accessible truths already discovered, what remains are often
subtle effects, some so delicate that they can be conjured up only
under ideal circumstances, using highly specialized techniques.
(Johnson 2014, para. 2)

As an example, Johnson cites Mina Bissell, a cancer researcher at
Lawrence Berkeley National Laboratory. In an article in the prominent science journal *Nature*, Bissell (2013) responded to the charge that biologists
are frequently unable to repeat each other's experiments, even when using
the same materials and methods. She writes:

[I]t is sometimes much easier not to replicate than to replicate
studies, because the techniques and reagents are sophisticated,
time-consuming, and difficult to master. . . .
     Many scientists use epithelial cell lines that are exquisitely
sensitive. The slightest shift in their microenvironment can alter
the results—something a newcomer might not spot. It is common for even a seasoned scientist to struggle with cell lines and
culture conditions, and unknowingly introduce changes that will
make it seem that a study cannot be reproduced. (paras. 3, 5)

C. Glenn Begley and L. Ellis (2012) reported in *Nature* that they and
their colleagues from the biotechnology firm Amgen could not replicate
forty-seven of fifty-three landmark cancer studies. Some of the results could

not be reproduced even with the help of the original scientists working in their own labs.[6] And in a leading article in *Forbes* magazine published in early 2014, biomedical scientist Henry Miller claims that several empirical studies show that 80 to 90 percent of the results coming from supposedly scientific studies in major journals fail to replicate (Miller 2014).

These findings provide a broader context for understanding the challenges involved in reproducing the results of parapsychological experiments. If psi effects are real, they are clearly subtle behavioral phenomena that may be sensitive to very small changes in experimental conditions. To withhold scientific acceptance until psi has been demonstrated to be universally reliable is likely to set an unrealistic standard that can never be attained.

Compounding matters are the unique epistemological issues involved in psi research and consciousness studies in general. As consciousness researchers from William James to Francisco Varela have pointed out, consciousness is not a phenomenon that easily lends itself to objective analysis, because the investigators themselves are not separate from the phenomenon being studied. In psi research, the very issue in question is whether human minds are nonlocally connected; thus, as noted earlier, to demand that results be universally repeatable irrespective of the attitudes and expectations of the experimenter is effectively to prejudge the question in dispute. It is in fact the case that the results of psi studies show clear differences between research teams, with much of the success achieved by experimenters known to be open to the possibility of psi effects.[7] Although these results raise suspicions among critics of experimenter error or fraud, the differences can also be explained in terms of experimenter psi, that is, "unintentional psi which affects an experimental outcome in ways that are directly related to the experimenter's needs, wishes, expectancies, moods, etc" (Kennedy and Taddonio 1976). The possibility that the experimenter may exert a psi influence over the data is, of course, not only plausible, but likely if the psi hypothesis is valid. The notion of experimenter psi raises broader questions about the nature of psi-conducive conditions generally, including whether the current epistemological assumptions of orthodox science may themselves be psi-inhibitory.

The combined results of psi studies involving meditation, hypnosis, relaxation, and the ganzfeld method strongly suggest that psi, if real, is a subtle signal whose detection is enhanced by reducing the "noise" produced by sensorimotor activity (Rao 2002). Other studies indicate that individuals who believe ESP to be possible tend to score higher than those who do not (the "sheep-goat" effect) (Palmer 1971, 1972; Schmeidler and McConnell 1973; Lawrence 1993), and that mutually positive attitudes between experimenters and participants are associated with highly significant positive results, whereas mutually negative attitudes between experimenters and participants correlate with significant negative results (Anderson and White 1956). Putting these elements together—a quiet mind, an open attitude, an ambiance of mutual positive regard between teacher and student—the conditions conducive to psi start to resemble the circumstances of a spiritual community engaged in meditative exercises. This resemblance makes sense when considering the widely held notion that the practice of spiritual disciplines like yoga and meditation can enable one to develop psychic capacities. These disciplines train the mind to attend to increasingly subtle aspects of experience, while dissolving the defensive postures and attitudes that keep the individual separated from deeper states of unitive awareness—states commonly reported to be highly permeable to the flow of nonlocal phenomena. In this light, the clinical setting of the laboratory, and a researcher's attempts to be "scientific" by adopting an "objective" stance toward the hypothesis, can be seen as probable psi-inhibitory factors. An open mind and a trusting heart among both experimenters and participants may be the equivalent of Galileo's telescope as some of the "instruments" necessary for the disclosure of knowledge in the domain of psi experience.

The possibility that the manifestation of psi phenomena may be connected to the attitudes and expectations of participants and experimenters exposes an inescapable tension between the objectivist epistemology of modern science and a participatory epistemology that appears to be emerging in psi research and other fields. An analogy can be made with cultural anthropology, which for decades has incorporated the concept of "participation observation" in its approach to ethnographic fieldwork. Participation observation is a method of data collection where the researcher attempts to develop an intimate familiarity with the social group he or she is observing by cultivating personal relationships with group members and participating in the group's social life (Kawulich 2005). The rationale is that only by taking part in the cultural matrix of the group can the researcher gain genuine access to the subject being studied. Consciousness-based phenomena like psi are arguably in a similar category, with their most intimate secrets revealed only to those researchers willing to participate directly in the subject under investigation.

Applying a participatory epistemology to psi research entails accepting, as parapsychologist Adrian Parker (2003) suggests, that "experimenter effects and psi-conduciveness are every bit as integral a part of the phenomena being studied as, say placebo effects are in psychological treatment" (p. 127). For Parker, embracing the reality of experimenter effects implies the need to develop more adventurous approaches to the design of psi studies:

> Experimenters with charisma and charm rather than psychology degrees could be employed to run the testing sessions whereas those with doctoral degrees retain responsibility for seeing that

the formal controls inbuilt in the procedure are followed and ensure that the ethical standards for interactions are met. (129)

What this discussion points to is the need for psi research to embrace multiple modes of knowing. Within the experimental sessions themselves, the cultivation of an atmosphere of trust in deeper dimensions of reality and in the possibility of something "magical" or "miraculous" taking place might greatly facilitate the appearance of psi phenomena. In the presession design and postsession analysis, more conventional rational modes of thought could predominate. As in participation observation in anthropological research, the ability of the psi researcher to maintain a balance between "insider" and "outsider" roles may be essential for the production of grounded knowledge in parapsychological studies. To combine in one approach an epistemology of trust and participation with one of critical rationality and discernment would clearly be a delicate operation, involving the risk that either mode of knowing might erode the integrity of the other. Yet nothing less than this degree of epistemological integration may be required to unlock the mystery of nonlocal mind–mind and mind–matter interactions.

DISTANT HEALING

Laboratory Studies

Distant healing has been defined as "a conscious, dedicated act of mentation attempting to benefit another person's physical or emotional well being at a distance" (Sicher et al. 1998, 357). This definition includes intercessory prayer (prayer for the benefit of another) and various other forms of spiritual healing. Anecdotes of distant healing are, of course, as old as humanity, with most indigenous cultures regarding spiritual healing as a natural fact of life, and, in the West, exemplified most famously by the stories of the healing miracles performed by Jesus. In the modern scientific tradition, research began in earnest in the 1960s with the pioneering work of psychologists Lawrence LeShan and Bernard Grad. One of Grad's earliest experiments tested the effect of human intention on the healing of plants. Experimenters deliberately damaged barley seeds by watering them with a saline solution. A healer held the beaker containing the saline solution and transmitted to it a healing intention before it was poured onto seeds in the experimental group. Seeds in the control group were watered by a beaker untouched by the healer. The experiment was repeated three times with similar results: The "treated" seeds grew faster than the untreated ones, with odds against chance of more than one thousand to one (Tart 2009, 173–174). Remote human intention has been shown to significantly influence the growth of fungus cultures (Barry 1968), bacteria cultures (Nash 1982), and yeast (Haraldsson and Thorsteinsson 1966). In nineteen of twenty-one experiments, the mental intention of healers was significantly correlated with the earlier recovery of mice from general anesthesia (Benor 2001, 312–316). Distant intention also has been found to have a significant effect on the rate of hemolysis of human red blood cells in test tubes (Braud 1988).

In the field of distant healing (as in most areas of medical science), there is no one "killer" study that has definitively established the phenomenon beyond doubt. Rather, it is only through the tying together of many strands of evidence that a convincing case can be built. Unlike many psi experiments, however, distant healing studies often do not lend themselves to meta-analytic review because there is usually too wide a variety between the types of healing interventions used and the healing outcomes measured to directly compare and combine data. Thus, systematic reviews of distant healing typically take the form of presenting examples of leading studies and adding up the number of statistically significant studies.[8]

Daniel Benor (2001) reviewed 191 controlled studies of distant healing and found that 124 (or almost two-thirds) of the studies demonstrated statistically significant effects. Of the fifty studies judged to be of excellent methodological quality, thirty-eight (or 76 percent) showed significant effects. In a comprehensive review of the quality of research on distant healing, Crawford, Jonas, and Sparber (2003) examined forty-five laboratory studies that met their inclusion criteria (which included the existence of randomization techniques, control interventions such as placebos, and publication in peer-review journals) and found quality scores ranging from 73 to 95 percent out of a maximum of twenty-two quality variables, with a mean score of 82 percent, indicating a generally very high quality for such studies.

Clinical Studies

Clinical trials involving distant healing on human patients have produced more ambiguous results. Several early studies resulted in significant outcomes. Randolph Byrd (1988) found that patients in a coronary care unit who were prayed for daily (by a group of devout Christians) scored significantly better than a control group on various global measures of progress, such as number of cardiac arrests, incidences of pneumonia, and need for antibiotics and diuretics. William Harris and his colleagues (1999) recorded similar results with another group of patients admitted to a coronary care unit. The experimental group that received prayers from a team of healers scored about 10 percent better than the control group on a global medical score summarized from a blinded, retrospective chart review at the end of each patient's stay. Sicher et al. (1998) found that AIDS patients who received distant healing for ten weeks from a team of healers of various traditions acquired significantly fewer new illnesses, had lower illness severity, significantly better reported moods, required fewer doctor visits, and had fewer days in the hospital than a control group.

However, two large, well-designed distant healing studies in the first decade of the 2000s showed no significant differences between experimental and control groups across most outcomes. In 2005, Mitchell Krucoff, a cardiovascular specialist at Duke University School of Medicine, designed a study involving nine medical centers in which all cardiac patients in the intervention group received prayers, with a subgroup receiving an extra "dose" of prayers from a second team of healers who prayed for the effectiveness of the prayers of the first team. No significant differences were found between the experimental and control groups, although recipients of the "double-dose" of prayers showed a positive trend on three of four outcomes at the six-month follow-up period. In 2006, Harvard professor Herbert Benson and others examined the effect of prayer on cardiac patients in six hospitals. Patients were randomly assigned to an experimental group (members of which received intercessory prayers from three Christian groups), a control group, and a third group whose members were told that they would receive prayer, but no prayers were in fact administered to them. At the six-month follow-up period no significant differences were found on any of the three specified outcomes (mortality, complications, and major events) between the experimental and control groups, with the third set of patients, who only believed they were being prayed for, showing negative outcomes.

However we might interpret these contrasting results, numerous commentators have highlighted important methodological issues inherent to distant healing clinical studies that may make it impossible to draw firm conclusions from the research. The primary issue is that it is virtually impossible in clinical studies to create a "pure" control group because patients in any control group have friends and/or family who will likely pray for them, especially if their condition is serious. As Targ and Thomson (1997) point out, in a hypothetical experiment to test the effect of prayer on a group of sick children "a woman 10,000 miles away praying for her sick baby 'and all other sick children' would contaminate any control group" (95). A distant healing study is therefore more likely to be a test of the amount or dosage of prayer—yet there is no reason to assume that with prayer, more is better. A related problem is that there is no way to be sure what "dose" of prayer has been applied because it is impossible to measure the quality or power of the prayers being offered. A spontaneous heartfelt prayer offered by a loved one might well have a greater effect than a standard prayer recited mechanically by a stranger, yet there is no way to monitor such qualitative differences in a distant healing study. Of course, these methodological issues cut both ways in the sense that neither studies showing significant effects nor those showing no effects can be taken to have conclusively determined the issue, because of the potential confounding factors just listed. As Larry Dossey (1997) suggests, to avoid these problems, distant healing research may need to focus predominantly on patients with modest health problems (because those with life-threatening conditions are more likely to have people praying for them) and easier-to-control laboratory studies of lower organisms.[9]

IMPLICATIONS OF PSI AND DISTANT HEALING RESEARCH FOR SUBTLE ACTIVISM

The results from distant healing laboratory research and several major lines of parapsychological studies, combined with the evidence from large case collections of spontaneous psi, suggest that nonlocal awareness is possible and has been demonstrated, at least for those willing to approach the data with an open mind. This evidence creates a prima facie case for consciousness being an irreducible feature of reality that is fundamentally nonlocal in nature. As such, psi and distant healing research provides support for the "strong" version of the subtle activism hypothesis, which emphasizes the nonlocal, field-like aspects of consciousness as the means by which certain consciousness-based practices might produce social benefits. If one individual can mentally transmit an image or thought to another—as apparently confirmed by the ganzfeld and dream telepathy experiments—it follows that many thousands of people simultaneously holding in their awareness an uplifting image (such as a world at peace) might have a subtle positive effect on society by transmitting to many others peaceful thoughts and feelings that presumably could lead to more peaceful decisions and actions. Nonetheless, most psi and distant healing studies have not specifically examined the potential social effects of consciousness-based practices. We now consider an important series of studies that has engaged directly with this issue.

THE MAHARISHI EFFECT

In the early 1960s, Maharishi Mahesh Yogi, founder of the TM movement, predicted that if as little as 1 percent of the population practiced TM, they would create an influence of harmony throughout the entire society. In the mid-1970s, with the introduction of the more advanced TM-Sidhi meditation technique and the discovery of the greater potency of group meditations, the prediction was amended: If just the square root of 1 percent of a population practiced the TM-Sidhi program in a group setting, they would have a measurable positive effect on the whole society. This formula came to be known as the "Maharishi Effect." It has been extensively tested in research spanning thirty years. As noted in chapter 2, twenty-eight studies on the Maharishi Effect have been published in academic journals, and another eighteen in research anthologies (Orme-Johnson nd-a). The results have consistently shown highly significant correlations between the practice of the TM-Sidhi program in large-group settings and improvements in a broad range of social indicators, including crime rates, auto accidents, fires, war deaths. The following sections summarize the evidence from a number of landmark studies in the series.[10,11]

Early Research: The "1 Percent" Cities

The research began in 1976 with a study by Borland and Landrith, who examined FBI statistics of yearly crime rates for eleven cities in the United States in which the number of people practicing TM had surpassed 1 percent of the total city population. "Practicing TM" meant that individuals were meditating twice a day for twenty minutes each session, usually in their own homes. Crime rates were chosen as a rough but accessible measure of social coherence. Borland and Landrith (1976) also examined crime rate statistics in eleven other cities chosen for their resemblance to the "1 percent cities" in population, region of the country, college population, and previous crime rates. From 1972 (the year the total number of meditators first surpassed 1 percent of the population in the experimental cities) to 1973 the crime rate increased in the "control" cities by an average of 8.3 percent, following the national average, whereas in the 1 percent cities, crime rates were found to decrease on average by 8.2 percent. The likelihood that this result occurred by chance was calculated at less than one in one thousand.

The first study published by an academic journal was by Dillbeck et al. (1981), who built on the Borland and Landrith study by including an additional thirteen smaller 1 percent cities (the first study had only included cities with populations exceeding 25,000) and by controlling for a number of factors known to influence crime that were not taken into account in the earlier study. An independent consultant selected the twenty-four control cities based on their statistical resemblance to the 1 percent cities in demographic variables known to influence crime rates, including population, population density per square mile, unemployment rate, income, median years of education, percentage change in residence each year, percentage of families below the poverty level, and percentage of people aged 15 to 29. The study found that, even after these factors were taken into account, the experimental effect reported in the original study remained: From 1972 to 1973, average crime rates in the control cities continued to climb, whereas average crime rates in the 1 percent cities dropped significantly. The study further found that average crime rates in the 1 percent cities continued to be significantly lower than in the control cities for the following six years.

The "Extended" Maharishi Effect

Two significant developments within the TM movement in the mid-1970s greatly increased the testability of the Maharishi Effect. The first was the introduction by Maharishi in 1977 of a more advanced meditation practice known as the TM-Sidhi technique.[12] The TM-Sidhi technique built on the experience of the basic TM method (whose essential goal is a state of resting in "pure consciousness") by introducing certain subtle thoughts, intentions, and activities that "make pure consciousness lively." The method is claimed to result in the emergence of certain *sidhis* or extraordinary abilities, the most renowned of which is "yogic flying," where the body spontaneously lifts up and hops forward, sometimes for long sequences, while the practitioner's mind remains in a deeply settled state. Because both the analysis of physiological changes in practitioners and their subjective reports suggested that the new technique was significantly more powerful than the basic TM method, it was hypothesized that a much smaller number of meditators practicing the TM-Sidhi technique would be required to bring about the Maharishi Effect.

The second development was the discovery that when large numbers of meditators practicing both the advanced TM-Sidhi technique and the basic TM method gathered together in one place, their effect on social indicators appeared to be exponentially greater than when people were meditating separately. The discovery was made by accident when 350 teachers of TM converged on Rhode Island in summer 1978, intending to teach TM to enough new students to raise the proportion of TM meditators in the total population to 1 percent, and then to measure changes in various social indicators. The 1 percent target was never reached, yet many significant changes were observed in the social indicators. The changes were attributed to the fact that the 350 teachers had been regularly meditating together, using the advanced TM-Sidhi technique, at their teaching headquarters over the summer.

This discovery led to the hypothesis of the "extended" Maharishi Effect: When just the square root of 1 percent of a given population practiced the TM-Sidhi technique together in a group setting, there would be a measurable positive effect on the total population. The total number of meditators that was hypothetically required to produce an effect for any given population was now small enough to be widely tested. For example, for a city of 1 million people, only one hundred meditators would hypothetically be needed to have an effect; for the entire world's population of seven billion, a little over eight thousand meditators would be needed.

Between 1978 and 1984, many "Super Radiance Assemblies" were held throughout the world.[13] Dillbeck and colleagues (1987) studied the correlation between three separate Super Radiance Assemblies and changes in crime statistics in nearby populations. These studies included a group of 3,500 in the Union Territory of Delhi, India during fall 1980, a group of 200 in Puerto Rico in April 1984, and a group of 1,200 in Metro Manila, the Phillipines in late summer and fall 1984. Two further Super Radiance Assemblies (one involving 350 meditators in Rhode Island in summer 1978, the other a group of 400 in the Phillipines from December 1979 to December 1981) were studied for their effect on composite quality-of-life indices.

Dillbeck employed a statistical tool known as time-series analysis (the particular type he used is called a Box-Jenkins procedure) to analyze the data. For complex social phenomena such as crime, even when one controls for numerous factors already known to influence crime rates (as in the earlier Dillbeck study), there are so many potential variables that might influence the rate that one might never be entirely confident that some unknown factor, rather than the independent variable, had not been the cause. A time-series analysis enables the creation of a mathematical formula that plots cyclical trends of data over a long period of time, thus taking into account all the different factors that have already been influencing the data, even where those factors are not known. When analyzing changes in data from an experimental period compared with a control period (e.g., comparing the period during an assembly with earlier or later periods), the time-series analysis eliminates that proportion of the change that would be anticipated from the cyclical trends that occurred in the same time period in previous years. The change in data that remains can thus be attributed more confidently to a new cause, such as the independent variable.

Applying this analysis to the changes in crime statistics that were observed during the periods of the Super Radiance Assemblies in Puerto Rico, Metro Manila, and the Union Territory of Delhi, Dillbeck found that in each case, crime rates dropped significantly during the intervention period (by between 11 and 12.1 percent). The study considered whether there were political events or changes in police policies or practices during the experimental periods that could have served as alternative explanations, but concluded that these factors could not account for the changes. The study also found statistically significant improvements in the composite quality-of-life indices in Rhode Island and Metro Manila during the experimental periods. The joint statistical probability that in all five cases this result had occurred by chance was calculated at less than one in a million. The

Journal of Mind and Behavior accepted this paper for publication after the editor obtained feedback from an independent expert in statistics that the mathematical methods applied in the study were appropriate and correctly applied (Dillbeck et al. 1987).

International Peace Project

As seen in chapter 2, the International Peace Project was a study designed to bring together two hundred TM meditators in Jerusalem in August and September 1983 to measure the impact of the meditation group on the war in Lebanon, as well as on a variety of other social indicators in Israel. It is one of the most significant of all the studies on the Maharishi Effect, in part because Yale's prestigious *Journal of Conflict Resolution* accepted it for publication, and in part because it has attracted the focused attention of several critics of the research. In contrast with the previous retrospective studies (in which Super Radiance Assemblies had gathered for various reasons and then statistics were examined after the fact), the International Peace Project was a prospective study, in which predictions of the results were made in advance and lodged with independent scientists in the United States and Israel.

Some of the more notable results include:

- War deaths in Lebanon dropped by an average of 76 percent during the 25 percent of days when there was highest attendance at the assembly.

- War deaths were especially low during a thirteen-day period in which group size was raised to a high level according to a preassigned schedule (average daily number of war deaths was 1.5 compared with 33.7 for the thirteen days immediately prior and subsequent to the experimental period).

- When all the variables were combined into a composite quality-of-life index, striking correlations can be observed with the attendance figures at the assembly (see Figure 2.1, p. 57).

- A "transfer-function" or "lead-lag" analysis to produce cross-correlations (performed at the request of one of the referees of the study for the *Journal of Conflict Resolution*) strongly supported the hypothesis that the direction of causation flowed from the Super Radiance Assembly to the changes in war deaths, car accidents, fires, and other variables, not the other way around (Orme-Johnson et al. 1988).

In a rare "editor's comment" to justify the journal's decision to publish the study, Duval (1988) remarked that "[t]he fundamental assumptions of a 'unified field' and a 'collective consciousness' are not within the paradigm under which most of us operate. Yet if one will, for the sake of argument, accept these premises as plausible, then the research conforms quite well to scientific standards" (814).

Effect of Multiple Super Radiance Assemblies on War Intensity in Lebanon

Davies and Alexander (1989) examined the effects of seven different Super Radiance Assemblies (including the International Peace Project group) held in various locations throughout the world from June 1983 to August 1985 on levels of conflict and cooperation in Lebanon. The assemblies were of sufficient size to exceed the threshold for a predicted effect on Lebanon, in accordance with the square root of 1 percent formula. The assemblies ranged in size from a gathering of 100 meditators in Beirut, Lebanon to three very large groups of 7,800 meditators in the United States. There were 93 days out of the 821 days included in the study in which the threshold size was reached or exceeded in the assemblies. An independent media content analyst was employed to examine eight international news sources for daily data on war deaths and injuries, and levels of cooperation and conflict (according to an independently established sixteen-point scale for rating events in terms of cooperation and conflict). The analyst was blind to the study's hypothesis and experimentally significant dates. The study found that, compared with the control days, during the ninety-three days when the assemblies were sufficiently large for a predicted effect on Lebanon there was an estimated 71 percent decrease in war fatalities, 68 percent decrease in war injuries, 66 percent increase in the level of cooperation between antagonists, and 48 percent reduction in the level of conflict. A time-series analysis was performed that precluded the possibility that the changes were due to seasonal cycles or pre-existing trends. Alternative explanations such as changes in weather or the possible effect of religious or national holidays were taken into account (e.g., Muslim holidays were shown to correlate with higher levels of cooperation, so these were included as part of the null model when assessing the effect of the assemblies).

Because of the large number of data points in the study and the very strong results, the probability that the result occurred by chance alone was extraordinarily low: less than 1 in 10 million trillion.

Washington, DC Demonstration Study

In 1993, a highly publicized "demonstration study" was conducted in Washington, DC to assess the effect of a Super Radiance Assembly on crime rates.

Predictions were lodged in advance with police officials and with a twenty-seven-member review board of scientists and public leaders. In June 1993, one thousand meditators arrived in Washington with the numbers steadily increasing to a peak of four thousand during the first week of July, where it stayed until the end of the month, when the group disbanded. Police statistics for homicide, rape, and assault were gathered for the experimental period and for the five-year period that preceded the study. For the previous five years, crime rates during the summer could be closely correlated with changes in temperature—the hotter the temperature, the higher the crime rates. In 1993, during the experimental period, crime rates dipped noticeably despite very high temperatures. The decrease was calculated as 23 percent less than what could have been expected based on a time-series analysis of previous trends. Other possible causes such as changes in police activities, lower temperatures, weekend effects, and increased rain were considered but rejected as alternative explanations. The probability that the result was due to chance was calculated as less than 2 in 1 billion (Hagelin et al, 1999).

Biochemical Effects of Group TM Practice in Nonmeditators

Walton, Cavanaugh, and Pugh (2005) studied the relationship between the number of participants in a large TM group in Fairfield, Iowa and levels of cortisol excretion and other physiological indicators of stress in six non-practitioners living or working in Fairfield up to twenty miles from the group. Previous research had established that the stress response usually entails increased secretion of the glucocorticoid cortisol. The hypothesis was that a proposed "psychoneuroendocrine" mechanism might help to mediate the observed social effects of TM group practice. The study found that an increase in the day-to-day size of the TM group was a significant predictor of reduced corticol excretion later that night in the nonmeditating participants. An increase in the TM group size was also a significant predictor of increased excretion rate in the subjects of 5-hydroxyindoleacetic acid, a precursor to serotonin that has been associated with reductions in anger, anxiety, and other negative emotions. The results thus support the hypothesis that group practice of TM reduces social stress by producing beneficial neuroendocrine effects in nonmeditators in the nearby population.

Qualitative Analysis of Responses to International Peace Project Research Findings

Harvard doctoral student Carla Brown (2005) examined responses to the International Peace Project research findings by interviewing thirty-five elite members of the Middle East policy community, including newspaper reporters, politicians, diplomats, and scientists. She found that more than

50 percent of those interviewed rejected the findings immediately without examining scientific merit. Stereotyping and prejudice were prevalent
causes for rejection. Twelve respondents considered the scientific evidence
minimally, and nine of those stated that science could not contribute to
social solutions. A small number of respondents did take into account the
scientific quality of the research, and indicated that they were likely to
consider further research along similar lines. The study demonstrates that
the Maharishi Effect research tends to be evaluated emotionally, rather than
rationally, by scientists, politicians, and the press.

CRITIQUES AND RESPONSES

One might expect that such a sustained and, in many respects, successful
(in terms of the number of studies published) attempt to achieve scientific
validation for a hypothesis that flies in the face of scientific orthodoxy
would not have gone unnoticed by skeptical observers. However, my search
of the literature revealed only four critiques that specifically focused on the
Maharishi Effect research.

The four works I found critical of the Maharishi Effect research vary
widely in their quality. Park and Stenger make highly polemical assertions
that contribute little to the scientific discussion of the phenomenon.[14]
Political scientist Philip Schrodt (1990) focuses on the International Peace
Project. He argues that the calculation of the independent variable (the
minimum size of the Super Radiance group required to create an effect per
the square root of 1 percent formula) failed to take into account relevant
neighboring populations in Syria and Jordan. He also claims that the experiment did not eliminate the possibility of reverse causation, namely, that
participants in the meditation group were more motivated to attend when
they believed the Maharishi Effect was working, from observing the news
of decreased war intensity. Finally, he argues that if a Box-Jenkins statistical
method is to be used, robust checking should be performed by testing for
the effects of "pseudo-interventions" on random days when the intervention
did not actually take place.

In response to Schrodt's first criticism (regarding how the threshold
size of the meditation group was calculated), Orme-Johnson, Alexander,
and Davies (1990) claim that in all research on the Maharishi Effect up
to that point, the square root of 1 percent formula had always been calculated by reference to political boundaries rather than geographical distance,
because the field effect was theoretically predicted to be mediated by qualitative factors such as closer personal ties, more frequent interactions, greater
homogeneity, and so on. As the size of the group increased, it was predicted
that Lebanon would be the first country affected due to the more intimate

and dynamic interaction between Israel and Lebanon brought about by the war. Orme-Johnson et al. also argue that, in any event, because six of the eight dependent variables were limited to Jerusalem or Israel, the meditation group would have influenced them even if the population were calculated by distance alone.

On the second issue of reverse causality, Orme-Johnson et al. argue that this was unlikely because the number of meditators who dropped in from the local area was quite small. Furthermore, they point out that there was also a clear relationship between group size and rates of daily crime, accidents, fires, and stock market performance, yet it is improbable that news of these changes would have influenced meditators' participation. Finally, they note that there was a thirteen-day period in which group size was raised to a high level (average of 197.1) according to a preassigned schedule independent of the level of fighting. During this time, the average number of daily war deaths was 1.5 compared with 33.7 for the thirteen day periods immediately prior and subsequent to the experimental period. It could not be said, they point out, that changes in war intensity could have caused the high level of participation during this period.

In response to Schrodt's third major criticism about the reliability of the Box-Jenkins Method, a "pseudo-intervention" was performed as a robustness check (as Schrodt had suggested) by using an RNG to randomize the sequence of the independent variable (i.e., the numbers indicating the size of the TM-Sidhi group), and no significant cross-correlations were found between the randomized independent variable and the war intensity data. Three other similar pseudo-interventions were performed with the same results (i.e., no significant cross-correlations were found).

Sociologists Evan Fales and Barry Markovsky (1997) aim their critique at the theory behind the Maharishi Effect. They argue that, although there are sometimes good reasons for publishing heterodox theories that fly in the face of established knowledge, in general such theories should be subject to especially careful scrutiny to reduce the inefficiency of the theory evaluation process. Fales and Markovsky claim that the Maharishi Effect theory is overly vague about key terms and processes and, as such, can only lead to crude predictions that cannot be precisely tested.[15] Furthermore, they argue that the results could plausibly be explained by the effects of several events that occurred at the time of the experiment, such as various Jewish holidays, summer heat, the resignation of Prime Minister Begin, or certain military operations.

In response to Fales and Markovsky's critique, Orme-Johnson (2009) argues that the assertion that the theory underlying the Maharishi Effect is "vague" and "ambiguous" is a subjective judgment of the authors, as is their characterization of the theory as "heterodox," because, in the social sciences, there is no generally agreed on "orthodox" theoretical position from which other theories may be judged to be "heterodox." The idea that the authors' subjective assessment of a supposed lack of theoretical clarity should take precedence over empirical data is, Orme-Johnson argues, exactly the opposite of the conventional practice of science, in which theories are created and modified according to the data. In response to Fales and Markovsky's claim that alternative variables could have accounted for the results, Orme-Johnson conducted a formal statistical analysis controlling for these events and found that, although some of the cultural/political factors did have an effect on the composite quality-of-life index examined in the study, these effects were independent of the effects of the meditation group and could not explain it.

ASSESSMENT

In my opinion, any fair-minded observer who examines carefully the Maharishi Effect research will have to give it its due. The effect has been successfully demonstrated in dozens of studies, many of which have been published in reputable scientific journals with rigorous peer-review processes. The experiments are based on publicly available data compiled by independent authorities who typically know nothing about the experiments. The results have been statistically significant to an extraordinary degree and the size of the effect often has been impressive. The research has controlled for alternative mundane explanations and cyclical trends. Although it is difficult for a nonexpert in statistics to penetrate the technical interpretations of the data, independent statisticians called on by leading journals have consistently approved the methods used in the studies.

The criticisms of the research have not revealed any significant technical or logical flaws that could explain away the results. As we have seen, Orme-Johnson deals convincingly with Schrodt's arguments about the possibility of reverse causality and the need for robust checking. Schrodt's claim that the threshold figure for the meditation group was calculated incorrectly (by ignoring the populations of nearby Syria and Jordan)—even if true— does not take away from the fact that empirical correlations were observed between the size of the meditation group and the dependent variables. Nor does Schrodt's argument account for the fact that, as Orme-Johnson points out, six of the eight dependent variables were located in Israel itself—meaning that, in theory, these variables should have been influenced by the meditation group even if the effect was calculated by distance alone.

Orme-Johnson's vigorous response to Fales and Markovsky's critique exposes the dubious grounds of the latter authors' argument that the evidence of the Maharishi Effect research can be rejected on the basis that its theory is improbable in light of the current state of orthodox knowledge in the field. As Orme-Johnson points out, not only would such an approach suppress the emergence of any novel sociological theory, the lack of a widely agreed on theoretical framework to sociology (or to the study of consciousness) renders meaningless Fales and Markovsky's claim that the Maharishi Effect is inconsistent with "prior knowledge." Furthermore, Orme-Johnson's statistical treatment of the events proposed by Fales and Markovsky as alternative causal factors demonstrates convincingly that these events alone cannot account for the experimental results.

The weakest aspect of the research is the fact that only scientists associated with the TM movement have produced it. Although the existence of an apparent vested interest in the success of the research does not by itself invalidate the findings, confidence in the results would obviously increase if researchers outside the TM movement were able to replicate them. Given the expense and complexity of transporting, feeding, and housing the considerable number of participants theoretically required to produce a measurable effect on large cities or nations, smaller-scale projects that target small towns or regional communities might be a more feasible approach to replication. Further research might also reveal whether the effect could be shown to work with other kinds of spiritual practices.

In their critique, Fales and Markovsky (1997) suggest that, "[p]resumably, if the material world can be influenced in purposive ways by collective meditation, inanimate detectors could be constructed and placed at varying distances from the collective meditators" (518). Precisely this approach has in fact been attempted by researchers associated with the PEAR laboratory as an extension of its research into RNGs, with intriguing results.

FIELD REG RESEARCH

In the early 1990s, researchers at the PEAR laboratory noticed that a continually running RNG (also called an REG) tended to yield anomalous data not only during periods of directed intention but also at other times when group attention was especially coherent. Field REGs were constructed for use with palmtop computers to test the hypothesis that situations that promote deep engagement or interpersonal resonance might elicit a "group consciousness" that could, in turn, have a measurable effect on the REG. The protocol for field REG experiments involves taking samples from two predefined categories of conditions. The experimental condition involves preidentified situations of high group resonance predicted to produce nonrandom behavior in the REG data. The control condition involves mundane situations where no special group coherence is likely. From a review of the results of early experiments, Nelson and his colleagues (1998) identified the following conditions as those likely to produce the most positive outcomes:

> Times and places that evoke unusually warm or close feelings of togetherness, with emotional content that tends to draw people together, where personal involvement is important but focused more toward a group goal involving a deeply engrossing theme, located at uplifting physical sites like the ocean or mountains, during creative or humorous moments, and enlivened with a sense of freshness or novelty. (cited in Radin 2006, 184–185)

In one case, a Shoshone medicine man, whose personal mission is to heal the sacred places of the American Indians, conducted a healing ceremony at a "power" spot near Devils Tower, Wyoming. He agreed to conduct a second "sham" ritual with much the same outward appearance at a control location. The real ceremony saw a steady cumulative deviation away from random data, with odds against chance of less than one in two hundred, whereas the sham ceremony resulted in data indistinguishable from chance. Other group situations tested include theater performances, large sporting events like the World Cup, and popular television broadcasts like the Academy Awards. By 2005, more than one hundred field REG experiments had been conducted whose results strongly suggest a correlation between periods of unusual group coherence and nonrandom fluctuations in the REG data. Furthermore, the effect size for successful field REG experiments have tended to be more than twice that found in the meta-analyses of individual RNG studies (Radin 2006).

GLOBAL CONSCIOUSNESS PROJECT

After researchers observed an unusual coherence between twelve independent field REG devices located across the United States and Europe during a widely promoted "Gaiamind" global meditation in January 1997 and again during Princess Diana's funeral in September 1997, the idea emerged to create a global network of continuously running REGs to test whether worldwide coherence was generated during other events that captured the attention of a large proportion of the world's population. The project was dubbed the Global Consciousness Project (GCP). The GCP network is comprised of about sixty-five active REG sites, many of which are in North and South America and Europe, but also in Australia, Fiji, Japan, India, Malaysia, Africa, China, and other places. Computers with custom software read the REG output and record one trial of two hundred bits each second continually over months and years. Every five minutes, the data from all the computers is automatically sent over the Internet to a central web server in Princeton, New Jersey, where the results are compiled and analyzed. The GCP hypothesis is tested by analyzing REG data from the network a few minutes before to a few hours after the occurrence of an "event of global interest." Events of global interest are those the GCP research team infers will capture a large percentage of the world's attention (based on prespecified categories or experience from prior experiments). By 2001, more than 66 percent of the GCP's formal tests showed a positive trend toward nonrandom behavior, with about 20 percent being statistically significant at $p < 0.05$. The cumulative results by 2010 of more than 350 global events revealed a steady overall deviation from randomness, with odds against chance of about a billion to one (Nelson and Bancel 2011).[16] Although the mean effect is small, it is highly statistically significant. These results suggest that the focused attention of thousands or millions of people around the planet may correspond with a subtle increase in physical coherence or order in the world.

Of particular relevance to the hypothesis of subtle activism, Nelson (2003) analyzed the cumulative deviation from chance recorded by the GCP network during seventeen meditation and prayer events focused on global harmony. He found a significant result with odds against chance of about three hundred to one (Figure 3.1). The parabolas corresponding to 5 percent

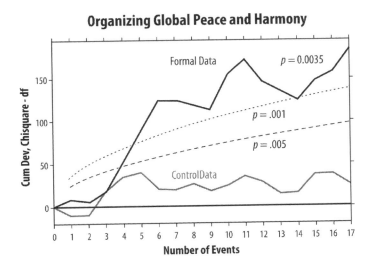

Figure 3.1. Response of Global Consciousness Project network to coordinated global meditation and prayer. Reprinted with permission from Nelson (2003).

and 1 percent probability are represented as dotted lines. The "control data" curve is based on a computer simulation that demonstrates what typical uncorrelated data would be expected to look like. The actual REG data is seen to be significantly anomalous.

Williams (2014) updated the data set used by Nelson to include 120 global harmony events and found an even more impressive cumulative result, with odds against chance of about six thousand to one (Figure 3.2).

Although the sample size in Nelson's report is small, Williams's analysis of 120 events is large enough for the statistics to become meaningful. The results suggest that the practice of global meditation or prayer may indeed subtly reduce the overall level of chaos or randomness in the world.

GLOBAL COHERENCE INITIATIVE

The Global Coherence Initiative (GCI) is a complementary project studying the interconnectedness between humanity and Earth's energetic systems. Through a global network of ultra-sensitive magnetic field detectors being installed at strategic locations around the world, GCI is conducting research on the mechanisms by which Earth's energetic fields affect human mental and emotional processes, health outcomes, and collective behavior,

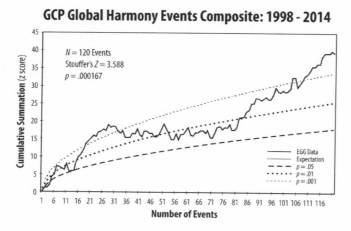

Figure 3.2. Updated analysis of response of Global Consciousness Project network to global harmony events. Reprinted with permission from B. Williams, (2014). *Global Harmony Events Composite: 1998–2014*. Retrieved from http://global-mind. org/papers/pdf/global.harmony.2014-Williams.pdf.

as well as exploring how collective human emotions and intentions may impact Earth's energetic fields. Data collected from solar and geomagnetic field detectors, and from human nervous system activity as reflected in heart rate variability (HRV), show that human physiological rhythms and collective behaviors are not only synchronized with solar and geomagnetic activity, but that disruptions in these fields can create adverse effects on human psychological, physiological, and social systems (e.g., Doronin et al. 1998; Pobachenko et al. 2006; Mikulecky 2007; Grigoryev 2009). Other solar and magnetic indices are correlated with improved HRV and mental and emotional states (Ertel 1998). GCI scientists believe this is likely due to a coupling between the human cardiovascular and nervous systems and resonating geomagnetic frequencies. Additionally, there is data support-ing the hypothesis that Earth's magnetic fields are carriers of biologically relevant information that connect all living systems (e.g., Persinger 1995, 2008; Montagnier et al 2011). As such, these fields may serve as conduits that allow our attitudes, emotions, and intentions to affect global events and the quality of life on Earth.

DISCUSSION

The claim of subtle activism is that certain intentional consciousness-based practices by individuals or groups can exert a subtle positive influence on the social realm. The principle of nonlocality is proposed to explain how it might work. Although quantum nonlocality is an accepted scientific principle, its application at the macroscopic level is controversial. We have reviewed four bodies of research that have investigated nonlocal phenom-ena at the level of our everyday world: parapsychology, distant healing, the Maharishi Effect, and the GCP. Meta-analyses of the principal lines of parapsychology research have consistently revealed small, yet highly statisti-cally significant effects that persist notwithstanding improved experimental controls and extreme scrutiny from hostile critics. Several large case collec-tions of spontaneous psi experiences show consistent, cross-cultural patterns that support the authenticity of the overall data. Almost two-thirds of 191 controlled studies of distant healing on a variety of living organisms have resulted in significant outcomes. Clinical distant healing trials are more ambiguous and potentially confounded by inherent methodological issues. More than forty studies on the Maharishi Effect have been published, including twenty-eight in peer-reviewed journals, with the results showing highly significant correlations between the practice of the TM-Sidhi pro-gram in large-group settings and improvements in a broad range of social indicators. The cumulative results of the GCP show a consistent correlation between the occurrence of "global events" and deviations from random behavior in the GCP REG network, with very large odds against chance. The GCP data on 120 global meditation and prayer events also reveals a statistically significant overall effect. The combined evidence strongly suggests that nonlocality is indeed not limited to the quantum realm but can also operate at the macroscopic level, and that the practice of techniques like meditation or prayer by large groups of people may have a measurable effect on levels of social harmony.

As noted earlier, the extent to which one tends to find this evidence convincing appears to depend greatly on one's ideological predispositions. Basic personality traits may also be determinative in this regard. Parapsychologist J.E. Kennedy (2005) points out that paranormal beliefs and experiences have been found to be associated with the intuitive, feeling personality dimensions of the Myers-Briggs type indicator, whereas skepticism appears to be linked with materialist, rational, pragmatic personality types. Kennedy argues that the demonstrated predominance of the latter personality types in leadership positions throughout society may be a major factor in institutional skepticism and resistance to psi.

Skepticism, of course, is one of the hallmarks of the scientific method. Yet, in the so-called psi wars, skepticism has all too frequently hardened into a quasi-religious scientific dogmatism that represents something close to the opposite of the scientific ideal of open-minded inquiry. Sociologist Marcello Truzzi, a co-founder of the skeptical organization Committee for the Scientific Investigation of Claims of the Paranormal (CSICOP) who left the organization in protest at its one-sided treatment of the paranormal, coined the term *pseudoskeptic* to describe those who assume for themselves the label *skeptic* when they are in fact dogmatic materialists. "Since skepticism properly refers to doubt rather than denial—nonbelief rather than belief—critics who take the negative rather than an agnostic position but still call themselves 'skeptics' are actually *pseudoskeptics* and have, I believe, gained a false advantage by usurping that label" (Truzzi 1998).

The number of extreme or 'pseudo' skeptics who have dedicated their careers to debunking paranormal claims is relatively small. Yet their arguments tend to resonate with a scientific establishment that shares their ideological commitment to mechanistic materialism. For example, influential scientific journals such as *Nature* and *Science* have published articles on parapsychology that incorporate some of the questionable rhetorical tactics of extreme skeptics, such as labeling parapsychology a pseudoscience or implying that positive data must be the result of cheating, incompetence, or fraud.[17]

Despite the apparent bias in orthodox science against paranormal or nonlocal phenomena, there is no doubt that science's understanding of consciousness is evolving rapidly. In particular, science is increasingly coming to appreciate the complexity of the relationship between mind and matter. For example, until relatively recently, most scientists understood mind or consciousness to be a mere epiphenomenon of the human nervous system, possessing no causal powers of its own. But numerous lines of research have now demonstrated instances of downward causation, where a change in mental state clearly appears to cause a change in physiology. Examples include the well-established placebo effect and the extensive research emerging from new fields like psychoneuroimmunology, neuroanthropology, and mindfulness neuroscience.

Many other scientific developments point to the existence of a complex and inextricable connection between perception and reality, consciousness and world. The revolution in physics brought about by quantum and relativity theory is probably the most well-known example in this regard. But one could also highlight significant developments within the philosophy of science in which thinkers such as Bachelard (1934), Popper (1968), Kuhn (1970), and Feyerabend (1975) have exposed the complex relationship between evidence and interpretation, showing that there can be no observations without a vast apparatus of pre-existing theory. Here too we could cite the influential enactive paradigm of cognition developed by biologist Francisco Varela, philosopher Evan Thompson, and psychologist Eleanor Rosch (1991), which regards mind, body, and environment as recursively linked or dynamically interdependent, with the process of cognition seen to be inseparable from an organism's embodied interaction with its environment, and the environment, in turn, seen to be itself shaped by these cognitively driven interactions in a process of coevolution. These and other developments have significantly undermined the core assumptions of materialism by demonstrating that mind or consciousness plays a much more active role in the shaping of physical reality than previously imagined.

Scientists have mostly tried to find ways to accommodate—or sidestep—these findings in a manner that keeps the basic materialist framework intact. But for science to embrace evidence of paranormal or nonlocal phenomena would seem to represent a crossing of the Rubicon, beyond which there could be no preservation of the materialist perspective. It is very difficult to imagine how evidence of nonlocal phenomena can be accounted for within an interpretation of consciousness as merely a byproduct of the human brain. Rather, the evidence presented in this chapter more straightforwardly suggests that consciousness should be regarded as a fundamental constituent of reality that is inherently nonlocal. A growing number of philosophers who take seriously the "hard problem" of consciousness (i.e., how to explain how subjective experience arises from a physical basis) have likewise concluded that consciousness simply cannot be reduced to material explanations. Philosopher Thomas Nagel (2012), for example, claims that "conscious subjects and their mental lives are inescapable components of reality not describable by the physical sciences" (41). The integration within science of an understanding of consciousness as a non-physical aspect of reality is obviously no small step, implying the resolution of a host of controversial issues pertaining to the relationship between science and spirituality. Indeed, such a development would likely be as revolutionary as any that has yet occurred in the history of science. Here is Nagel on this point:

> [W]e should expect theoretical progress in this area to require a major conceptual revolution at least as radical as relativity theory, the introduction of electromagnetic fields into physics—or the original scientific revolution itself . . .
>
> And it cannot consist (merely!) in a revision of the basic concepts of physics, however radical—as happened with the introduction of electromagnetic fields or relativistic space-time. . . . [S]omething must be added to the physical conception of the natural order that allows us to explain how it can give rise to organisms that are more than physical. (42, 46)

Given the radical nature of the theoretical shift required, it may take more than intellectual factors to bring it about. Although empirical evidence of the kind presented in this chapter is clearly significant, it frequently seems less decisive in producing a change of heart on these issues than firsthand, personal experiences of deeper realities, as can occur in spontaneous mystical states, near-death experiences, psychedelic journeys, vivid psychic encounters, and so on. As Kuhn noted, paradigm shifts tend to be more akin to sudden conversion experiences than rational processes. Perhaps the deepening global crisis will become so extreme that at some point it will lead to a collective transfer of allegiance away from the ideology of materialism, a worldview that increasingly appears implicated in the self-destructive trajectory of modern society. My own motivation for advancing the concept of subtle activism is not merely to make an intellectual point, but to encourage the development of projects that allow people from all parts of the planet to experience directly and profoundly their underlying connectivity with each other and with the whole of reality. I am convinced that these kinds of shared experiences could contribute to shifting the cultural paradigm at least as much as further empirical studies. The development of a theoretical framework that cogently accounts for the evidence is also crucial to achieving more widespread acceptance of the reality of nonlocal or paranormal phenomena. Let us, then, turn our attention to theory and examine several models that help explain how subtle activism might work.

CHAPTER FOUR

FOUNDATIONS OF SUBTLE ACTIVISM

How might subtle activism work? How could the consciousness-based activities of an individual or group possibly influence vastly complex modern sociopolitical systems without any direct communication through conventional channels? The notion of a transcendent intelligence or underlying ground of being that is responsive to human prayer, ritual, and other spiritual practices is, of course, an ancient idea that has been central to most of the world's cultural and religious belief systems. Yet such a concept runs counter both to our regular perception of the everyday world (which seems on the surface to consist of separate material objects) and to the currently orthodox scientific view that assumes a physical basis for all phenomena. As noted in chapter 3, however, various well-known developments in physics throughout the twentieth century brought forth a picture of reality at its most fundamental level that was radically—and bizarrely—at odds with the materialistic assumptions of modern science. These findings not only pointed to the profound interrelatedness of things at more basic levels of reality but also suggested that consciousness may be more deeply intertwined with the physical universe than previously assumed.

In chapter 3 we looked at how these developments in physics supported the scientific investigation of various kinds of phenomena that appear to demonstrate the principle of nonlocality in the everyday world and we examined several of the main lines of research in this regard—parapsychology, distant healing, the Maharishi Effect, and the Global Consciousness Project. These and other efforts have contributed a substantial body of empirical data that supports the hypothesis that consciousness is not reducible to a property of the brain but may in fact be a nonlocal phenomenon. However, an important reason why most scientists continue to disregard such evidence is the absence of a broadly accepted theoretical framework that could account for the findings. In this chapter, I consider several theoretical systems that offer explanations for nonlocal phenomena and, specifically, for how consciousness-based practices may influence events in the sociopolitical realm. But first, let us look at the current status of the scientific understanding of consciousness in general.

WHAT IS CONSCIOUSNESS?

Consciousness seems to be irreducibly mysterious. Although it is the most intimate and familiar part of our being, it is very difficult to understand and articulate what it actually is. Many believe that consciousness represents the most conspicuous obstacle to a comprehensive scientific understanding of the universe. Unlike in most other fields, the problem goes beyond the absence of certain theoretical details. Science simply has no explanation at all for how consciousness fits into the natural order. Richard Frackowiak and seven other leading neuroscientists write:

> We have no idea how consciousness emerges from the physical activity of the brain and we do not know whether consciousness can emerge from non-biological systems, such as computers. . . . At this point the reader will expect to find a careful and precise definition of consciousness. You will be disappointed. Consciousness has not yet become a scientific term that can be defined in this way. Currently we all use the term *consciousness* in many different and often ambiguous ways. Precise definitions of different aspects of consciousness will emerge . . . but to make precise definitions at this stage is premature. (Frackowiak et al. 2004, 269)

As Frackowiak et al. indicate, part of the problem is that the term *consciousness* is used to mean many different things. K. Ramakrishna Rao (2002) identifies as many as thirteen different meanings of consciousness in both everyday thought and the scientific literature. As Rao points out, the Western scholarly tradition has tended to regard *mind* and *consciousness* as virtually interchangeable terms, or to regard consciousness as an aspect or species of the mind, namely, that part of the mind accessible to individual awareness (in contrast to unconscious or subliminal aspects of mind). Eastern traditions, on the other hand, have tended to distinguish clearly between mind and consciousness, with consciousness regarded as a nonphysical, autonomous, and irreducible aspect of reality, whereas mind is seen as a subtle form of matter (Rao 2002).

Despite the variety of meanings given to consciousness, it is generally accepted that it refers in some way to the subjective dimension of experience. Our mental and physical functioning does not occur in the dark, but is accompanied by conscious experience. As many philosophers have pointed out, conscious experience, or subjective awareness, is not reducible to third-person observations, but is only comprehensible from the first-person perspective: "it [subjective awareness] only exists as experienced by some 'I,' some human or animal that has the experiences" (Searle 2000, 4). In a seminal paper "What is it like to be a bat?" Thomas Nagel (1974) argued that an organism has conscious experience if "there is something it is like to be that organism" (166). The expression "what it is like to be" is an attempt to capture the ineffable feeling of subjective awareness. We cannot know from the outside if a bat has consciousness, for example, because all of its physical characteristics do not tell us what it is like for a bat to be a bat. This difficulty in explaining subjective awareness in terms of physical processes has come to be known as the "hard problem" of consciousness (Chalmers 1996). It is "hard" because, for a growing number of philosophers and scientists, it is impossible to imagine how any experimental findings could, even in principle, explain the emergence of subjective experience.

Many writers identify dual aspects of mind or consciousness. Chalmers (1996), for example, makes a distinction between *phenomenal* and *psychological* concepts of mind. The former refers to conscious or subjective experience, where the mind is characterized by the way it feels, e.g., "what it is like" to see green or to feel love or to be a bat. The latter is the explanatory basis for behavior, where the mind is characterized by what it does, e.g., the mental state of pain results in an aversion reaction to the object that caused the pain. The phenomenal aspects of mind constitute what is commonly understood as "consciousness." The difficulty in explaining phenomenal aspects in terms of neural processes is the "hard problem" of consciousness. The psychological aspects of mind have been the traditional focus of study in mainstream psychology, and may or may not be accessible to consciousness. These aspects can largely be explained in objective terms without reference to subjective awareness.

HISTORY OF THE SCIENTIFIC STUDY OF CONSCIOUSNESS

While Western philosophers have pondered the nature of consciousness since the pre-Socratics, the modern attempt to study it systematically is usually traced to Descartes. Descartes sharply distinguished between mind (or consciousness) and body, arguing that they are two distinct substances. Although he affirmed the self-evident reality of the mind, he excluded it from the scope of modern science, arguing that science should restrict its analysis to mathematically precise quantitative descriptions of external realities extended in space. One important consequence of this interpretation is that consciousness was largely dismissed as a serious topic of scientific investigation until quite recently. Cartesian dualism came to be a prevalent, commonsense view throughout the modern world. Yet the innate human desire for a unified world picture that accounts for both mental and physical phenomena inevitably brought challenges to the dualist conception.

For several centuries after Descartes, this challenge came primarily in the form of idealism, the view that the mental realm is the ultimate reality, with the material world in some way reducible to it. Anglo-Irish philosopher George Berkeley advanced this perspective in the early eighteenth century and it dominated nineteenth-century philosophy, mostly through such German idealists as Immanuel Kant, Johann Fichte, Friedrich Schelling, G.W.F. Hegel, and Arthur Schopenhauer. By the early twentieth century, however, idealism had become largely supplanted in Western academic thought by materialism, which sought to establish a unified conception of reality from the opposite pole, the physical realm. Materialism holds that only the physical world is fundamentally real and that mental phenomena emerge as the result of material interactions.

Psychology, as the study of the mind, has always had an inherent interest in consciousness. Several of its pioneers, such as Gustav Fechner, Hermann von Helmholtz, and William James, treated the subjective aspects of consciousness seriously and embraced introspective or phenomenological methods to investigate them. However, mainstream psychology took a strongly materialistic turn near the start of the twentieth century with the emergence of behaviorism, which analyzed all mental states in terms of certain kinds of associated behavior. Behaviorist schools of psychology thoroughly rejected the introspective approach, essentially ignoring or denying the dimension of subjective awareness altogether. By the late 1950s, several inherent limitations of behaviorism had become widely recognized, not the least of which was the fact that, in bypassing conscious experience, it seemed to leave out precisely that which is most important to us as human beings. Since then, it has been displaced by various theories of mind—identity theory, functionalism, computationalism—all of which retained an essentially physicalist framework, although in increasingly sophisticated forms.[1]

In recent decades, a distinctly biological approach to the study of consciousness has emerged, in large part due to the development of several "functional neuroimaging" technologies, such as high-resolution electroencephalography and functional magnetic resonance imaging. These techniques allow researchers to observe with increasing precision the brain's activity in association with various tasks or stimuli. They have yielded an abundance of information that explains many of the functions studied in traditional psychology—perception, language, emotion, learning and memory, decision making—in terms of neural activity in the brain. Largely as a result of these developments, the past few decades have seen an explosion of interest in consciousness studies. Considered scientifically irrelevant for several centuries, consciousness has suddenly become the subject of intense interdisciplinary attention, drawing researchers from such diverse fields as cognitive science, neurobiology, neuropsychology, physics, philosophy, transpersonal psychology, and theology.

Most contemporary scientists assume that the success of neuroscience in identifying many of the neural correlates of mental functioning will soon translate into a neurobiological explanation of all mental properties, including subjective awareness itself. However, as a growing number of philosophers have pointed out, even if the neural correlates of conscious experience could somehow be identified, they would not be the same thing as the actual first-person experience of consciousness itself. Regardless of how complex the neural networks of the brain might be, they remain biological structures that must be described in third-person language. As Paul Ingram (2007) states:

> As fruitful as research into the neural correlates of consciousness may be, at best scientists can only report on a series of correlations between physical brain states and phenomenal experiences reported by subjects in first person language. Of course, neurological third-person descriptive accounts of these correlations are empirically important, but if the resulting explanations are given exclusively in neurological terms, they will, by the nature of the case, be unable to specify what are the phenomenal *qualia*[2] that subjects experience. Reductive physical accounts simply are not able to do justice to first-person/third-person distinctions. (105)

Among those convinced that phenomenal experience cannot be reduced to physiological structures are a number of thinkers who argue that the scientific understanding of consciousness will be incomplete unless it includes first-person experience as an explicit component alongside third-person observations. Neuroscientist Francisco Varela (1996), for example, has proposed the concept of "neurophenomenology," a method that combines physiological data with first-person phenomenological reports as a way to bridge the "explanatory gap" between physical properties and conscious experience. To develop this method, Varela and Shear (1999) examine a wide range of approaches to the disciplined study of subjective states of consciousness, from phenomenology to meditation. These approaches include a number of theories and methodologies emerging from Asian meditative traditions, such as Buddhism, Vedanta, and Yoga. In justifying their inclusion of Eastern perspectives, Varela and Shear point out that these traditions have accumulated a vast amount of expertise in cultivating the mind's introspective capacities from centuries of effort to develop systematic first-person methodologies. Furthermore, note Varela and Shear, many of their observations are expressed in terms not significantly different from phenomenological psychology. Thus, "[i]t would be a great mistake of western chauvinism to deny such observations as data and their potential validity" (6).

Similarly, K. Ramakrishna Rao (2002) argues persuasively that, although Eastern views on consciousness have spiritual connotations that are alien to the Western scientific mind, their traditions provide "a rich harvest of profound phenomenological accounts, a useful classification of a variety of conscious states, and the development of valuable techniques for enhancing human potential and wellbeing" (325). As a result, Rao maintains, Eastern traditions offer an important complementary perspective to the Western outlook that, if included in a more integrative approach, may help us to better understand consciousness in all its facets.

Although the value of embracing first-person methodologies and Eastern perspectives on consciousness is far from universally accepted, there can be little doubt that the failure of Western science to resolve the "hard problem" of consciousness leaves the question of consciousness fundamentally open. Consequently, an increasing number of thinkers in the field recognize the need to explore many different kinds of ideas about the nature of consciousness, including some that lie beyond the metaphysical suppositions of orthodox science. The wide-ranging nature of the following survey of theoretical foundations of subtle activism can thus be understood in the context of the fluid and open state that currently characterizes the field of consciousness studies.

THEORETICAL PERSPECTIVES EXAMINED IN THIS CHAPTER

We start our survey of theoretical approaches to subtle activism with a consideration of the theory of "Vedic Defense" developed by Maharishi Mahesh Yogi, founder of the TM movement. Maharishi's theory draws from ancient Vedic knowledge about the nature of consciousness and contemporary developments in unified quantum field theories to explain how the practice of TM by large groups may positively influence levels of social harmony. Next, we consider biochemist Rupert Sheldrake's hypothesis of formative causation and theory of morphic fields. Originating as a biological theory to explain the development of forms in plant and animal species, Sheldrake's theory of morphic fields extends the field concept to a number of contexts, including human societies. Religious studies professor Christopher Bache incorporates Sheldrake's framework into a theory of collective healing by individuals in nonordinary states of consciousness. Bache's theory of collective healing and Maharishi's theory of Vedic Defense amount to two models that specifically attempt to explain how consciousness-based practices may support collective or social transformation. As we will see, although there are important differences between these approaches, they also share a considerable number of overlapping concepts. After identifying these areas of common ground, I point out further parallels with theories from other disciplines, including physicist David Bohm's theory of holomovement and the implicate order and Carl Jung's psychological theory of the collective unconscious. I also look at similarities with Dion Fortune's esoteric model of magical activism. Finally, I draw from the similarities in all these approaches to sketch a broad outline of common principles that could form the basis of a general hypothesis of subtle activism.

MAHARISHI'S THEORY OF VEDIC DEFENSE

Maharishi Mahesh Yogi is undoubtedly one of the most influential figures in popularizing Eastern spiritual traditions in the West and his TM is probably the single most extensively researched meditation technique (Orme-Johnson and Farrow 1977). In chapter 2, I gave a brief overview of Maharishi's theory of Vedic defense, the conceptual framework that underlies the Maharishi Effect. In this chapter, we consider the model in greater detail.[3]

To recall, the Maharishi Effect refers to the claim that the practice of TM and other advanced Vedic practices by a large group equal to or greater than the square root of 1 percent of any given population will result in a measurable positive influence throughout the entire population. The starting point for the theory is Maharishi's contention that the source of all violence, negativity, conflict, and other problems in society is stress in the collective consciousness of the nation and the world. Before we examine what Maharishi means by "collective consciousness," it is important to understand his concept of consciousness itself. For Maharishi, consciousness is not simply a by-product of individual human nervous systems but is the most fundamental field of nature. The Vedic teachings describe pure consciousness as an unmanifest, unbounded, and all-pervading field of pure intelligence. Maharishi and the TM researchers argue that this conception of consciousness is consistent with the latest findings of quantum physics, in particular with the development in the late twentieth century of various unified field theories. As Maharishi and the TM researchers tend to strongly emphasize the parallels between the findings of modern physics and the principles of Vedic wisdom that underlie the Maharishi Effect theory, it will be helpful here to briefly summarize certain aspects of the (now well-known) story of the remarkable evolution of modern physics.[4]

One of the most significant and unexpected developments of quantum physics in the twentieth century was the "disappearance" of hard matter as the assumed basis of reality. Our evolving understanding of the basic "building blocks" of nature took a crucial step away from Newton's concept of matter as "solid, massy, hard, impenetrable, moveable particles" when, in the early twentieth century, it was discovered that the space between the subatomic particles was unimaginably greater than had been previously thought. This discovery led scientists to view apparently solid, stationary material objects like tables and chairs as actually composed of vast spaces of emptiness and billions of electrical charges swirling around at a blinding pace.[5] However, with Heisenberg's uncertainty principle and other developments, even this notion came to be viewed as overstating the substantiality of matter. Heisenberg discovered that whenever scientists attempted to pin down a single subatomic particle (like an electron), it disappeared from their grasp. One could measure an electron's position, for example, but then one would not have any precise knowledge of its momentum. Or one could measure its momentum, but have no clear idea of its position. Or one could develop a statistical approximation of both position and momentum, but then not have a precise sense of either one. Such behavior should not follow, of course, if subatomic particles were "solid, massy, and impenetrable" as in Newton's vision. As physicists continued to delve ever deeper into the nature of quantum reality, they concluded that subatomic particles have no real, autonomous existence, but rather are local vibrations or fluctuations of an underlying quantum field. As Capra (1975) said:

> [t]he quantum field is seen as a fundamental, physical entity; a continuous medium which is present everywhere in space. Particles are merely local condensations of the field; concentrations of energy which come and go, thereby losing their individual character and dissolving into the underlying field. (196–197)

Just as a wave in the ocean appears to have its own reality, but is not in any way separate from the water around it, so too are subatomic particles viewed as continuous with the underlying quantum field. Indeed "particles" are now typically described in quantum mechanics as "waves" (partly in reference to the probability distribution of their various features).[6] Moreover, the quantum field itself has no physical or material reality. With this view, the idea of solid matter vanished altogether. Einstein put it bluntly:

> We may therefore regard matter as being constituted by the regions of space in which the field is extremely intense. . . . There is no place in this new kind of physics both for the field and matter, for the field is the only reality. (cited in Capek 1964, 319)

Or as philosopher of science Karl Popper said, in modern physics, "materialism has transcended itself" (Popper and Eccles 1977, 7).

Further research revealed that quantum fields themselves have a "state of least excitation," or a vacuum state. The vacuum state can be explained in terms of the level of excitation of subatomic particles. Research showed that an electron, for example, can be very active or relatively sedate. When it relaxes below a certain level, it simply drops out of existence altogether. Some writers offer an analogy with a tuning fork—when it has almost stopped vibrating, the musical note it was producing ceases to exist. Similarly, when an electron has almost stopped vibrating, the electron itself ceases to exist. It returns to the state of least excitation of the field, also called the vacuum state because there are no real particles in it. Although the vacuum state is empty in the sense that it has nothing within it, it is also the source of all subatomic particles and thus is a field of infinite potential.

A further development noted by the TM researchers has been the attempt by physicists since the 1930s to devise various "grand unified theories" (GUT) to provide a unified picture of the functioning of all the forces and fields of nature (including attempts to develop a single model to explain both Einstein's relativity theory and the findings of quantum physics). Although no GUT is currently universally accepted among physicists, Oates (2002) argues that many leading models incorporate a mathematical concept known as supersymmetry to account for all four of the natural forces in nature (electromagnetism, gravity, strong, and weak force). These supersymmetric theories all include a notion of a "superfield"—one unified field that contains within it all the force and matter fields in nature.[7]

On the basis of these developments, Maharishi and the TM researchers argue that the best understanding from modern science is converging with ancient Vedic teachings about the fundamental nature of reality. For example, Oates (2002) points out the remarkable similarities between the Vedic notion of consciousness as an "unmanifest, unbounded, and all-pervading field of pure intelligence" and the following description by physicist E.C.G. Sudarshan of the vacuum state:

> The vacuum state is transcendental and unmanifest, yet it is the source of all manifestation. It is omnipresent and all-pervasive, since it underlies all of the various excited (or active) states of the universe. Further, it is nonspatial, nontemporal, immutable, and absolute. According to the quantum field theory, the vacuum state represents perfection—it is the level where orderliness is perfect and entropy [randomness and disorderliness] is zero. (cited in Oates 2002, 104)

Indeed, Maharishi and the TM researchers go so far as to claim that the unified field that physicists have proposed as the basis of physical reality is none other than the objective, mathematical description of the unified field of consciousness described in the ancient Vedic literature. In support of this contention, they point out that, like consciousness, the quantum vacuum has no material reality, yet displays many features of intrinsic intelligence, such as inherent creativity, orderliness, and, especially, the property of self-interaction or self-referral—a characteristic identified in the Vedic texts as the very hallmark of consciousness.[8] Oates (2002) argues that the idea that the unified field proposed by physics is in fact a field of consciousness is also supported by the discovery in physics of the inextricable bond between mind and matter at the quantum level. According to the dominant Copenhagen interpretation of quantum physics, the interconnection between observer and observed was demonstrated by the discovery that the act of measurement of subatomic particles appears to codetermine which aspects of subatomic reality are transformed from probabilities to actualities. For example, if a physicist chooses to measure the position of a subatomic particle, position will manifest. If the particle's spin is measured, spin will manifest. Before measurement, the position or spin (or any other quality) of the subatomic particle can be described only as a mathematical probability—it has no actual, manifest reality. Subatomic reality is thus seen as inherently indeterminate or amorphous, with its form codetermined by the way it is measured, or observed. This discovery has led many physicists to conclude that consciousness must be fundamentally interwoven with physical reality at all levels. As subatomic particles seem to "know" when and how they are being measured, nature seems to display qualities of consciousness, at least at that level of physical reality. Thus, the TM researchers (as well as other physicists) argue, it seems logical to assume that the underlying quantum field that gives rise to those particles must also be characterized by consciousness.

For the TM researchers, the significance of the claim that the unified field—whether in physics or Vedic science—is a field of consciousness is that, being consciousness, it can in principle be experienced by anyone. Human intelligence and nature's intelligence are seen as two aspects of an underlying unity, having their common source in the unified field. The practice of TM or other advanced Vedic techniques is said to allow an individual to experience a transcendental state of consciousness, regarded as a direct experience of the unified field that underlies all reality. When an individual has such an experience, he or she is said to "enliven the field" and to thereby automatically radiate an influence of harmony to others in the vicinity. The TM researchers claim that this "action at a distance" is explainable by either of the two long-distance mechanisms inherent to all quantum fields: (a) field effects, i.e., "the long-range propagation of influences through wave-like perturbations of the underlying field" (as in radio or television); and (b) infinite correlation, i.e., those long-range correlations that are instantaneous and unaffected by even astronomical distance (such as the phenomenon of nonlocality or quantum entanglement) (Oates 2002, 146).[9] Or, in Maharishi's words: "Tickle it [the unified field] here and it laughs over there" (cited in Oates 2002, 142).

Let us now return to Maharishi's claim that the primary influence on the quality of social life is the level of stress in the collective consciousness of society. Maharishi defines the collective consciousness of a social group as simply "the wholeness of consciousness of the entire group" (Orme-Johnson and Dillbeck 1987, 209). Each level of society (e.g., family, city, state, nation, world) is conceived by Maharishi as having its own field of consciousness, with its own unique characteristics. According to Maharishi, there is a reciprocal relationship between individual and collective consciousness, whereby each individual is seen to influence the collective consciousness of society and in turn to be influenced by it. At the basis of all levels of individual and collective consciousness is the unified field, the field of pure consciousness. Because the unified field is seen as the most fundamental level of individual and collective consciousness, Maharishi maintains that it is implicitly present in the foundation of society at all levels. According to Maharishi, the unified field just needs to be enlivened in the consciousness of individuals for it to infuse social life with its qualities of peace and invincibility. Governments alone cannot create significant peace in society, Maharishi argues, because they are simply mirrors of the collective consciousness. For him, the quality of the national consciousness will inevitably determine the quality of the national government, not the other way around. Therefore, he concludes, the most effective way to bring about genuine peace in society is to focus on improving the coherence of the national consciousness.

As for how a relatively small group of meditators could influence an entire population, Maharishi and the TM researchers use an analogy with physical systems governed by wavelike interactions, such as laser light. Orme-Johnson and Dillbeck (1987), for example, point out that in such systems the influence of elements that are acting coherently is proportional to the square of their number, while the influence of elements that are acting incoherently is only proportional to their number. In the case of lasers, for example, Orme-Johnson and Dillbeck note that when the coherent emission of photons exceeds the square root of the total number of photons, the entire system undergoes a phase transition in which all the photons begin to interact coherently, generating the laser light. It was largely on the basis of this principle that Maharishi and the TM researchers developed the square root of 1 percent formula to describe the threshold proportion of any given population that would have to be engaged in the practice of TM to create a measurable influence of harmony.

SHELDRAKE'S HYPOTHESIS OF FORMATIVE CAUSATION AND THEORY OF MORPHIC FIELDS

Through a series of books, biochemist Rupert Sheldrake (1981, 1988, 1991) has argued that all living systems inherit a kind of collective memory that is created by the repeated behaviors of previous members of their species. His proposal was originally formulated as a biological theory to describe how the forms of plant and animal species developed from birth and were stabilized in adulthood. In the first half of the twentieth century, several biologists had proposed the existence of "morphogenetic fields" as a way to explain how form develops in living systems. Borrowing from the field concept increasingly used by physicists, these biologists conceived of morphogenetic fields as invisible regions of influence that were specific to each plant and animal species and which contained ordering principles that shaped the development of individual members of each species. Sheldrake's hypothesis of formative causation assumes the existence of morphogenetic fields, but builds on previous theory by arguing that their structure is determined not by transcendent ideas or timeless mathematical principles (in a Platonic or Pythagorean sense), but by the actual forms and habits of previous similar organisms. Sheldrake thus conceives of the morphogenetic field of each species as a kind of cumulative memory of the species. Each member of the species is influenced by the species field, claims Sheldrake, and in turn contributes to the field, potentially influencing future members of the species. Because morphogenetic fields are nonmaterial, the species memory is not transferred through any genetic or physical mechanism, but, according to Sheldrake, by a process he calls "morphic resonance"—the influence of like upon like. Just as the strings in certain musical instruments will tend to vibrate when other strings of similar frequencies are sounded, Sheldrake proposes that present-day organisms are influenced by previous similar organisms through morphic resonance. However, unlike acoustic resonance (and other forms of resonance already known to science), Sheldrake maintains that morphic resonance does not involve a transfer of energy from one system to another, but rather a nonenergetic transfer of information. Morphic resonance thus involves a kind of action at a distance in both space and time, in which past patterns of activity influence the behavior of subsequent similar systems.

An important feature of Sheldrake's theory is that, by conceiving of the ordering principles in morphogenetic fields not as immutable laws but as the cumulative habits of past organisms, he leaves open the possibility for fields to continue to evolve. As noted, Sheldrake emphasizes not just the influence of the species field on the individual but the contribution of the individual to the field. Sheldrake claims that whatever is learned by the individual is incorporated into the morphogenetic field of the species, making it easier for future members of the species to learn the same behavior. Sheldrake argues that this hypothesis is empirically testable because it is possible to observe the rate a new skill is learned by all members of a species once some individual members have already learned the skill. Several experiments have indeed produced results consistent with the hypothesis.[10]

In defending the extension of the field concept into the realm of living systems, Sheldrake points out that, despite the increasing use of the field metaphor within physics (including the articulation of various kinds of quantum matter fields), the atomistic or mechanistic paradigm has continued to hold sway over many other areas of science, including biology. Sheldrake argues that the use of mechanistic models is especially inappropriate for the study of living organisms. Following Alfred North Whitehead and other process philosophers, he endorses instead "the philosophy of organism" in which all of nature is seen as fundamentally alive and governed by organic principles.[11] From this perspective, Sheldrake maintains, there is no reason why organisms at all levels of complexity should not have corresponding fields. The assumption that the known fields of physics are adequate to explain all the phenomena of life, including organisms of higher complexity, is, for Sheldrake, simply a hangover of scientific reductionism—the belief that anything can be understood in terms of its smallest constituent parts. Consistent with the organismic philosophy and systems theory, Sheldrake proposes a "nested" hierarchy of fields—fields nested within fields nested within fields—and does not assume that the lower level fields have a privileged place in the system. At each level, the field is seen as an irreducible whole unto itself, while containing parts that are themselves wholes. For example, the morphogenetic fields of species can be seen to contain fields of individual organisms, which contain fields of organs, which contain fields of cells, and so on, with the species field itself nested in fields of still higher order. Indeed, going beyond biological theory, Sheldrake introduces the term *morphic fields* to refer to a number of types of organizing fields in addition to those of morphogenesis, including animal and human behavioral fields, human social and cultural fields, and mental fields.

Sheldrake's discussion of the morphic fields of human societies and cultures has special relevance for the hypothesis of subtle activism. In justifying his proposal, Sheldrake notes that the idea that societies are wholes greater than the sum of their individual parts has been almost universally accepted in all cultures, and that even the modern West—with its mechanistic and reductionistic mindset—has not seriously challenged this view. In the spirit of the organismic philosophy, Sheldrake argues that human cultures can

be compared with living organisms in the sense that they have forms that
are inherited and reproduced over and over, are largely self-organizing, and
change and evolve. He points out that the metaphor of society as organism has indeed been adopted in some form by many of the main schools
of modern social theory.[12] Sheldrake also notes that the idea of invisible
organizing principles that determine and sustain social forms has been a
feature of social theory since its inception, despite contemporary models
describing these principles in prosaic terms like patterns of relationship,
social structures, and social consensus. Sheldrake argues that the contemporary theories face the same difficulty confronted by earlier ones of having to
explain these organizing principles either by reducing them to mechanisms
within individual brains (which seems implausible) or by associating them
with some version of eternal Platonic forms (which seems inconsistent with
the historical reality of social change). For Sheldrake, thinking of societies
in terms of morphic fields provides an explanation for social patterns and
structures that is more plausible than reductionistic theories, while more
able than idealist models to account for social change.

Moreover, Sheldrake notes that many prominent sociologists and
psychologists have supported the notion that societies might possess something like a collective or group mind. For example, French sociologist Emile
Durkheim coined the term *conscience collective* (collective consciousness) to
describe "the set of beliefs and sentiments common to the average members
of a single society which form a determinate system that has a life of its
own" (cited in Sheldrake 1988, 247). Sigmund Freud wrote:

> I have taken as the basis of my whole position the existence of
> a collective mind, in which mental processes occur just as they
> do in the individual . . . Without the assumption of a collec-
> tive mind, which makes it possible to neglect the interruption
> of mental acts caused by the extinction of the individual, social
> psychology in general cannot exist. (cited in Sheldrake 1988, 221)

American social psychologist William McDougall (1920) similarly
stated that "we may fairly define a mind as an organized system of mental
or purposive forces; and, in the sense so defined, very highly organized
human society may properly be said to possess a collective mind" (9). Finally,
and perhaps most relevantly, Carl Jung, with his theory of the collective
unconscious, conceived of a layer of the psyche that owed its existence not
to personal experience but primarily to cultural inheritance (we return to
Jung in more detail later in this chapter).[13]

Sheldrake also points out that the experience of being part of a group
mind that transcends its individual members has been widely reported in

a variety of everyday settings, such as team sports, musical concerts, and other kinds of group activities. For example, Sheldrake refers to sports writer Michael Novak, who writes:

> When a collection of individuals first gels as a team, truly begins to react as a five-headed or eleven-headed unit rather than as an aggregate of five or eleven individuals, you can almost hear the click: a new kind of reality comes into existence at a new level of human development. . . . For those who have participated in a team that has known the click of communality, the experience is unforgettable, like that of having attained, for a while at least, a higher level of existence. (Novak 1976, 135–136)

Sheldrake argues that conceiving of human societies in terms of morphic fields incorporates the group or collective mind concept, but also provides a way for explaining how cultural patterns and structures are maintained from generation to generation.[14] In his view, human language, thought, customs, and other cultural patterns are stabilized by self-resonance with a society's own past and by morphic resonance with previous similar societies. According to this hypothesis, new social and cultural fields emerge through the course of human history and then become increasingly habitual through repetition. Sheldrake maintains that the tradition of virtually all indigenous societies to use mythic stories as a way to teach ideal human behavior is consistent with this theory: Through myth, human activities are stabilized by their similarity with past patterns of activity, which are seen to have been repeated continuously all the way back to the time of the original mythical ancestors. Similarly, Sheldrake points out that the function of many rituals (in traditional or modern cultures) is to establish a connection with the past by repeating formalized patterns of activity in close conformity to the way they have been done over the generations. Sheldrake argues that the idea of morphic resonance explains why there is such a widespread belief in the need for present-day cultural rituals to closely follow the form of those in the past—the more similar they are, the stronger the resonant connection between the past and present participants in the ritual.

As with other kinds of fields, Sheldrake conceives of different levels of social fields arranged in a nested hierarchy, for example, family or tribal fields nested in regional or national fields, which are nested in a human species field (which is nested in still higher-level fields), with each level capable of influencing and being influenced by each other. Although morphic fields can evolve through the contributions of their individual members, Sheldrake acknowledges that they generally have a conservative effect and thus cannot in themselves entirely account for the phenomenon of social and cultural change. Over time, as the habitual patterns that characterize the morphic field are repeated over and over, the inherent creativity of the field is reduced. But how can we account for the emergence of a new field the very first time? Sheldrake argues that we can think of these creative leaps in three ways.

The first regards them as emerging "from below," with matter, life, or nature seen to possess an inherent creativity that allows for the synthesis of pre-existing patterns into new, more complex forms. The second supposes that new fields originate from within pre-existing higher-level fields, which are seen as the more fundamental source of creativity. A third approach, favored by Sheldrake, proposes that creativity is an interactive and evolutionary process, with the more inclusive higher-level field being somehow the source of the new field, but itself being modified by the new patterns of organization that the new field forms within it. Sheldrake acknowledges that the chain of reasoning involved in the two latter approaches ultimately leads us back to some kind of primal universal field as the source of all creativity and, consequently, into the realm of metaphysical speculation and/or to a recognition of the limits of conceptual thought.[15]

BACHE'S MODEL OF COLLECTIVE HEALING BY INDIVIDUALS IN NONORDINARY STATES OF CONSCIOUSNESS

In *Dark Night, Early Dawn*, religious studies professor Christopher Bache (2000) incorporates Sheldrake's theory into his hypothesis that, in certain profound states of inner work, the therapeutic effect of the healing process extends beyond the psyche of the individual to aspects of various collective levels of consciousness in which the individual is embedded. Bache was prompted to develop his theory largely because he had noticed that some elements of his own intense process of self-exploration, involving many years of psychedelic therapy, did not seem to fit with transpersonal psychologist Stanislav Grof's cartography of the psyche, which, Bache claims, focused primarily on individual transformation. Grof (1976, 1985, 1988) had developed a map of consciousness based on sixteen years of clinical experience with thousands of patients involving the therapeutic use of psychedelic substances, especially LSD, and, later, a therapeutic method called "holotropic breathwork." Although a lengthy summary of Grof's work is not necessary here (the interested reader is referred to any of Grof's books listed in the reference section), it is helpful for our purposes to outline the three general realms of consciousness that Grof identified on the basis of his clinical observations: the psychodynamic, the perinatal, and the transpersonal.

Grof found that initial sessions of patients undergoing psychedelic therapy usually involved their re-living of earlier and earlier biographical

experiences that broadly corresponded with Freudian psychoanalytic principles (he called this domain of experience the psychodynamic realm). As
patients continued their work, however, Grof found that they typically
moved even further back into an extraordinarily intense encounter with
the process of their biological birth. Grof identified a relatively predictable sequence of experiences that tended to accompany this process, with
a dramatic confrontation with physical and psychospiritual death being the
central experiential motif. The final stage of the process regularly involved
an experience of total annihilation, followed almost immediately by an
unexpected rebirth into radically expanded states of consciousness, usually
involving a variety of profound archetypal and mystical unitive experiences.
Grof called the realm related to experiences of the birth, death, and rebirth
process the "perinatal" ("surrounding birth") and the realm related to experiences of archetypal and mystical states of consciousness the "transpersonal."[16]

Although Bache's early work in his own psychedelic therapy mostly
meshed with Grof's model, at a certain point he found his experiences
seeming to diverge from the theory. In particular, Bache started to wonder
why his experiences at the perinatal stage of his work consistently involved
forms of suffering that were primarily collective, not individual, in nature.
For example, Bache (2000) reports experiencing "the torment of thousands
of beings tortured to their breaking point and then beyond" or pain that
"somehow comprised all of human history" (64–65). Bache points out that
Grof himself had noted that perinatal experiences could frequently take on
a collective scope, yet he tended to present his findings within a framework that emphasized personal transformation. After trying and failing to
interpret his experiences of collective suffering in terms of an individual-
centered model, Bache eventually concluded that the suffering needed to be
understood in the context of collective evolutionary history. For Bache, the
episodes of collective suffering were of such enormous scope that something
larger than personal consciousness seemed to be involved. He proposes that
this "something larger" might be the "species mind" of the human race. Just
as traumatic experiences can accumulate in the memory of an individual,
Bache suggests that the unresolved agony of human history might live on
in the collective memory of the species mind. And just as working through
painful personal memories can bring therapeutic release for the individual,
Bache argues that so might conscious engagement of collective trauma (by
an individual in a very expanded state of consciousness) bring healing to
the species mind.

Although he makes a sophisticated case for the epistemic value of his
direct experience of the species mind in psychedelic states of consciousness,
Bache also grounds the concept theoretically in Sheldrake's hypothesis of
formative causation and his associated theory of morphic fields. Slightly

modifying Sheldrake's theory, however, Bache maintains that the species mind, as one layer of a vast cosmic intelligence he calls "Sacred Mind," contains within it not just the species memory but also inherent creative capacities of enormous scope. That is, Bache, like Sheldrake, sees morphic fields embedded in higher-order fields reaching back to a unified universal field, but he emphasizes more than Sheldrake does the intrinsic creativity and agency of the intermediate fields, due to their permeability to the universal intelligence. Also, whereas Sheldrake holds that morphic resonance does not involve a transfer of energy from one system to another, Bache maintains that the notion that an individual can facilitate some kind of therapeutic discharge at the level of the species mind does imply the transfer of some form of energy, even if that energy is only psychic or mental. Although Bache acknowledges that the difference here may be merely semantic, he is open to the possibility that some processes of morphic resonance do involve an energetic transfer of information.

AREAS OF OVERLAP AND DIFFERENCE

It might already be obvious that there are several significant areas of conceptual overlap between these theories. At the most basic level, they each claim that beneath the surface appearance of separate material objects there exist one or more invisible dimensions of reality that connect all the parts together in a more fundamental unity, and that these invisible dimensions can be conceived of as "fields" that possess properties of consciousness. Both Sheldrake and Maharishi explicitly propose the existence of a number of different social fields (e.g., family, city, state, nation, world) that are themselves seen to be embedded in a universal unified field, the creative source of all reality. (Sheldrake focuses on the intermediate fields, with the universal field very much in the background; for Maharishi and the TM researchers, the reverse is true. We return to this important difference shortly.) All the models share the understanding that there is a reciprocal relationship between the individual and the collective field, that is, the individual and the field are seen to mutually influence each other (the capacity of the individual to influence the collective field is obviously a crucial element in any theory of subtle activism). Sheldrake's theory of morphic resonance also seems to fit well with Maharishi's explanation of precisely how an individual can influence the collective through the practice of TM. Maharishi maintains that when the unified field is "enlivened" in the consciousness of individuals (through the practice of TM and other advanced Vedic techniques), the social fields in which those individuals are embedded are automatically infected with the qualities of the unified field, because that field is the basis of all individual and collective consciousness. Such a process can be understood in terms of morphic resonance—the unified field being seen as common for all people, when it is activated in one person it begins to vibrate in another.

A place of common ground between Bache's theory and Maharishi's approach is the concept of a kind of threshold that must be crossed in order for individuals or groups to influence the collective in any significant way (i.e., via consciousness-based methods). For Maharishi and the TM researchers, the threshold is expressed quantitatively through the square root of 1 percent formula. Bache describes a qualitative threshold in terms of a certain level of depth in psychedelic work in which the subject expands beyond his or her individual identity to access collective dimensions of suffering and redemption.[17] Bache and Maharishi also agree that one reason why an individual or group can potentially influence an entire society is the disproportionate effect of coherent forms of consciousness (as accessed in meditation or psychedelic states) compared with ordinary consciousness.[18]

However, there are also some important differences between these approaches. As we have noted, Sheldrake embraces the organismic philosophy developed by Whitehead, and his theory contains several principles from that model that are largely absent in Maharishi's approach. For example, Sheldrake explicitly rejects the reductionistic tendency of modern science to explain all the properties of complex organisms in terms of the properties of their parts. He includes in this criticism the assumption that the known fields of physics are fundamental, with the fields of higher organisms seen as merely derivative. Instead, Sheldrake maintains that at each level of complexity organisms possess an organic unity that is irreducible to lower levels. Accordingly, he proposes that the morphic fields of systems at all levels of complexity should be seen as fundamental, rather than as derivative of the fields of physics. In contrast, Maharishi and the TM researchers, as we have seen, essentially equate the unified field discovered by physics with the transcendent field of consciousness described in Vedic teachings as the basis of all reality. Although Maharishi also refers to the concept of intermediate social fields, these fields are merely a footnote to his primary focus on the unified field, and their ontological status and value is not clarified. Although many theorists in addition to Maharishi have pointed out the uncanny parallels between the discoveries of modern physics and principles of Eastern mysticism, numerous critics have argued, in agreement with Sheldrake, that such an approach is reductionistic and fails to distinguish between fundamental levels of reality.[19]

The most prominent of these critics in transpersonal studies is American philosopher Ken Wilber. Briefly, Wilber defends the perennialist notion of the "Great Chain of Being," which describes reality as a "spectrum of consciousness" composed of different levels or dimensions, the most important of which are the material, the mental, and the spiritual.[20] He maintains that each level needs to be approached through a different epistemology, summarized as the "eye of flesh" for knowledge of the material world, the "eye of reason" for knowledge of the mental world, and the "eye of contemplation" for knowledge of the transcendent realm. Wilber argues that the new physics has simply discovered the interconnectedness of physical reality—the bottom rung in his "Great Chain"—which cannot be equated with the multidimensional unity described by mystics.

In defense of Maharishi and the TM researchers, they have been careful to point out that the scientific method cannot provide direct, experiential knowledge of the underlying unity revealed by its mathematics—for that, meditation is required (Oates 2002, 117–118). Also, as Capra (1985) argues, it is possible that Wilber's approach reifies the distinctions between the various levels, which in reality are complexly interwoven and interdependent. From this perspective, insights about the nature of reality at the physical level are not without significance for our understanding of the other levels. Nonetheless, the very strong emphasis placed by Maharishi and the TM researchers on the findings of physics to justify their theory does tend to reinforce the reductionistic assumption that physics is in a privileged position to explain the entire cosmos, and on this point, Sheldrake clearly takes a different view.

Another difference worth noting is that Sheldrake is deliberately nonspecific about the nature of the primal unified field in which the intermediate fields are seen as ultimately embedded, whereas Maharishi definitively identifies it with the transcendental ground of being described in Vedic literature. Sheldrake does acknowledge the existence of some kind of primal field to explain the ultimate source of creativity in the cosmos. His primary focus not being metaphysics, however, he does not devote much ink to the idea and leaves its nature relatively unspecified. For Maharishi, on the other hand, the unified field is the central concept of his philosophy and, although he uses the discoveries of physics to support it, his primary reference is the system of knowledge contained in ancient Vedic teachings. As we saw earlier, the Vedic literature describes the unified field as an "unmanifest, unbounded, and all-pervading field of pure intelligence responsible for all expressions of the laws of nature, in which all the laws of nature are located." TM researcher David Orme-Johnson (nd-c) maintains that the notion of a single unified field of consciousness at the source of existence is a core tenet of the "perennial philosophy," the purportedly universal system of thought said to have endured over many centuries in all parts of the world. Like the defenders of the perennial philosophy, Maharishi and the TM researchers claim not only that all mystical and contemplative traditions share a similar experiential insight into the ultimate nature of reality, but also that this understanding accurately represents the objective truth of existence. Unlike perennialists, however, the TM researchers tend to emphasize the Vedic teachings in particular as the most complete body of knowledge and, through modern TM research, the most scientifically validated one, implying its objective superiority to other contemplative paths, even those that share its nondual, monist metaphysics.

The Vedic teachings espoused by Maharishi undoubtedly constitute one of humanity's most profound systems of thought. His theory of Vedic Defense possesses, to my mind, a high degree of internal coherence and logic. Yet if our aim is to construct a general model of subtle activism that is as broadly inclusive as possible (a necessary goal, I believe, in our postmodern pluralistic world), it would be inappropriate to adopt an exclusively Vedic or even perennialist framework notwithstanding the claims of those systems to possess universal truth and appeal. Although the philosophical issues involved in a discussion of the limitations of perennialism are complex and cannot be comprehensively treated here, a summary of philosopher Jorge Ferrer's (2001) incisive critique should be sufficient to illustrate its potential pitfalls for our purposes.

At the heart of Ferrer's argument is his charge that the perennialist stance perpetuates the "Myth of the Given" in spiritual studies, that is, the belief in a singular, pregiven ultimate reality that can be objectively known by any human mind sufficiently emptied of its subjective distortions. In connection with this objectivist approach, Ferrer claims that perennialism also tends to privilege a nondual monist metaphysics resembling the Neo-Platonic Godhead or the Advaitin Brahmin. One of the difficulties with this approach, Ferrer points out, is that it does not adequately account for the apparently irreducible diversity of ultimate spiritual realities reported by mystics across traditions. For example, as Stephen Katz (1978) made clear in his influential paper "Language, Epistemology, and Mysticism," Jewish, Christian, Buddhist, and Hindu mystics (among others) regularly describe their experiences of ultimate reality in strikingly variable terms that cannot be equated with each other unless one adopts an a priori stance that assumes all mystical experience to be identical. Ferrer maintains that, in practice, perennialism can tend toward intolerance of spiritual views inconsistent with its metaphysical vision, frequently by incorporating such alternative views within a perennialist scheme that ranks spiritual traditions in relation to their commitment to an Advaitin-like nonduality, the assumed pinnacle of spiritual realization. In the context of subtle activism, for example, the problem of adopting a perennialistic framework is made clear if we consider the degree to which a sophisticated theologian like Walter Wink (see chapter 2) would feel welcomed within an approach that implied that the realization of an impersonal ground of being was an objectively deeper insight into reality than an encounter with a personal God. Obviously, such a dilemma would only be exacerbated if the basic framework of subtle activism were associated with a specific tradition, such as India's Vedic system of thought. As an alternative to perennialism, Ferrer (2001) proposes a participatory vision of spirituality that involves going beyond objectivism and subjectivism "towards the recognition of the simultaneously interpretive and immediate nature of human knowledge" (142). Such an approach incorporates a participatory epistemology that, according to Ferrer, is well described by Tarnas (1991) in the following terms:

> In this view, the essential reality of nature is not separate, self-contained, and complete in itself, so that the human mind can examine it "objectively" and register it from without. Rather, nature's unfolding truth emerges only with the active participation of the human mind. . . . On the one hand, the human mind does not just produce concepts that "correspond" to an external reality. Yet on the other hand, neither does it simply "impose" its own order on the world. Rather, the world's truth realizes itself within and through the human mind. (434)

Ferrer (2001) argues that when this epistemological vision is applied to spirituality, the idea of a specific pregiven ultimate reality cannot be maintained. Instead, he advances a view that "no pregiven ultimate reality exists, and that different spiritual ultimates can be enacted through intentional or spontaneous creative participation in an indeterminate spiritual power or Mystery" (151).[21]

Following Ferrer, I suggest that subtle activism would be well served by regarding the creative source as irreducible to any particular conception, with multiple spiritual realizations possible through human–divine co-creation. This approach has the advantage of supporting, as Ferrer puts it, a "more relaxed spiritual universalism" that welcomes the variety of ways in which the sacred can be expressed in the world. By embracing this framework, subtle activism could thus invite the participation of the widest possible variety of spiritual traditions, an especially relevant consideration in the context of global meditation and prayer events that aim to bring together practitioners from many different cultures and spiritual paths.

Notwithstanding these important differences, it is clear that the models we have examined are basically in alignment with each other in relation to the following principles that are fundamental for a theory of subtle activism:

1. Beneath the surface appearance of separate objects, there is a universal field of consciousness that is seen as an underlying ground and creative source of everything in existence.

2. Human individuals are embedded in this field, as well as in various kinds of social fields that correspond with different social units (family, city, nation, species, planet, etc.).

3. Individuals both influence these collective fields and are influenced by them.

4. The mechanism by which individual influence occurs can be explained in terms of morphic resonance (the influence of like upon like).

How might these principles be congruent with theories from other disciplines?

PARALLELS IN PHYSICS: BOHM'S THEORY OF HOLOMOVEMENT AND THE IMPLICATE ORDER

David Bohm, an American physicist who worked in the early part of his career with both J. Robert Oppenheimer and Albert Einstein, developed a model based on his theoretical investigations in quantum physics in which reality is regarded at its most fundamental level to be an undivided whole in a perpetual state of flow and change. He called this flow the *holomovement*. The "movement" part of the term refers to Bohm's idea that all of reality is dynamic process. Bohm (1980) pointed out that our patterns of thought and language tend to create fixed concepts that make dynamic processes seem like static entities. Keepin (1993) provides a simple example. The paper on which this text is printed appears to be static, however, we know that it is in a constant process of change and is evolving at all times toward dust. For Bohm, therefore, the paper would more accurately be described as "papering." All of reality, including thought itself, is, for Bohm, in a state of dynamic flux, and apparently stable structures are simply temporary abstractions out of the totality of which they are a part. The "holo" in holomovement refers to Bohm's belief that reality is in some essential way comparable to a hologram, in the sense that each part of reality is seen to contain information about the whole. Putting these concepts together, the holomovement can be understood, as Keepin (1993) puts it, as a dynamic flow in which "every portion of the flow contains the entire flow." Or, in Bohm's words, it refers to "the unbroken wholeness of the totality of existence as an undivided flowing movement without borders" (Bohm 1980, 172).

Bohm conceived of the holomovement as consisting of two main aspects: the explicate order and the implicate order. The physical universe that we perceive with our senses—the explicate order—was regarded by Bohm as only a tiny fraction of the whole, with the deeper implicate order being the more fundamental reality. Bohm proposed that material objects are simply the surface projections of the much vaster implicate order, "unfolded" out of the underlying field of wholeness. He also extended his theory beyond physical reality. Both matter and consciousness, in Bohm's view, are abstractions from the implicate order, which he saw as their common ground. In all this, it should be stressed that Bohm's model was originally developed as a result of his expert grasp of quantum theory and that the concepts of holomovement and the implicate order are rigorously grounded in the experimental evidence of quantum mechanics.

The implications of Bohm's theory for the hypothesis of subtle activism should be clear. Through his notion of the implicate order, Bohm provided another way for us to conceive of an underlying dimension of reality through which we are all connected and, presumably, through which we might be able to exert a nonlocal influence on others across space and time. Grof (1985), for example, in reviewing Bohm's model, writes that, "If the basic assumptions of the holonomic theory about the explicate and implicate order reflect reality with a sufficient degree of accuracy, it is conceivable that certain unusual states of consciousness could mediate direct experience of, and intervention in, the implicate order. It would thus be possible to modify phenomena in the phenomenal world by influencing their generative matrix" (90–91).

PARALLELS IN PSYCHOLOGY

When we considered Sheldrake's hypothesis of formative causation, I noted that several prominent sociologists and psychologists (including Durkheim, Freud, and Jung) subscribed to the view that societies possess something like a group or collective mind, a position compatible with the concept of social fields proposed by Sheldrake and Maharishi. German psychologist Gustav Fechner (widely regarded as one of the founders of modern experimental psychology) and American philosopher and psychologist William James also proposed the existence of some kind of collective consciousness underlying the phenomenal world. Fechner was principally concerned with developing methods to measure sensory thresholds, that is, the lowest levels at which a stimulus can be detected by the senses. Based on his own direct experience of a deeper layer of consciousness in which all minds were connected, Fechner believed that if an individual's sensory threshold could be sufficiently refined, he or she would experience the "general consciousness" underlying the apparent separateness of individual minds on the surface.

James distinguished between the standard "productive" theory of consciousness, which assumes that consciousness is created by various complex chemical interactions in the brain, from a "transmissive" theory, which holds that consciousness transcends and pre-exists the brain, with the brain's role being to mold consciousness into various forms (see Barnard 2008). James argued that the notion that the brain receives, directs, and transmits consciousness is just as coherent with empirical evidence as is the idea that the brain produces different states of awareness. As James pointed out, just because there is an observable correspondence between changes in the neurochemistry of the brain and changes in consciousness, it does not necessarily follow that the changes in the brain cause the corresponding change in consciousness. It is equally credible, James maintained, that changes in the brain's chemistry might "open the door" to previously inaccessible levels of consciousness that "exist ready-made in the transcendental world" (cited in Barnard 2008, 6).[22]

Yet it is Jung's theory of the collective unconscious (which I have thus far only mentioned in passing) that provides the most comprehensive psychological model in support of Sheldrake and Maharishi's notion of social fields and Bache's concept of collective healing in deep inner states. Jung (1981) found uncanny parallels between the content of his patients' dreams and images and motifs from mythological traditions that could not possibly have been known to the dreamers, suggesting the existence of a layer of the psyche that was collective and universal in nature.[23] With the evidence of synchronicity—those striking occasions when two or more independent events without any apparent causal connection appear nonetheless to form a meaningful pattern—Jung argued that the archetypal patterning that characterized the collective unconscious was more like a "universal substrate" that permeated the environment than a merely psychological phenomenon.

Although Jung regarded the collective unconscious as common to all humanity, he maintained that it could be differentiated into racial or national subunits. He wrote, "[n]o doubt, at an earlier and deeper level of psychic development . . . all human races had a common collective psyche. But with the beginning of racial differentiation, essential differences are developed in the collective psyche as well" (Jung 1981, 149). Jung's student Marie-Louise von Franz (1985) elaborated on this point by identifying at least three levels in the collective unconscious (Figure 4.1): a "group unconscious" associated with families, tribes, clans and so on, a "common unconscious" associated with national units, and finally an unconscious common to all humanity, comprised of "the sum of those universal psychic archetypal structures that we share with the whole of mankind" (20).

Sheldrake maintains that von Franz's analysis is consistent with the notion of morphic resonance because members of particular social groups are likely to be more similar to former members of the same social groups than to members of groups from different races and cultures, yet they share with the members of all groups certain characteristics as part of a universal

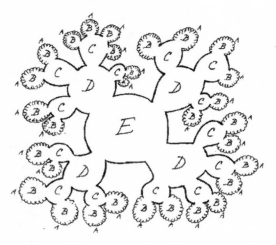

Figure 4.1. The structure of the unconscious. A: ego consciousness; B: personal unconscious; C: group unconscious; D: unconscious of large national units; E: universal archetypes. From von Franz (1985).

human heritage. The following statement by von Franz makes clear that her (and therefore Jung's) approach is also in close agreement with Bache's theory of collective healing in deep inner work (and thus with the hypothesis of subtle activism):

> Whenever an individual works on his own unconscious, he invisibly affects first the group and, if he goes even deeper, he affects the large national units or sometimes even all of humanity. Not only does he change and transform himself but he has an imperceptible impact on the unconscious psyche of many other people. (von Franz 1985, 17)

PARALLELS IN ESOTERIC THOUGHT

Dion Fortune's esoteric theory of magical activism also seems generally in tune with the frameworks set out in this chapter. In addition to being a teacher in the esoteric traditions, Fortune had attended psychology courses at the University of London and was aware of Jung's work. Her theory appears to have incorporated Jungian concepts within an overarching esoteric framework. To recall from chapter 2, Fortune believed that a nation possesses something akin to a collective mind comprised of two aspects: the "group mind" and the "group soul." The group mind represents the more transitory, malleable aspect located in current public opinion and thought; the group soul is the older, more stable layer built up by centuries of accumulated experience. Fortune likened the group mind to the conscious part of an individual's mind and the group soul to an individual's unconscious. Her conception of the group soul clearly corresponds with (and perhaps incorporates) Jung's notion of the collective unconscious, differentiated into national or racial units. Because the group soul can be seen as a kind of "collective memory" of the national mind, it is also consistent with Sheldrake's idea of a social morphic field. Her division of the collective mind into two levels is also in close conformity with Bache's extension of Sheldrake's theory into teaching and learning.

Applying these ideas on a smaller scale, in *The Living Classroom* Bache (2008), following Sheldrake, proposes the existence of "learning fields" in the university classroom that "reflect and embody the cumulative learning of all the students through the years who have ever taken a specific course with a specific professor" (53). Bache distinguishes two layers of the learning field: the "course field" and the "class field." The course field is that part of the field that holds the accumulated learning of all the students who have ever taken the same course with the same professor (thus it corresponds with Fortune's "group soul"). The class field (analogous to Fortune's "group mind") is the layer of the field created by the current group of students. Bache regards the class field as the "outer membrane" or the "living edge" of the larger course field. Similarly, we can understand the "group mind" in Fortune's model to represent the "living edge" of the older "group soul." Both Bache and Fortune regard the older, stable layer of the field as the energetically more powerful level, while acknowledging that the current layer is nonetheless capable of influencing the overall field. Such a view is in accordance with Sheldrake's hypothesis that the learning of current individual members of a species contributes to the ongoing evolution of the species' morphic field, although over time, and with many repetitions of similar patterns, the field exerts an increasingly powerful influence over present behavior.

Fortune's understanding of precisely how her group's magical activities were able to influence the national mind also seems consistent with Sheldrake's notion of morphic resonance. To recall, Fortune proposed that the primary task of her group's work was to create a channel to allow spiritual forces to transmit certain archetypal ideals and symbols into the collective consciousness of the nation. Because these ideals were seen to underlie the group soul of the nation, they were regarded as deeply harmonious with national tradition.[24] By coming together as a group and meditating on these archetypal thought-forms, Fortune maintained that her network created a "miniature collective subconscious," which enabled access to the corresponding level of the national mind. Here we see two expressions of the principle of morphic resonance. The transmission of information from Fortune's group to the English collective mind was seen to be possible because of the similarities between the archetypal symbols visualized by the group and the ideals of the national tradition, and between the collective unconscious created by the group and the collective unconscious of the nation.[25]

Fortune's approach also suggests an alternative to Bache's proposal regarding the capacity of individuals to facilitate collective transformation through spiritual methods. The path that Bache describes seems to require the individual to be willing to experience suffering of extraordinary intensity and scope in order to affect collective change. Much of this intensity can arguably be attributed to Bache's method of self-exploration, because entheogenic substances are renowned for surfacing unconscious material at much faster rates than most other methods. However, some of the intensity also might be connected to the extent of the psychic "stretch" that seems to be involved when a solitary individual opens up to collective levels. Referring back to von Franz's diagram (Figure 4.1), we might speculate that a very large, almost heroic, amount of inner work may be the price that an individual practitioner is required to pay to directly access and transform collective layers of consciousness in a relatively short amount of time (i.e., levels C, D, and E). Yet Fortune's proposal suggests that members of a group may have immediate access to level C in von Franz's model (the group unconscious of families, tribes, clans, etc.) and, by morphic resonance, with at least level D (the national unconscious)—without, apparently, having to endure an ordeal comparable to that recounted by Bache. By making this point I am not meaning to unfavorably contrast Bache's approach with that of Fortune. I fully appreciate that they are very different methods that cannot be compared side by side. I simply want to suggest that it might be easier to access certain levels of the collective psyche in the context of group, rather than individual, work. Indeed, in *The Living Classroom*, Bache himself makes the point that highly coherent group fields can function as a kind of amplifier, extending the reach of its members further into the collective intelligence than would be possible for individuals alone. To continue in this line of thought, we could speculate that a large, well-organized global meditation, involving people of many different races, religions, and cultures, might provide direct access to level E in von Franz's model, the universal unconscious common to all of humanity (arguably equivalent to Bache's notion of the "species mind").

A GENERAL HYPOTHESIS OF SUBTLE ACTIVISM

As seen in chapter 2, subtle activism can be practiced in many different forms and by a wide variety of religious and spiritual traditions. Accordingly, it is unlikely that any one conceptual model will perfectly accommodate these diverse perspectives. However, if we summarize the salient points from the theoretical frameworks considered in this chapter, we can construct a broad list of metaphysical principles that could form the basis of a general hypothesis of subtle activism:

1. Despite the appearance of radical separateness, there is a common underlying ground and creative source of all reality. Following Ferrer (2001), this creative source can be described as a mystery that is irreducible to any particular conception, yet is capable of being experienced through human co-creative involvement in the form of various spiritual realizations. As an example, one can think of this mystery as a unified field that underlies both the human mind and the natural world. Such terms as *God, the Tao, Brahma, the Void,* and others have also been used by the world's wisdom traditions to describe this mystery.

2. Social units (e.g., families, tribes, nations) can be conceived of as collective organisms with collective minds. These collective minds are comprised of at least two layers—the portion created by the presently living members of the social unit, and the (usually much bigger) portion created by the habits, behaviors, and mental patterns of all the previous members of the social unit. The part created by the living members can be compared with the conscious mind of an individual; the part created by nonliving members is like the individual's unconscious mind.

3. The collective mind of a social unit—including both conscious and unconscious portions—also can be described as a social field. Social fields (or collective minds) are arranged in a nested hierarchy, for example, family or tribal fields nested in regional or national fields, nested in a human species field, which is nested in still higher fields. All of these fields are themselves embedded in the ultimate creative source of reality.

4. Individual humans are embedded both in the ultimate creative source as well as in various social fields, including family, national, and species fields. There is a reciprocal relationship between the individual and these fields, that is, each individual is influenced by but also contributes to the collective memory of the field.

5. Morphic resonance is a key principle that explains how an individual or small group can influence the social field through consciousness-based practices. When an individual or group, through meditation, prayer, or other form of consciousness-based practice, makes experiential contact with aspects of the social field shared by all members (e.g., national archetypes, pure consciousness, or collective wounds), the individual or group enlivens or—in the case of collective wounds—helps heal those aspects for everyone in the field.

6. A certain threshold of influence must be crossed to affect the social field in any significant way. This threshold might be achieved quantitatively in terms of numbers of practitioners (e.g., Maharishi's square root of 1 percent formula), or qualitatively as in the level of depth, coherence, or intensity of the inner work.

Admittedly, these principles include some concepts that are not at present scientifically testable. However, as noted by Kennedy (1994), "[s]cientists and skeptics should be careful not to claim that beliefs are false when actually they are untestable" (73). Concepts outside the domain of science at a given time can still be valuable in stimulating creative thinking on a topic, and may generate ideas that become testable at a later time. Given the radical uncertainty that characterizes current scientific knowledge about the nature and origins of consciousness, it seems especially appropriate to remain open to a broad range of ideas on the subject.

In chapter 2 we considered examples of subtle activism in relation to a variety of social fields, ranging from the field of a local community (in the example I gave of shamanism), to the fields of cities (in many of the Maharishi Effect studies), the fields of nations (the Sarvodaya Peace Meditations and Fortune's "Magical Battle of Britain"), and the planetary field (the Harmonic Convergence). As indicated in chapter 1, a number of philosophers and scientists believe that one of the deepest narratives underlying our historical moment is the need for humanity to develop a more integrated planetary civilization. In this context, it is only natural that a major focal point of contemporary subtle activism will be on the level of the planetary field. In the following chapter, we consider in more detail the possible nature of an integrated planetary consciousness, how it might come about, and the potential role that subtle activism could play in supporting such a development.

CHAPTER FIVE

SUBTLE ACTIVISM AND THE EMERGENCE OF PLANETARY CONSCIOUSNESS

In the first part of the sixteenth century CE, Copernicus and his followers proposed that the Earth was a planet that revolved around the Sun. At around the same time, the European voyages of discovery and conquest demonstrated unequivocally that the Earth was round and ushered in a new era of unprecedented levels of communication and exchange between the peoples of every continent. As noted by French philosopher Edgar Morin (1999), these events mark the dawn of not just the modern period but what might also be called the Planetary Era. Ever since, the net of interconnections between the peoples and cultures of the world has continued to be woven together in increasingly tight and complex patterns.

Trade and cultural exchange between Europe, Asia, and the Americas increased dramatically in the seventeenth century with the rise of the English, Dutch, and French maritime trading companies and the establishment of the first European settlements in the Americas. The Industrial Revolution in the eighteenth and nineteenth centuries greatly empowered the dynamics of European imperialism and enabled the massive waves of European migration to the colonies in the Americas, Australasia, South Africa, and other regions. In the twentieth century, the advent of radio, television, the telephone, and the Internet allowed instant worldwide communication of news and events from anywhere on the planet. With the invention of the airplane and the development of commercial airlines, international travel became accessible and common. Wars became global, involving not just armies but also regular citizens from every inhabited continent. International political, legal, and economic institutions were established to monitor and enforce norms of international behavior (e.g., the United Nations, the International Criminal Court, the World Bank, the International Monetary Fund, the World Trade Organization, etc). Economic activities became increasingly integrated into a highly interdependent global economy. In the latter part of the twentieth century, ecological concerns of global scope emerged for the first time, leading to extensive international dialogue and cooperation to attempt to develop globally coordinated responses (e.g., the "Earth Summit" in Rio de Janeiro in 1991, and the climate change conferences in Kyoto in 1997 and in Copenhagen in 2009).

For many, this seemingly inexorable tightening of the many diverse fibers of human existence into a texture that, despite frequent ruptures and ongoing internal tensions, increasingly functions as an interdependent whole points to the potentially imminent emergence of an integrated planetary civilization and, with it, an associated planetary consciousness. A number of evolutionary-minded thinkers (including, as seen in chapter 1, Teilhard de Chardin and Thomas Berry) regard the shift to a planetary perspective as perhaps the most important narrative underlying our moment in history and a profoundly significant step in the evolution of consciousness. But what do we mean, exactly, by the term planetary consciousness? Is it a realistic possibility? And could there be a role for subtle activism to support its emergence?

DEFINITIONS AND CONCEPTS OF PLANETARY CONSCIOUSNESS

If we look at the idea of planetary consciousness from the perspective of an individual, we could describe it as a state of consciousness in which a person identifies on some level with the entire human species and/or the entire community of life on Earth. If we "identify" with a particular group, we tend to see ourselves as having something in common with the other members of that group and we are thus likely to extend care and compassion to those members. For example, Wilber (1995) defines *worldcentric identity* as "the capacity to distance oneself from one's own egocentric and ethnocentric embeddedness and consider what would be fair for all peoples and not merely one's own" (227). In this view, a person's circle of care (and presumably their identity) extends beyond members of their own biological family, ethnic group, or nation to include all human beings.

We could extend our definition even further to argue, as Brian Swimme (2003) and Thomas Berry (2009) do, that a truly planetary perspective means we see ourselves first and foremost not just as members of the human family but as earthlings in interdependent relationship with all the human and nonhuman members of the Earth community. Similarly, Lawrence Hagerty (2000) defines planetary consciousness as "a state in which one is as closely attuned to issues that affect *all* life on this planet as one is to one's own personal affairs" (x). Whether our global view encompasses the human species or the whole Earth community, however, it is unlikely that such a perspective will replace our particular cultural identity, but will rather complement it. Thus we might imagine, as David Spangler (1984) suggests, a transnational or planetary culture existing side by side with a person's ethnic or national culture, with both enriching the other.

In addition to understanding planetary consciousness in individual terms, we can consider it from the perspective of the whole of which the individual person is a part. If we consider the entire human species or the entire Earth community, for example, the emergence of planetary consciousness in more and more individuals could be seen as a case where the collective "being," previously slumbering, now starts to become aware of itself through individual human consciousness.

In this regard, James Lovelock's (1979 1988) Gaia theory is central to an emerging recognition that the Earth is a whole, self-regulating system. Lovelock proposed that the Earth's living matter functions like a single self-sustaining organism that keeps its systems in a "meta-equilibrium" broadly conducive to life. In developing his theory, Lovelock observed that various systems crucial for life on Earth appear to have always maintained a certain homeostasis that supports life. For example, since the beginning of life on Earth, the average temperature of most of the Earth's surface has remained between 60°F to 100°F—the optimal range for life—despite the fact that in that time, our sun, following the pattern of a typical star, would have increased its energy output by about 30 percent. Similarly, geological evidence shows that the concentration of salt in the world's oceans has remained relatively constant at around 3.4 percent—again, the ideal amount for life—despite the fact that more salt is continuously being deposited into the oceans by rivers. The amount of oxygen in the Earth's atmosphere is also ideally suited to life, despite computer calculations showing that, were the Earth's atmosphere maintained only by random chemical reactions, we should expect it to have a chemical composition similar to that measured on planets without life, such as Mars and Venus. On the basis of these and other apparently homeostatic behaviors of the Earth's biosphere, Lovelock proposed the concept of Gaia as a complex feedback system that seeks to maintain an optimal physical and chemical environment for life on Earth. Although the mainstream scientific community distanced itself from what it regarded as the teleological implications of Lovelock's initial hypothesis, the core idea that the biosphere profoundly shapes the inorganic environment, rather than merely adapts to it, with the two forming a continuous, self-sustaining whole, is now widely accepted.

The primary significance of Gaia theory for the awakening of planetary consciousness is the image it provides of the Earth as a single living organism. As T. Berry (2009) notes, Gaia theory

> establishes the basis for a new type of religious experience different from but profoundly related to the religious-spiritual experience of the earlier Shamanic period in human history. . . . The sense of awe and mystery that was evoked in the earliest human awakening to the universe is beginning to awaken once more within this new context of scientific understanding. (115)

Along with the first footage of Earth taken from outer space by the Apollo astronauts (which, synchronistically, occurred at about the same time that Lovelock was first formulating his hypothesis), Gaia theory has seeded the collective imagination with the image of the Earth as a living being. In this light, we might say that Gaia theory is an expression of the Earth's self-recognition via human scientific awareness. Even Lovelock himself, who has been careful to refute attempts to use his theory as support for the notion that the Earth is a sentient, conscious entity, acknowledges the spiritual significance of his hypothesis when he says that "a theory of the Earth that sees it behaving like a living organism [is] inevitably theological as well as scientific" (Primavesi 2000, xi-xii).

We can also recall Teilhard de Chardin's idea that the noospheric web of thought being spun ever more tightly around the globe is creating a new planetary membrane that will eventually start to function as a single, organic unity. Because of the continuing growth in human population on a finite sphere along with the ever-increasing complexity of the global communications network, Teilhard foresaw an inevitable "closing of the spherical thinking circuit" to form a

> harmonized collectivity of consciousness equivalent to a sort of super-consciousness. The idea is that of the earth not only becoming covered by myriads of grains of thought, but becoming enclosed in a single thinking envelope so as to form, functionally, no more than a single vast grain of thought . . . the plurality of individual reflections grouping together and reinforcing one another in the act of a single unanimous reflection. (Teilhard 1959a, 251–252)

As seen in chapter 1, Teilhard regarded this development as simply a natural extension of the evolutionary process and, in particular, a higher form of a process of "moleculization" whose first phase was the formation of proteins up to the stage of the cell, and whose second phase was the formation of individual cellular complexes, up to and including the human. "First the vitalization of matter, associated with the grouping of molecules; then the hominization of Life, associated with the supergrouping of cells; and finally the *planetization* of Mankind, associated with a *closed* grouping of people . . ." (Teilhard 1959b, 108).

Peter Russell (1983) proposes that the growth of the noosphere can be understood as the evolution of a global brain. Just as the brain of a human embryo develops in a two-stage process—an initial population explosion of embryonic nerve cells followed by a phase of growing interconnectivity between the cells—Russell claims we can observe similar trends with regard to human development on the planet. In particular, with the ongoing human population explosion and the exponential increase in interconnectivity between humans through the ever-more sophisticated worldwide communications network, Russell maintains that the human presence on the planet increasingly resembles a planetary nervous system or brain. Just as the development of the neo-cortex is linked to the emergence of human conscious self-awareness, so, argues Russell, might the development of a global "brain" be associated with the emergence of Gaian self-awareness.[1]

Hagerty (2000), on the other hand, contrasts the noosphere (Russell's global brain) with what he sees as a pre-existing Gaian mind: an ancient, slow-moving intelligence involved in the regulation of life on the planet since the beginning.[2] Hagerty proposes that we conceive of the mind of Gaia as a "meta collective consciousness" composed of the consciousness of everything on the planet. In Hagerty's view, the noosphere (the entirety of human collective consciousness) is just one component of the Gaian mind, which also consists of the collective consciousness of minerals, plants, and animals. Moreover, Hagerty contends that the noosphere is a part of the Gaian mind that seems to have "slipped away." Although the human collective consciousness is clearly an aspect of Gaia, Hagerty argues that we have become dissociated from the ground of our being, as evidenced by our gross mistreatment of the biosphere, the physical foundation of our very existence. The obvious implication for Hagerty is the need for the human noosphere and the Gaian intelligence to harmonize.

Whether or not one is prepared to accept the notion of a Gaian or noospheric mind, what seems undeniable is that, in the face of growing global ecological concerns, an increasing number of people sense the need to adopt a Gaian worldview, which recognizes the interconnectedness of all life on the planet. Yet in a world still controlled by economic and political systems with powerful vested interests in maintaining the existing order, and with the continued existence of many forms of religious and national fundamentalism that vigorously resist any move to a global perspective, it is clear we have not yet crossed the threshold to a genuinely planetary age. Let us consider in more detail, then, what might be needed to transform the vision of planetary civilization from dream to reality.

OWNING THE SHADOW

A first step may be to acknowledge what philosopher Sean Kelly (2010) calls the "planetary shadow," by which he means the unprecedented global suffering associated with the legacy of Western colonialism and industrial capitalism in the modern era. Before we can come together in mutual recognition of our common humanity, we will need to face squarely the distressing facts of the past and present suffering of billions of poor and oppressed peoples and countless thousands of nonhuman species, for whom the initial five centuries of the Planetary Era (in its broad sense) have brought mostly tragic and brutal loss. Such an examination of conscience may lead to, as Tarnas (2001) puts it, a "fundamental moment of remorse . . . a sustained weeping and grief" for the devastating harm the dominant culture has inflicted on all those at the margins of its singular vision.

To embrace such a perspective is to acknowledge our complicity in participating to varying degrees in a global system that perpetuates such widespread and unequally distributed suffering. After all, it is not only businesses and governments that have a vested interest in maintaining the status quo. Almost everyone in the developed world contributes to the profits of transnational corporations—and thereby perpetuates the suffering of others—because we do not want to give up our comfortable lifestyles. In a real sense, as S. Kelly (2010) says, "we *are* those we oppose" (130). Recognizing this truth will hopefully lead us to question our tendency to readily affix blame on some *other* group or category of persons whom we assume, unlike us, make their bad choices maliciously or deliberately. However, rather than using this insight to turn our blame inwardly in self-judgment or to give up our efforts in despair, it might ideally lead us to see that we are all fundamentally in this together. This does not mean, of course, that we should not resolutely or even fiercely confront destructive or lazy behavior—whether in ourselves or in others—yet we might strive to do so within an overarching context of compassion, given the complexity of the task we all face in negotiating the transition.

EMBRACING DIFFERENCE

As noted earlier, philosophical postmodernism, especially as represented by thinkers like Michel Foucault, Jacques Derrida, and Jean-Francois Lyotard, has tended to criticize "grand meta-narratives" for purporting to be universal while in fact expressing particular culturally and historically situated—and typically privileged—viewpoints that, knowingly or not, serve to reinforce hierarchies of power and maintain ideological elites. Instead of universal systems of thought, postmodern philosophy has emphasized locality, otherness, plurality, and difference. These principles have profoundly influenced the academy, especially in the humanities, and also have permeated the contemporary sociopolitical milieu, providing a source of liberation for large numbers of previously marginalized groups and individuals. In this light, proposals for a common or unified planetary consciousness might be viewed with suspicion as yet another "totalizing unity" that promises emancipation, yet which in fact perpetuates oppression. A particular concern might be that specific individual or cultural needs will be papered over by a quasi-religious appeal to the salvific potential of the (higher, more significant) collective reality. Given the fate of marginal individuals and cultures in twentieth century totalitarian states, which made exactly these kinds of appeals, such concerns are understandable. Economic globalization is another instance where the imposition of a system of supposedly universal application and benefit has in practice resulted in the exploitation of marginal groups and cultures and the general suppression of difference. Yet not only does the global ecological crisis present the human species with an evolutionary imperative to develop a universal and not merely local perspective, it is through the integration of postmodern insights themselves that we can start to reconstruct a genuinely inclusive planetary vision.

Central to such a vision will be a more complex understanding of the relationship between the part and the whole, one that honors differentiation and distinctness as vital components of any authentic wholeness. In this regard, we would do well to be guided by S. Kelly's (1993, 2010) notion of "complex holism," which he proposes as a meta-principle for the development of a planetary wisdom. While drawing partly from Hegel's "logic of the Absolute" and Jung's concept of the Self as *complexio oppositorum*, S. Kelly finds particular inspiration for his proposal in French philosopher Edgar Morin's "paradigm of complexity." Morin (1977) suggests three interrelated principles inherent to an understanding of complexity: the dialogic, recursivity, and the holographic principle.[3] Although all three principles have relevance for our discussion, I want to draw special attention to Morin's (1977) definition of the dialogic: "the association of two principles which are at once complementary, concurrent, and antagonistic" (80). Kelly notes that the yin-yang symbol and the wave-particle duality of quantum physics are prominent examples of the principle. As Kelly points out, the antagonistic quality in the dialogic makes clear that although the associated principles may combine in creative and synergistic ways, they also retain their relative independence and cannot be reduced simplistically one to the other, or resolved in a final synthesis. In the context of our present discussion, the dialogic principle implies that a complex understanding of planetary consciousness will recognize a dynamic balance between the individual and the whole (and between diversity and unity). In this regard, the proliferation of diverse individual and cultural narratives that has emerged from postmodern critiques of supposedly universal knowledge claims can be seen as an essential precursor to, and ongoing component of, any truly planetary perspective. On the other hand, our commitment to locality and difference risks becoming dogmatic and limiting unless we can also be open to the possibility of our many diverse views finding common ground in a wider or more encompassing context.

This new common context, however, is not the abstract and singular vision of universality that characterized the Enlightenment project and which demanded the sacrifice of difference to a predetermined notion of unity. The collective envisioned here is a concrete and practical universality, based on the fact of planet Earth being our common home, and a dynamic multitude, which constantly adapts to reflect changes in its many diverse parts. Such a reality is not imposed unilaterally from above but (in conjunction with inspired leadership) emerges spontaneously from the voluntary participation of individuated persons and cultures that recognize the advantages of collaborative engagement. Not only does this form of collectivity permit diversity, it actively encourages it to maximize the collective intelligence of the whole.[4]

IDENTIFYING RESISTANCE

Despite the fact that we can observe a general trajectory over the past several centuries toward an increasingly interconnected human presence on the planet, we must acknowledge the continued dominance of political and economic structures that powerfully resist the transition to a planetary or Gaian consciousness. Although we might want to share William Irwin Thompson's (1985) optimistic view that, like a star that flares into a brilliant supernova just before it dies, the apparently intensified expression of these forms in recent years signals their imminent decline, they still represent the central influence in contemporary society and thus remain a force with which we must reckon.

Although nearly all of the mechanistic assumptions of the modern worldview have been seriously challenged and deconstructed in virtually every academic discipline over the course of the twentieth century, the absence of a widely accepted framework to take the place of the old paradigm has permitted many of the old ideas to continue to serve as the basis for our social, economic, and political affairs, although in increasingly incoherent and problematic ways. For John Turnbull, one of the most insidious expressions of the mechanistic paradigm—and one of the greatest impediments to the spread of a Gaian worldview—is the neoliberal economic ideology that underpins our current economic system. Turnbull (2007) describes neoliberalism as:

> the belief that there should be as few restrictions as possible on the operations of businesses and the economy in general; that government should privatize all but its core functions, such as defense and the judiciary; and, at the international level, that overseas markets should be opened up by the use of political, economic, or diplomatic pressure. (42)

As Turnbull notes, underlying these beliefs are the assumptions that all human beings are singularly concerned with maximizing their personal consumer choices (thus transforming "decent, well-rounded citizens into gluttonous . . . consuming machines"), that material wealth is the most important measure of individual and collective well-being, and that economic growth can continue indefinitely (i.e., natural resources are assumed to be infinite).

This ideology works against the uptake of a truly planetary, or Gaian, perspective in numerous ways. Whereas a Gaian worldview sees human society as embedded in the larger Gaian system, the neoliberal ideology assumes the economy to be somehow independent from nature, which it regards as little more than a source of raw materials (that can never be exhausted) and a dumping ground for society's waste. Whereas a Gaian perspective encourages humans to recognize that, as part of an interconnected system, their actions have far-reaching consequences that must be taken into account, economic globalization (based on neoliberal assumptions) transports those consequences (for some) to far-away places where they can easily be forgotten. And whereas a Gaian worldview celebrates and works to preserve the many diverse expressions of human and nonhuman life on the planet, neoliberalism demands that all cultures and species adapt to its single prescribed way of life or simply perish.

Although the staunchest advocates of this ideology are those with the greatest vested interest in the current system (i.e., the leaders of large corporations and industries), governments and politicians are also deeply invested in maintaining a favorable relationship with the business community. As Turnbull points out, were politicians to challenge directly the root assumptions of the dominant ideology—for example, by enacting laws that required companies to pay for the full costs of doing business, including damage to the environment—campaign contributions would dry up, financial markets would react, and it would play badly in the corporate media, consequences no politician who wants to be re-elected can easily ignore.[5] Perhaps most insidiously of all, the system is further maintained by the unwillingness of virtually all of us in the developed world to sacrifice the comforts of our lifestyles—comforts that have been passed down to us by virtue of our membership of societies that have created and most benefited from the current economic system. In light of these mutually reinforcing dynamics, the further spread of a truly planetary or Gaian perspective will remain limited unless we are able to reform our democratic systems of government so that the real interests of people are placed before corporations. Reform of this kind will first require, of course, that the collective consciousness of the people be so transformed as to demand such a change.

In addition to the lingering, and still dominant, assumptions of modernity that permeate our economic and political structures, there is another posture that even more blatantly opposes any move toward a genuinely planetary age: the regressive stance of religious fundamentalism. Such a stance involves an attempt to reinstate a premodern identity by rejecting the process of secularization associated with the modern scientific worldview. This orientation is not to be confused with postmodern critiques of the limitations or one-sidedness of modern science and rationality but rather amounts to a return to a naïve or precritical epistemological approach. Needless to say, the intolerance shown by fundamentalist groups to those who do not share their views is a significant obstacle to the emergence of a more integrated planetary perspective.

In recent years, we have witnessed the startling ascension to the world stage of especially virulent forms of fundamentalism, most notably in the global spread of radical Islamic terrorism and the rise to power of the extreme Christian right in the United States. Again, although we might optimistically interpret such manifestations in the context of the rising planetary culture as the convulsions of a dying world order, they represent a reality with which we still need to contend. Whether we should relate to these forces by opposing them with fierce strength and moral clarity, extending them extraordinary compassion and understanding, or in some other fashion, is not always clear. Perhaps the frequently confounding nature of this dilemma is like the grain of sand in our planetary oyster, with our sincere attempts to grapple with it providing a spur to the development of the collective moral and spiritual intelligence necessary to bring forth the pearl of planetary consciousness.

SIGNPOSTS OF AN EMERGING ORDER

Notwithstanding the repressive power of these conservative elements, however, it is hard to deny that evidence of an emerging planetary culture is all around us. As Teilhard (1959a) pointed out, although we can usually identify a definitive birth moment of a new evolutionary level, we can also recognize in the earlier stage a long period of preparation during which components of the emerging order appear in trace form. Like the "first light" before dawn, as S. Kelly (2010) puts it, there are many features of our times that seem to anticipate an imminent collective shift toward planetary awareness.

Morin (1999) lists a number of these features in *Homeland Earth*: the persistence of a global nuclear threat; the emergence of a planetary ecological consciousness (made explicit by the 1992 Earth Summit in Rio, and, we can now add, by the Kyoto and Copenhagen climate change conferences in 1997 and 2009 respectively); the recognition by the West of the Third World (whereby its problems, previously ignored by the colonial powers, are increasingly recognized as problems of the entire planet); the development of a global civilization (one of the byproducts of economic globalization which, Morin argues, for all its cultural and environmental destructiveness, is also providing common customs and lifestyles that lift barriers to mutual comprehension between people and nations); planetary "teleparticipation" (the power of television—and, we can now add, the Internet—to bring catastrophic events from around the world into people's homes, arousing empathy and the feeling of belonging to the same global community); and the view of Earth from the moon (seen live by a large portion of humanity during the Moon landing and forever after providing a common image of our shared planetary home).

We can add to this list several other notable factors. First, there is the emergence of the movement for "Global Justice" (to adopt George Monbiot's [2006] term), a diverse, grassroots, and explicitly global movement that opposes the exploitative effects of economic globalization on developing nations and the natural world. The most visible manifestations of the movement include the dramatic public demonstrations staged in major cities in recent years to protest the policies of the World Trade Organization and other leading institutions of the international economic system (most famously in Seattle in 1999 and Genoa, Italy, in 2001), and the World Social Forum, held annually in Brazil to provide a space for an extremely diverse coalition of tens of thousands of participants to develop alternatives to the neoliberal agenda. Second, we can recall the massive worldwide demonstrations on February 15, 2003 to protest the imminent U.S. invasion of Iraq. With an estimated 6 million to 10 million people marching in rallies in up to sixty countries, this unprecedented display of coordinated global action inspired *New York Times* columnist Patrick Tyler to declare that world public opinion had emerged as the "second superpower." Central to the organization of both the February 15, 2003 protest and the demonstrations of the Global Justice movement were the unprecedented grassroots networking capacities provided by the Internet. The development and exponential growth of the Internet with its provision of virtually instant access to an unprecedented and ever-growing store of collective knowledge and information, has itself seemed to many to foreshadow a quantum leap in the evolution of consciousness. Indeed, for those familiar with Teilhard's work, the Internet has appeared to represent something like the mechanical apparatus of the noosphere, that "organized web of thought" Teilhard foresaw one day encircling the globe.[6] We can also note the staging of several significant globally coordinated music concerts in recent decades (e.g., Live Aid, Live 8, and Live Earth), which not only brought together enormous global audiences but also focused the world's attention on significant humanitarian and ecological crises, thereby inspiring the global community to relate to these issues as matters of collective concern. Finally (although many other examples could be given), there is the development of the Earth Charter, the most significant attempt yet to develop the ethical foundations of a "just, sustainable, and peaceful global society." The product of a highly collaborative, decade-long worldwide dialogue about shared values and common goals, endorsed by thousands of organizations and governments, the Earth Charter seeks to inspire in all people "a sense of global interdependence and shared responsibility for the well-being of the human family, the greater community of life, and future generations." Although the Earth Charter is not legally binding, its supporters claim that, in the eyes of many international lawyers, it is acquiring the status of a "soft law" document that is morally binding on governments that endorse it, and that can form the basis for the development of actual laws.

CROSSING THE THRESHOLD

What might it take for humanity to make the transition to a truly integrated planetary civilization? Peter Russell (1983) and Christopher Bache (2000) build on insights from systems and chaos theory into the nature of dissipative structures to speculate on how a new level of organization might emerge for the human species. In the 1970s, Belgian chemist Ilya Prigogine coined the term *dissipative structures* to describe open, self-organizing systems that maintain their internal organization far from thermodynamic equilibrium. They are called dissipative structures because the entropy, or disorder, they produce is dissipated to the environment. Examples of dissipative structures include galaxies, cyclones and hurricanes, and all living systems. Dissipative structures are capable of retaining their internal organization despite changes to their external environment so long as the fluctuations in energy flow remain within certain limits. If the fluctuations are too extreme, the system is driven into instability or crisis. Sometimes the system simply collapses, unable to adapt to the new conditions. In other cases, however, the crisis can result in the emergence of new levels of self-organization. For example, in the primitive stages of life on Earth, a food crisis for the early bacterial cells resulted in the development of photosynthesis—the capacity to catch photons from the Sun and use them as food. These crisis periods are called bifurcation points, moments of truth when a system can either adapt or perish. Chaos theory informs us that when a system approaches a bifurcation point it becomes highly sensitive to input. Tiny influences can have vastly amplified effects due to the presence of complex feedback loops. Chaos theorists Briggs and Peat (1990) explain:

> A bifurcation in a system is a vital instant when something as small as a single photon of energy, a slight fluctuation in external temperature, a change in density, or the flapping of a butterfly's wings in Hong Kong is swelled by iteration to a size so great that a fork is created and the system takes off in a new direction. (143)

Russell and Bache argue that human society, confronted by a looming global crisis of many dimensions, increasingly resembles a dissipative structure facing a bifurcation point. As these authors acknowledge, civilizational collapse is certainly conceivable, yet chaos theory suggests another possibility: that human society, in the right circumstances, might rapidly re-organize into a fundamentally new form. The question is, what might induce such a shift?

In the context of today's highly complex and unstable global situation, chaos theorist David Peat (2008) proposes the concept of "gentle action" as a way to support intelligent systemic change. In his book *Gentle Action*, Peat argues that although our financial, economic, social, and ecological systems have become enormously complex and thus inherently unpredictable, governments and organizations still tend to take action based on the traditional mechanistic assumptions that exact prediction and control is always possible and that issues can be solved by focusing only on the most obviously problematic part of a system. Yet, Peat claims, when our actions are more rigid and simplistic than the systems we seek to influence, not only are our efforts doomed to failure but they frequently become part of the problem. In contrast, Peat recommends the intelligent application of subtle or minimal interventions that apply to the system as a whole. For example, as a first step toward transforming a complex system Peat encourages a practice of "creative suspension" and "alert watchfulness." Such an approach does not involve overt action but allows the deeper dynamics of the system—its rigidities, fixed positions, unexamined assumptions, and so on—to become apparent. By bringing these dysfunctional patterns to awareness and no longer feeding them energy, Peat maintains that they are allowed to dissolve while providing space for the inherent creativity within individuals and groups to develop new and more flexible approaches that are better adapted to their environments. In this way, Peat (nd-a) claims, the organization or group effectively dies to its old self and is reborn in a form "as sensitive, subtle and intelligent as the systems and situations that surround them" (section, The Dilemma of Action, para. 7). At the global level, Peat (nd-b) similarly argues that our planet does not need violent revolutions or highly structured government programs imposed from above but "a new action that is sensitive and highly intelligent" (para. 27).

SUBTLE ACTIVISM AND PLANETARY CONSCIOUSNESS

It should be apparent that the approach of subtle activism as outlined in this book is deeply congruent with Peat's proposal and could potentially support an organic reconfiguration of society in a fashion similar to the process just described. In these turbulent times, there seems clearly to be a need for gentle forms of intervention that relax the grip of individual and collective egoic patterns and allow for a more universal perspective to arise. Anthropology professor Ian Pratiss (nd) maintains that the shift that is called for at the collective level parallels the process of individual spiritual development, which he describes as "a pilgrimage from the 'I' of ego-attachment to the 'I' of our true nature—that boundless consciousness that harbors no separation." To continue the analogy, it should be noted that individuals on a spiritual path do not tend to finally resolve their issues through increased efforts at the level of the personality but by a shift in identity whereby they realize their inherent connection to the whole. Similarly, so might our global problems resist resolution until various kinds of bounded identities (individual, cultural, religious, ethnic, national) become permeable to a more encompassing planetary point of view. The practice of subtle activism may help to support this transition by gently softening these types of boundaries. The following account by Bache (2000) of a profound experience he had in the context of psychedelic therapy illustrates how this might occur:

> Just as my previous work had mediated the experience of collective anguish out of the collective field, my current task now seemed to be to mediate the experience of no-self into the collective surround. I experienced this primarily in terms of a flow of energy moving through me into the species-mind. To the extent that this flow took cognitive form at all, it took the form of becoming comfortable with the loss of boundaries. This had many aspects

to it—being comfortable surrendering the boundaries of race, the boundaries of socioeconomic distinctions, the boundaries of nationality, the boundaries of religion. Wherever we had drawn boundaries around ourselves in history, there was fear. I seemed to be mediating a calming energy that encouraged the dissolving of these boundaries and the softening of these fears. . . . Soothing energies moved through me and reached into the human field, making it a bit easier for persons to relax and yield to the flow of historical events that were challenging and dissolving the unreal divisions humanity had drawn upon itself. (223–224)

Peat's proposal for acts of "creative suspension" or "alert watchfulness" before engaging in more active or forceful interventions in complex organizations finds a particular echo in the approach of subtle activism to social and political systems. For example, consider the "Gaiafield attunement" practice that has emerged as a core method for my own Gaiafield Project.

In a Gaiafield attunement practice, participants cocreate a contemplative space that focuses on a pressing collective issue (e.g., the outbreak of war, a significant natural disaster, a major election, etc). Participants are invited first to center themselves in their own experience, then to connect with the other participants and the "field" of the group, and with the presence of the sacred in various dimensions, including the Earth itself, or Gaia. The group is then guided to bring its collective attention to the worldly situation in question and to hold the issue in silent contemplation for an extended period (usually about twenty minutes). The final step is to invite participants to share any insights or guidance that may have arisen for them in the meditation. The practice can be applied in a range of contexts, from a small local group meeting face-to-face to a teleconference or audio webcast involving thousands of people from many different countries and cultures around the world. The idea is to create a field of awareness that holds the situation in all its complexity, allows the emergence of deeper levels of the group's collective intelligence and creativity, and creates a channel for the flow of inner energies into the world. Although the decision makers and stakeholders most directly involved in the situation will usually not be part of such a practice, the wisdom generated by this approach could, through the principle of morphic resonance, contribute to a collective psychic environment in which a deeper, more holistic perspective on the issue becomes slightly more accessible to all. (As seen in chapter 3, the considerable scientific evidence of nonlocality gives us reason to believe that this kind of gentle action could indeed exert genuine influence.)[7]

Even if one is unwilling to accept the potential nonlocal influence of this practice, however, there can be little doubt that bringing thousands of people from many different countries together in contemplative practice grounded in a shared concern for humanity or the Earth (as can occur in the largest form of the practice) would be inherently meaningful—at a minimum for the participants involved. Thomas Berry (2009) writes, "the entire dynamics of the modern world is, to an increasing degree, throwing people and societies together in close exterior proximity but without the capacity for interior communication" (27). Although, as Berry points out, we should take care to avoid an "overly facile" unification in an undifferentiated religious or spiritual context, there is a genuine need for the establishment of what Berry calls "common spiritual spaces" that allow for a deeper communion between peoples and traditions.

I already noted in chapter 1 the potential significance of the practice of global meditation and prayer for the evolution of planetary consciousness. Here I would just like to observe that although there might be many ways to experience planetary awareness, a global meditation and prayer event is an expression of that consciousness in arguably its most distilled form. Planetary consciousness is the very essence of the practice, constituting both its subject (in the form of the worldwide group of participants) and its object, meeting in an act of sustained self-reflection. In this light, we could speculate that global meditation and prayer events may be planting seeds of the coming world deep in the fertile soil of the collective psyche. French poet Charles Peguy said, "Everything begins in mysticism and ends in politics"—meaning, as William Irwin Thompson puts it, that politics is just the clean up operation after a social transformation has been introduced by visionaries and artists. "Finally, when everybody can see it, it gets its political representation" (Thompson 1985, para. 12). So too with the transition to a planetary civilization. One of the most meaningful tasks of our times, then, may be to evoke experiences of planetary communion of such sublime joy that an unspoken vow is made, from the most intimate heart of humanity, to persevere through the trials ahead, to heal the wounds of our collective past, and to accept the pain that must accompany the birth of planetary awareness.

CHAPTER SIX

CONCLUSION

There were two broad objectives for this book. The first and primary goal was to introduce the concept of subtle activism as an innovative approach to social change, emerging from the intersection of spirituality and activism. In this regard, my intention was to present subtle activism as a generally meaningful way of relating to the world, regardless of historical context. To further this objective, I defined subtle activism in chapter 1 as "practices of spirit or consciousness intended to support collective transformation." I distinguished it from the more common spiritual focus on individual growth and from other forms of socially engaged spirituality—namely, those that tend to view spirituality as a resource to inform action in the world, but not as a form of action in its own right. In chapter 2 we looked at numerous stories involving the use of spiritual practices for collective benefit by many of the world's major religious traditions, suggesting the universal appeal of what I call subtle activism. Drawing from several lines of scientific research—parapsychology, distant healing, the Maharishi Effect, and the Global Consciousness Project—I presented in chapter 3 a substantial body of empirical evidence that supports the principle of nonlocality that underlies the hypothesis of subtle activism. In chapter 4 we examined several theories that have been proposed as a way to explain how it might work—including Maharishi Mahesh Yogi's theory of Vedic defense, Rupert Sheldrake's hypothesis of formative causation and theory of morphic resonance, and Christopher Bache's model of collective healing by individuals in nonordinary states of consciousness—and I summarized the common principles of these (and a few other) approaches into a rudimentary model of subtle activism.

Alongside this primary goal, however, the book also had a secondary objective: To propose that subtle activism may have an especially meaningful

role to play at this particular moment in history. My original interest in
the idea of subtle activism emerged from a deep desire to somehow bring
the transformative wisdom of spirituality into the public realm to serve as
a healing balm for the interconnected social, economic, ecological, and
spiritual crises that confront us in our times. To better understand the historical significance of these enormous challenges, I presented the evolution
of consciousness frameworks of Teilhard de Chardin, Thomas Berry, and
Richard Tarnas. These authors share the view that the period we are living
in represents a potentially crucial turning point in the evolution of consciousness, one that calls for a fundamentally new understanding of who we
are and how we relate to each other, the planet, and the cosmos. In this
context, I proposed that the practice of subtle activism may have a vital
role to play in supporting the transition toward the more integrated planetary consciousness called for by Teilhard and Berry and the re-enchanted
worldview emphasized by Tarnas.[1]

I also highlighted the contemporary relevance of subtle activism by
arguing that it represents a natural extension, in the domains of activism
and spirituality, of an integral and participatory perspective now emerging
in many fields of thought. In terms of activism, I noted that, whereas the
conventional modern view tends to conceive of activism as an externally
oriented activity involving direct confrontation with the social and political forces one wishes to change, subtle activism incorporates the integral
understanding that there is an interior and an exterior dimension to all
phenomena, including social and political realities. In regard to spirituality,
I suggested that subtle activism can be seen as a creative component of an
emerging integral approach to spirituality that seeks to encompass all the
dimensions of our lives, including our participation in social and political
realities as well as individual inner experience.

Although some will no doubt be quick to dismiss the hypothesis of
subtle activism as an ungrounded expression of new age spirituality, such an
interpretation would be to misconstrue the integrative thrust of the proposal.
I have emphasized, for example, that subtle activism should not be seen as
an approach that, on its own, will magically solve all the world's problems.
Rather it should be viewed as a creative complement to more orthodox
strategies as part of an integrative approach to social change. In this context, one of the most significant contributions of subtle activism may be to
introduce into the often highly polarized milieu of social and political work
a spirit of greater possibility and a reminder of a deeper common ground
shared by all people, regardless of their surface differences.

An area that deserves further attention is the development of ethical
criteria that could help us to distinguish more from less desirable forms of
subtle activism. In chapter 2, I posed several questions about the nature

of subtle activism, e.g., is it an essentially neutral force that can equally serve positive and negative ends or does it lend itself more readily to the actualization of universal spiritual values such as love, peace, and joy? However, because these questions raise complicated theological and philosophical issues concerning the nature of good and evil, I left them open—thus I recommend a more thoughtful treatment of this topic in the future.

It is important to note too that subtle activism is not simply an intellectual concept but an emerging practice passionately embraced by an increasing number of people who want to participate in the healing and awakening of our world. For those who are inspired by the ideas of this book and want to find venues for engaging in the practice of subtle activism, appendix 1 provides a list of recommended organizations and initiatives.

Confronted by the vast extent of suffering on the planet, it can be easy to feel helpless about what we, as human individuals, can do to make a meaningful difference in the world. Subtle activism is not a substitute for the more overt actions we might feel called to take, but it does represent a creative response to the world situation that may enable many people to remain engaged who might otherwise become passive and despairing. Whatever the future holds, I believe that this kind of engagement may be crucial in mitigating human suffering and optimizing the unfolding of collective reality. It is my hope that, as more people participate in this work and the technology continues to advance, we will see the emergence of a growing number of high-quality subtle activism initiatives that will allow the presence of love and wisdom to increasingly permeate the collective heart of humanity.

APPENDIX 1

SUBTLE ACTIVISM RESOURCE LIST

The following entries describe leading organizations and initiatives in the emerging field of subtle activism. The list includes organizations involved in education and training, research, events, networking, and developing practices.

1 Giant Mind
http://1giantmind.org
1 Giant Mind's mission is to reduce and prevent stress-related lifestyle disease and mental illness by empowering people worldwide with learn-to-meditate programs, resources, and research. They envision a calmer, happier, healthier world where meditation is as commonplace as basic personal hygiene, exercise, and a healthy diet.

Bell and Todd: Source Power Art
http://www.bellandtodd.com/
Bell & Todd create empowered mandalas, sourced in Nature, for use in personal and collective healing and transformation. Their images are a source of visual empowerment for many global subtle activism events. They create custom mandalas for organizations involved in world change. Bell & Todd also offer subtle activism training for individuals and groups.

BeThePeace
http://bethepeace.com
On the annual UN International Day of Peace (September 21), BeThePeace functions as a central "portal" through which hundreds of organizations worldwide join together to create one of the world's largest global prayer and meditation events for peace.

Brahma Kumaris

http://www.brahmakumaris.org/index_html

http://www.brahmakumaris.org/us

Brahma Kumaris offers meditation training combined with programs of spiritual development, interfaith collaboration, and community service. "We recognize that a deeper understanding between faiths, based on acceptance and respect, will contribute to a culture of peace and non-violence. We facilitate activities with people from a wide variety of faith-based traditions and cultures to experience and appreciate the essence and diversity of their lifestyles."

Center for Mind-Body Medicine (CMBM) Global Trauma Relief Program

http://cmbm.org/global-trauma-relief/about-gtr/

CMBM combines modern science, wise tradition, and human connection to train people in self-care skills and then, to teach those skills to others. "We are teaching thousands to heal millions– and by teaching the teachers first, we see individuals, families and communities everywhere reconnecting with themselves and one another to embrace the richness of our human experience."

Children of the Sun Foundation

http://childrenofthesun.org

Children of the Sun is a nonprofit public foundation initiating conscious evolution through activities that build unity and global coherence. Their programs are helping to catalyze a worldwide Goodwill Movement to shift mass perception into a worldwide reflection of global peace and cooperation among all people, on every level and walk of life.

Common Passion

http://commonpassion.org/hompage

Common Passion is a global social collaborative of individuals and communities "who share compassion as a common passion." Their mission is to create social and environmental harmony through faith- and science-based applications of collective consciousness. They orchestrate global meditations and prayer events with all faith and wisdom traditions.

Compassionate Seattle

http://www.compassionateseattle.org

Compassionate Seattle evolved out of the 2008 five-day event, Seeds of Compassion, which brought His Holiness the 14th Dalai Lama and other spiritual leaders to visit the city. In 2010, Compassionate Action Network was launched as part of Compassionate Seattle's mission to build a global network where self-organizing groups can connect and collaborate to awaken compassion within themselves, others and the world.

Compassion Games
http://compassiongames.org
Compassion Games promotes and shares games that are designed to benefit society. Compassion Games and activities have social impact, help people to try new things, and build relationships and trust. They believe that when you engage with others on behalf of others, you will feel it in your heart and gain a greater connection to your community.

David Spangler
http://www.davidspangler.com/subtleactivism.htm
David Spangler is an American mystic and spiritual philosopher who teaches subtle activism as part of his incarnational spirituality approach. Incarnational spirituality emphasizes the sacredness of our everyday lives and the uniqueness of each individual's spiritual and creative capacities. Spangler uses subtle activism as a way for people to engage with the world via subtle energies and spirit.

Alliance for the Earth/Earth Treasure Vase Global Healing Project
http://earthtreasurevase.org
Inspired by an ancient Tibetan Buddhist tradition, the Earth Treasure Vase Global Healing Project brings healing and protection to the Earth by filling consecrated clay vessels with prayers and offerings, and ceremonially burying them in the Earth in collaboration with indigenous elders, young activists, and grassroots leaders in places where healing and protection are most needed around the planet.

Earthdance Network
http://www.earthdance.org/story/
Earthdance is a world of communities, working and playing together to create a culture of peace, through music and dance events, synchronized global link-ups, and social activism. More than just an epic party, Earthdance is a flash forward to an alternative peaceful future. Earthdance's synchronized Prayer for Peace represents the focal point of their annual global celebration.

Gaiafield Project
http://gaiafield.net
The Gaiafield Project develops subtle activism practices, theories, and programs, and works with like-minded groups to co-create local, national, and global networks of subtle activists to support a shift to a planetary culture of peace. They believe that in our turbulent times there is a deep need for fostering greater coherence in the energetic fields that underlie communities at every scale.

Global Coherence Initiative

http://www.glcoherence.org

The Global Coherence Initiative is a science-based, co-creative project to unite people in heart-focused care and intention, to facilitate the shift in global consciousness from instability and discord to balance, cooperation, and enduring peace.

Global Consciousness Project

http://noosphere.princeton.edu

The Global Consciousness Project is an international, multidisciplinary collaboration of scientists and engineers who collect data continuously from a global network of physical RNGs located around the world. Their purpose is to examine subtle correlations that may reflect the presence and activity of consciousness in the world. They hypothesize that there will be structure in what should be random data, associated with major global events that engage people's minds and hearts.

Global Peace Initiative of Women (GPIW)—Contemplative Alliance

http://www.gpiw.org/contemplative-alliance.html

Launched by GPIW in 2008, the Contemplative Alliance is an interspiritual movement grounded in contemplative practices and approaches with the goal of heightening awareness and generating actions to address the critical issues of our times. They bring together contemplative organizations and individuals from across religious, faith, and worship traditions, for contemplative practice and dialogue. Their vision is that individuals and organizations, acting from a place of deep inner wisdom, can advance the well-being of the global community.

Heart Mastery/Institute of HeartMath

http://heartmastery.com

HeartMastery, a division of HeartMath LLC, is dedicated to empowering people through the intelligence of their hearts in order to better navigate these changing times. HeartMastery programs and products enable people to live more rewarding, healthy, and productive lives personally, professionally, and in benefit to the world. See also, Institute of HeartMath: http://www.heartmath.org

Institute of Noetic Sciences (IONS)

http://www.noetic.org

IONS, founded in 1973 by Apollo 14 astronaut Edgar Mitchell, is a research, education, and membership organization whose mission is supporting individual and collective transformation through consciousness research, educational outreach, and engaging a global learning community in the realization of our human potential. IONS conducts, sponsors, and collaborates on leading-edge research into the potentials and powers of consciousness, exploring phenomena that do not necessarily fit conventional scientific models while maintaining a commitment to scientific rigor.

International Day of Peace/Culture of Peace Initiative
http://cultureofpeace.org/idp
Since 1982, the UN International Day of Peace, also known as "Peace Day," has been observed on September 21 and has provided opportunities for individuals, organizations, and nations to practice peace and create practical acts of peace during that twenty-four-hour period. Thousands of groups, a majority of the world's nations, and millions of people now participate in some way annually.

MedMob
http://www.medmob.org
MedMob uses the flash-mob concept to create both planned and spontaneous public meditation events around the world. Their intention is to create an environment for people from all religions, all worldviews, and all experience levels to join together in meditation, to help improve the world.

Satyana Institute
http://www.satyana.org/about_new2.html
The Satyana Institute is a nonprofit service and training organization. Its mission is to support individuals, communities, and organizations to combine the inner work of the heart with outer service in the world. The name *satyana* comes from two sanskrit roots: sat, which means truth or being, and also refers to action aligned or suffused with spirit; and yana, which means vehicle. So "satyana" means a vehicle for action infused with the grace of spirit.

Thomas Huebl
http://thomashuebl.com
Thomas Huebl is a contemporary mystic based in Germany whose focus is on the development of a new "Culture of We" and on the practice of timeless wisdom. Thomas facilitates large-scale healing events in various cities to address collective human issues, such as the Holocaust. His intention for such events is to help people heal and integrate aspects of the collective shadow that are handed down from generation to generation.

Transcendental Meditation (TM) Practice and Research
http://permanentpeace.org
The above link is for the Maharishi University of Management's Institute of Science, Technology and Public Policy at MIU, under the direction of John Hagelin. The purpose of the institute is to identify, scientifically evaluate, and implement proven, prevention-oriented, forward-looking solutions to critical national and global problems. The institute works in close cooperation with universities, research institutes, government and private foundations, and business and industry.
http://www.truthabouttm.org
The above site, curated by longtime TM researcher and advocate, David Orme Johnson, also provides information and links about TM studies on the individual and societal effects of the TM meditation practice.

Transformative Change
http://transformativechange.org/about-us/what-we-do/
Transformative Change (XC), an initiative of social visionary and Buddhist teacher Rev. Angel Kyodo Williams, is dedicated to bridging the inner and outer lives of social change agents, activists, and allies to support a more effective, more sustainable movement of justice for all. XC brings the practice of presence to community-based visioning, strategizing, and organizing for cohesive, sustainable social transformation. Marrying social activism to a deep, sustained personal practice cultivates the sensibilities in individuals necessary for them to become embodied agents of conscious social change.

Unify
http://unify.org
Unify.org is a platform created to support organizations and people who are organizing global synchronized movements of good in the world. Unify supports global synchronized events such as Earth Day or Peace Day and has developed a platform to support coherence and unification during such days.

Winter Feast for the Soul
http://www.winterfeastforthesoul.com/index2.php
The Winter Feast is an annual online forty-day retreat as a synchronized period of practice where participants become part of a shared dream for a consciousness of oneness and peace on the planet. They embrace all forms of practice that bring an individual to a period of stillness in their daily life. The commitment to forty minutes of practice each day for the forty-day period of the Feast allows people to have a life-changing experience of the importance of stillness. In that space, the promptings of the Inner Divine are found and loving kindness and compassion flow naturally into daily life.

World Peace Prayer Society

http://www.worldpeace.org/index.html

The World Peace Prayer Society offers a variety of practices, ceremonies and initiatives to spread the message and prayer, "May Peace Prevail on Earth," throughout the world. Activities include the World Peace Prayer Flag Ceremony, the Peace Pole Project, Peace Pals Project, and more.

World Prayers

http://www.worldprayers.org/index.html

The World Prayers Project gathers and presents historic and contemporary world prayers in a unified, multifaith online archive, sending thousands of prayers a day to people around the world. Their mission is to improve human relations by celebrating the many forms of prayer and honoring the benefits of spiritual, cultural, and natural diversity.

Zen Peacemakers

http://zenpeacemakers.org

The Zen Peacemakers Order is a spiritually based approach to social engagement based on three Buddhist tenets: Not knowing, Bearing Witness, and Loving Actions. The Bearing Witness program involves listening deeply with the entire body and mind to social situations of suffering, giving rise to spontaneous actions of love and compassion.

http://zenpeacemakers.org/zpo-bearing-witness-training-program/

APPENDIX 2

SUBTLE ACTIVISM

═══════════════════════════════════════

Science, Magic, or Religion?

Unlike most spiritual approaches, subtle activism purports to have a real effect on the world at large. To the extent that one might seek to make empirical claims (or even to hold empirical hopes) about the nature of this effect, one would inevitably be drawn into the realm of quantitative science to explain it. For example, the use of empirical methods by the TM researchers to study the Maharishi Effect makes sense in the context of their claim that the practice of TM in a large-group setting equal to or greater than the square root of 1 percent of any given population will result in a measurable positive influence throughout the population.

Another possibility, however, is to maintain that, although subtle activism might have an impact on the world, its effects are too subtle or nonlinear to be explained by current empirical methods. For example, the results of a subtle activism project might be recognized by sensitive observers in the form of strikingly symbolic correlations between the project and subsequent events in the world, yet empirical science is ill equipped to measure such correlations. From this perspective, it is arguable that subtle activism is more akin to a form of magic. Religious studies professor David Hufford (2003) defines magic as "the production of effects in the natural world through the influence of the supernatural, that is, spiritual causality" (297). Although Hufford's definition expresses a popular traditional view and is therefore a reasonable place to start, a precise concept of magic as distinct from religion and science has long been the subject of contentious academic debate. Because this discussion sheds light on where subtle activism belongs within these three categories, it is worthwhile to spend some time outlining the broad contours of the debate.

The typical distinctions used by anthropologists in the early part of the twentieth century to contrast magic negatively with religion and science have long been discredited as products of Western ethnocentrism. For example, magic has traditionally been compared with science on the basis that, although both claim to offer knowledge that can be used to attain control over the environment, magic attributes the outcome to supernatural influences, whereas science emphasizes naturalistic explanations. However, in practice it is frequently difficult to distinguish the natural from the supernatural. For instance, as anthropologists Wax and Wax (1962) rhetorically ask, in what category should one place the belief, common to a number of indigenous cultures, that a baby's illness is caused by the negative emotions of his or her mother being transmitted through the breast milk (especially in light of contemporary perspectives emerging from the field of psychoneuroimmunology)? Magic has been negatively compared to religion, on the other hand, as being essentially coercive or manipulative in its relations with the supernatural realm in contrast with the "supplicative" and worshipful attitude said to be characteristic of religion. However, this distinction too has been widely criticized as meaningless because it is impossible to perceive in most cases the extent to which someone is being "manipulative" or "supplicative" in his or her communion with supernatural forces. For example, on what basis could one discern the supposed differences in attitude between a "religious" prayer for a good harvest and a "magical" ritual for a successful hunt? In light of the collapse of these traditional distinctions, the question has been raised as to whether it even makes sense to retain a concept of magic at all (Versnel 1991).

Esoteric scholar Wouter Hanegraaf (1998) argues, however, that a consensus seems to have been forming since the 1960s that magic can be best understood in terms of its distinctive worldview, rather than by the nature of its rites or practices. The worldview commonly associated with magic is seen as "participatory" in that humans are regarded as embedded in an enchanted cosmos, without a rigid separation between humans and things. From this perspective, certain actions can have immediate (i.e., nonlocal) effects unmediated by physical causality because of a perceived correspondence between different aspects of the universe. Along these lines, Hanegraaf notes the argument made in the 1960s by Dutch scholar of religion Jan van Baal that too much emphasis had been placed on the supposed belief in the pragmatic effectiveness of magic (as if magic were a substitute for practical action) at the expense of recognizing what van Baal saw as its more fundamental role, namely, to express and reconfirm a view of the world in which the element of mystery is valued. Van Baal argued that the effect of a magical spell, for example, "evokes the weird atmosphere of mystery, in which things have power, in which things are more than they are and hold out to man danger and promise at the same time" (cited in Haneagraaf 1998, 82–84). As Hanegraaff points out, the persistence of magic in the modern world is difficult to understand if it is primarily seen as a way to achieve practical results—for in that case it would have to compete with science—but it makes sense if we consider the contrast the magical worldview provides to the disenchanted modern perspective. According to this approach, magic becomes less competitive with science (because these two realms are not seen to share a common worldview within which a valid comparison could be made) and more a special case of religion (i.e., religion with a participatory worldview).

Although this perspective has much to recommend it, Hanegraaff is right to note that it seems to leave the distinction between magic and religion relatively vague. I believe that the common perception that magic is more centrally concerned than other forms of religion with achieving effects in the natural or social world is a valid distinction that follows naturally from an interpretation of magic as religion within a participatory framework. To recall, Matthews and Matthews (2003) claim that "the magician of any time seeks to bring the inner impulse to the outer world" (10). We also saw that, in the enchanted cosmos of the primal human, the spiritual attention of the shaman or magician tends to extend "out" into the natural world at least as much as it moves "up" toward transcendent spiritual realities. In both the primal and esoteric versions of magic and enchantment, a holographic worldview involving correspondences between inner and outer worlds leads naturally to an emphasis on the manifestation of spiritual realities in the world as the primary craft of the shaman or magician.

In contrast, various developments in the evolution of religion in Western culture led to the formation of a dominant religious worldview that came to emphasize transcendent rather than immanent spiritual realities, with radical implications for religious expression. Tarnas (2006), for example, identifies the following key religious developments that contributed to the formation of the modern Western religious worldview:

1. The "discovery of transcendence" in the period 800 to 200 BCE (called by Karl Jaspers the Axial Age).

2. The Biblical emphasis on humanity's special relationship to a monotheistic and transcendent supreme being.

3. The Reformation's rigid desacralizing of the world in favor of the human being's exclusive spiritual loyalty to God.

In the modern religious worldview, the human being is seen to be in a unique relationship to a transcendent divinity that is separate from the created world, a world whose particular features are increasingly perceived as having no special correspondence with spiritual realities.[1] Within this framework, religious and spiritual experience became increasingly confined to a private, internal encounter between individuals and transcendent spirit. Religious practice in the modern era, then, has tended to involve a movement "in" toward private, interior experience and a movement "up" (or "beyond") toward a transcendent spiritual reality, but not, typically, a movement "out" toward immanent sources of spirituality in the social or natural world. What I am suggesting is that a key trait that distinguishes magic from other forms of religion is its emphasis on manifesting spiritual realities in the world in contrast with the focus on communing with or realizing transcendent spiritual realities that has characterized the dominant orientation of world religions since the Axial Age. An emphasis on manifestation typically involves an engagement with immanent spiritual realities and a corresponding "this-worldly" spiritual focus, whereas an emphasis on transcendence tends to lead to a more "other-worldly" spirituality.[2] Unlike the traditional distinctions of early anthropologists that were used negatively to compare magic with religion, however, I maintain that a focus on manifestation is simply the natural expression of religion in a culture with an enchanted cosmology, whereas an emphasis on the transcendent realm is a religious expression to be expected in a culture with a disenchanted worldview.

By this definition, subtle activism could accurately be described as a form of magic. One of the central claims of this book is that subtle activism is a natural application of a widely re-emerging participatory, holistic worldview in the arenas of both activism and spirituality. As noted in chapter 1, Jorge Ferrer's (2001) participatory account of human spirituality, for example, reframes spiritual or transpersonal phenomena as "multilocal participatory events" (in contrast to individual inner experiences) that can take place "in the locus of an individual, a relationship, *a collective identity* or a place" (2–3)—a perspective clearly conducive to subtle activism's focus on collective sociopolitical realities. Indeed, the main innovation subtle activism introduces to contemporary spirituality is precisely its extension of the modern focus on individual inner experience to a concern for the spiritual dimension of sociopolitical phenomena and for the sociopolitical dimension of spiritual phenomena. As I have argued, such a movement of spirit into the world is a natural religious expression in the context of a re-enchanted view of the cosmos, and, I suggest, a feature that helps to distinguish magic from other forms of religion. The designation of subtle activism as magic seems especially apt given Hanegraaff's (1998) convincing thesis that the participatory perspective is a central element of New Age or New Paradigm thought, and that the intellectual and spiritual foundations of that movement lie primarily in Western Esotericism, a tradition that, as Hanegraaff notes, is virtually synonymous with *magia*. This categorization (subtle activ-ism as magic) is also supported by the fact that neo-paganism—considered by Hanegraaff to be a specialized subset of the New Age movement and defined as "a religious movement based on magic in the sense of a certain ritual practice which expresses a comprehensive [participatory] worldview" (84)—has been a major pioneer in the field of subtle activism through its development of various forms of "magical activism."[3]

However, the picture becomes more complicated when we consider that even new forms of religious expression that explicitly embrace a re-enchanted view of the cosmos, although they may revitalize the imma-nent dimension of spiritual reality, have nonetheless usually emerged in the context of Judeo-Christian cultures, and thus will have often been sig-nificantly influenced by the dominant strain of Western religious thought and its emphasis on the transcendent dimension of spirit. Even contem-porary approaches that are expressly magical or pagan, for example, while in many respects repudiating orthodox Christianity and the conventional Western religious worldview, tend to display influences of the mainstream tradition. For example, York (1996) maintains that, in contrast to ancient paganism's conception of divinity as radically plural, neo-paganism tends to be duo-theistic (divinity as God-Goddess) or a qualified polytheism that is essentially "monist with polytheistic manifestations" and, as such, rep-resents merely an updating of "an essentially Christian attitude." Pearson (2007) similarly argues that Christianity is the real invisible player in the development of modern Wicca, and concludes that a Christianity that has been constructed as wholly "other" by some Wiccans is a product of the imagination. Indeed, if we go back to the esoteric tradition of Renaissance Europe, we can already observe the blending of elements from mystical Christianity with the practice of the "occult sciences" (magic, alchemy, and astrology). Some prominent modern occult teachers such as Dion Fortune also incorporate Christian teachings within an esoteric framework. Other notable contemporary expressions of this particular vein of spiritual syncre-tism include "Christopaganism" and the Santo Daime Church (which com-bines elements of South American shamanism with mystical Catholicism).

One way to comprehend this impulse to incorporate the notion of a transcendent God within essentially pagan, nature-based spiritual frameworks is by analogy with Tarnas's (2006) analysis of the evolution of the Western worldview. To recall, Tarnas maintains that any shift to a *re*-enchanted view of the cosmos will not be simply a return or regression to what Luc-ien Levy-Bruhl called the participation mystique of the primal human, but rather an integration of that perspective with the positive dimensions of the modern quest for autonomy in a synthesis that includes both developments. Similarly, in relation to the evolution of the Western religious worldview, we might expect that religious expression within a re-enchanted cosmology will entail not merely a return to the magical perspective of the shaman, but an integration of that approach with all we have learned from the long process of differentiating and communing with the transcendent dimension. We might thus expect to see the emergence of panentheistic spiritual forms that equally emphasize transcendence and immanence, realization and manifestation, mysticism and magic.[4] And this, finally, is how I believe we can best understand the contemporary emergence of subtle activism. Although some practices of subtle activism focus on a movement of spirit out toward immanent spiritual sources in the world, and others emphasize a movement up (or beyond) to a transcendent divine source, most appear to incorporate a mixture of the two approaches. For example, Sufi mystic Vaughan-Lee talks about the need for humans, in exercising their spiritual power for the healing of the world, both to enact "the will of the Absolute" and to awaken the soul of the world by recognizing the divine light hidden within matter. Religious studies professor Christopher Bache (2000) describes many collective healing experiences involving transcendental states of consciousness, but also others that emphasize immanent spiritual realities such as "Earth Consciousness" and various layers of the "species mind." The "Gaiafield Attunement" group practice that has emerged in our own events at the Gaiafield Project involves contact with both a transcendent spiritual source and with immanent dimensions such as the intelligence located in nature. Although we saw in chapter 2 that subtle activism can be practiced in various contexts, I believe we are now in a position to recognize contemporary subtle activism, in the strictest sense, as an emerging panentheistic spiritual impulse that occurs most coherently within a participatory spiritual framework and a re-enchanted view of the cosmos.

NOTES

INTRODUCTION

1. The words *spiritual* and *consciousness* are notoriously difficult to define. I discuss what I mean by these terms in chapter 1.

2. For example, and of particular relevance to our topic, from the earliest days of the Internet, many spiritually oriented individuals and groups immediately grasped its potential to help facilitate profound experiences of global communion through meditation and prayer events involving large numbers of people in all parts of the world. Since the birth of the Internet, several large, well-planned global meditation events have indeed occurred (e.g., the Gaiamind event of 1997, the Global Interfaith Prayer Vigil of 2003, and the annual spiritual observances on September 21, the UN-designated International Day of Peace). Here we can see how the novel opportunities provided by the increasing sophistication of the global telecommunications network are converging with the pressures of the global crisis to bring forth creative forms of spiritual activity in the public realm that go beyond the traditional focus on individual growth.

3. Indeed, it may be primarily through the emergence of what might be called postmodern spiritual expressions—and not merely through a reassertion of Enlightenment values—that we will be able to develop a truly comprehensive response to the surprisingly robust attacks on modernity by fundamentalist religion in recent years (mainly in the forms of Islamic extremist terrorism worldwide and right-wing Christian fundamentalism in the United States). Postmodernism in this context can be understood simply as the impulse to go beyond the limitations of modern thought while honoring its genuine achievements. See Griffin (1997, xi-xiv) for a helpful discussion on constructive versus deconstructive postmodernism.

4. See chapter 3 in E. Kelly and colleagues (2009) *Irreducible Mind* for an extensive overview of phenomena where a change in mental state appears to cause a change in physiological state.

5. On the surface, it would appear that this research provides support for the view that the social effects of meditation practice do occur in a linear, mechanical fashion. But it is also possible that the TM research captures only that part of the total effect that can be measured empirically. There could be additional effects that occur via the principles of resonance and affinity I have described, but that are not (and probably cannot in principle be) included as relevant data within the parameters of conventional empirical studies. In any event, the Maharishi Effect is

theoretically predicted by the TM researchers to be mediated by qualitative factors such as the closeness of the personal ties between the meditators and the affected population, which suggests an alignment with my position (see Orme-Johnson et al. 1990).

      6. The prototypical statement is from Marx: "religion is the opiate of the masses."

      7. See Tart (2009) for a classic statement of the "Western Creed" of materialism that we are socially conditioned to accept as unquestionable truth:

> I believe in the material universe as the only and ultimate reality, a universe controlled by fixed physical laws and blind chance; I affirm that the universe has no creator, no objective purpose, and no objective meaning or destiny; I maintain that all ideas about God or gods, enlightened beings, prophets and saviors, or other nonphysical beings or forces are superstitions and delusions. Life and consciousness are totally identical to physical processes and arose from chance interactions of blind physical forces. (28)

CHAPTER ONE: THE INNER DIMENSION OF SOCIAL AND PLANETARY TRANSFORMATION

      1. By focusing on the West, I do not mean to imply that the story of Western development is normative for the whole world. However, apart from the fact that, being Western, it is the only tradition immediately accessible to me, the values, attitudes, and assumptions of the West (along with its scientific, technological, and economic influence) have clearly played a disproportionate role, for better or for worse, in shaping the contemporary global situation.

      2. Indeed, feminist, postcolonial, and poststructural scholars have criticized the rational epistemology of the modern West as disembodied, cognicentric, ethnocentric, and masculinized (see Ferrer and Sherman 2008).

      3. Hanegraaf's analysis of New Age Religion dates the movement to the early 1970s (emerging as an heir to the 1960s counterculture) and characterizes it by the fact that its exponents all express a critical view of modern Western culture by presenting alternatives derived from a "secularized esotericism" (520). Hanegraaf considers New Paradigm thought to be an essentially American subset of New Age Religion that focuses on defining, in theoretical terms, the components of the new worldview that is believed to be taking shape in our times.

      4. As Hanegraaf (1998) notes, the German Idealist/Romantic philosophers introduced the modern emphasis on development or evolution to a framework otherwise highly consistent with the enchanted worldview of esoteric Renaissance thought.

      5. Panentheism refers to the belief that God or the Divine is both immanent in creation and transcendent to it.

      6. Berry uses a new term *Ecozoic Era* to convey the radical nature of the shift that will have occurred when humans learn to live in a "mutually enhancing" relationship with the rest of the community of life on Earth.

7. The term *subtle activism* was coined in 2005 by philosopher Sean Kelly (nd) in his paper "The Hidden Face of Wisdom: Toward an Awakened Activism." In 2006 and 2012, Sean and I co-taught a course entitled "Subtle Activism: Theory and Practice" at the California Institute of Integral Studies. The term also has been adopted by David Spangler to describe an approach he previously called "inner" or "energy" activism. John Heron (2006) refers in passing to subtle activism in his book *Participatory Spirituality: A Farewell to Authoritarian Religion* (53–55), as does transpersonal theorist Jorge Ferrer (nd) in his paper "Embodied Spirituality: Now and Then." Spangler, Heron, and Ferrer give the term much the same meaning as I do. I am not aware of anyone else yet using the term.

8. See Ferrer (2001) and Ferrer and Sherman (2008) for a definitive explication of a participatory understanding of spirituality. By embracing a participatory approach, however, I do not mean to imply that all practices will be equally effective in supporting collective transformation. The relative effectiveness of different practices in this regard is something to be discovered through a process of trial and error.

9. An exception is the case of practices intended to support individuals or small groups in key public positions (e.g., prayer for the US president or members of Parliament). The key distinction in those cases is not between individual—collective but between private—public.

Also, by "collective transformation," I do not mean only the human social or political realm. The "collective" here includes the entirety of what Thomas Berry refers to as the "Earth community," including all its human and non-human members. For example, a practice intended to bring healing to an ocean following a large oil spill would be, in my view, an expression of subtle activism.

10. See Rothberg (1993, 106).

11. Others (e.g., Varma 1972; Starhawk 1979; Orme-Johnson et al. 1988; Hagelin 1998; Bache 2000 Oates 2002; Howell 2002; Fortune 1993; S. Kelly, nd; Vaughan-Lee 2005; Heron 2006; Spangler 2008) make similar claims.

12. At least, rational norms became the ideal for conduct in the public realms. In practice, less rational influences continued to predominate, though these factors were not usually religiously motivated.

13. As Spangler (2008) notes, it is not an either/or situation. An ideal subtle activism program, for example, might entail a committed group of individuals engaging consistently in a series of highly focused practices, punctuated by one or two "peak" events involving thousands of people across the planet.

14. Peter Russell coined the term in his book *The Global Brain* (see Russell 1983).

CHAPTER TWO: SUBTLE ACTIVISM AND SPIRITUALITY

1. That is, the greater effectiveness of having large numbers of meditators gathered in one place, compared with the effect of people meditating separately in their own homes.

2. Note that this approach is sometimes also called the "Maharishi Technology of the Unified Field." For simplicity's sake, I refer to the entire research as the Maharishi Effect.

3. A chronological history of the research is well summarized in Aron and Aron (1986), Oates (2002), and Wallace (2005). David Orme-Johnson's website (http://www.truthabouttm.org) is also an excellent resource for research on the Maharishi Effect.

4. The term *iddhis* is the Pali version of the Sanskrit *siddhis*.

5. Obviously, the Christian metaphysical vision of a personal God who intervenes in worldly affairs in response to human prayer differs significantly from the Vedic concept of an impersonal field of consciousness that behaves more or less predictably in accordance with natural laws. Both of these approaches can be contrasted with the shamanic cosmology of lower, middle, and upper worlds filled with a wide variety of spiritual entities and the esoteric focus on divine intermediaries like angels and Ascended Masters. It is important to acknowledge that these differences are nontrivial and present a challenge to developing a concept of subtle activism broad enough to encompass as many different approaches as possible. In chapter 4, I argue that a participatory understanding of human spirituality has the advantage of supporting, as Ferrer (2001) puts it, a "more relaxed spiritual universalism" that welcomes the variety of ways in which the sacred can be expressed in the world without denying their real differences.

6. "Hermeticism" has two different meanings in esoteric scholarship. In the narrow sense, it is used to refer to the original Alexandrian texts attributed to the legendary Hermes Trismegistus and the literature directly inspired by these texts (e.g., "neo-Alexandrian Hermeticism"). However, it is also used more generally as a virtual synonym for the term *Western esotericism* (Faivre 1992, 3).

7. For a detailed map of the lineage of the Hermetic tradition see Faivre (1992) and Matthews and Matthews (2003).

8. To construct this broad overview of the field, I am drawing heavily from the work of Antoine Faivre, professor emeritus at the Sorbonne University of the History of Esoteric Currents in Modern and Contemporary Europe Studies. Faivre is widely considered the world's foremost intellectual authority on the subject of Western Esotericism.

9. Faivre (1992) also mentions two other "nonintrinsic" characteristics that frequently appear with the four intrinsic features: "transmission" and "the practice of concordance." Transmission is the idea that esoteric wisdom can and ought to be transmitted directly from master to disciple. The practice of concordance involves the tendency among esoteric practitioners to try to realize commonalities between different traditions, with a view to achieving a kind of illumination and all-encompassing gnosis or knowledge.

10. "Magic," in this context, is understood as the application of the knowledge of Nature's hidden order (e.g., the use of stones, metals, and plants for the reestablishment of physical or psychological harmony) but also often includes the idea that suffering Nature herself can participate in salvation through human intentionality (Faivre 1992).

11. The notion of mediation is considered by Faivre to be the principal feature that distinguishes esotericism from mysticism—mystics, in general, being more concerned with transcending all intermediate forms in their quest to experience total union with God or the Absolute, whereas esotericists, according to Faivre, seem to be more interested in contact with intermediaries.

12. For the case of George Washington, see the George Washington Papers at the Library of Congress for examples of original correspondence, viewable online, between George Washington and various Masonic Lodges. In these letters, Washington is addressed as "brother" and he refers to God as the "Great Architect of the Universe," a common Masonic reference (see, e.g., ::, Accessed November 19, 2014).

13. Fortune's interpretation of Nazism exactly mirrored that of Carl Jung, who wrote, in his famous essay "Wotan," that the "unfathomable depths" of the character of Odin (aka Wotan), the Norse "God of storm and frenzy," explained more of Nazism than all economic, political, and psychological factors put together (Jung 1970, 373).

14. Fortune's statement was made in a letter dated September 21, 1941. At the time, German forces occupied or controlled most of continental Europe (and were poised to capture Kiev in the Soviet Union); the Japanese had yet to attack Pearl Harbor, and the United States had not formally entered the war.

15. Note, however, that the massive antiwar global demonstrations on February 15, 2003—and many other expressions of overt political activism at the time—were also unsuccessful in achieving a peaceful outcome.

CHAPTER THREE: SUBTLE ACTIVISM AND SCIENCE

1. See, e.g., the cases of Leonara Piper, Daniel Home, and Ted Serios, discussed in Griffin (1997, 51–66).

2. In his comprehensive review regarding the psychology of paranormal belief, psychologist Harvey Irwin (1993) noted that "much of the skeptical research on the topic seems to have the implicit objective of demonstrating that believers in the paranormal are grossly deficient in intelligence, personality, education, and social standing" (6).

3. *Ganzfeld* is a German word meaning "whole field."

4. Selective reporting, or the "file-drawer" problem, refers to the possibility that an unknown number of unsuccessful experiments may not be reported, leading to inflated estimates of overall significance, because the unreported data cannot be included in meta-analyses of the research. The charge can be refuted, however, by calculating the number of unreported unsuccessful studies that would need to have been performed to reduce the combined result of a meta-analysis to a nonsignificant level. If that number is unreasonably large, it is fair to conclude that the significant result is not due to selective reporting.

5. In this regard, we have already seen the admission by skeptic psychologist Ray Hyman that the anomalous effects found in recent remote viewing and ganzfeld experiments could not reasonably be ascribed to chance (or to selective reporting or inappropriate statistical analysis). It is also relevant to note the admission by lifelong skeptic Carl Sagan (1995) that:

At the time of writing [1995] there are three claims in the ESP field which, in my opinion, deserve serious study: (1) that by thought alone humans can (barely) affect random number generators in computers; (2) that people under mild sensory deprivation can receive thoughts or images "projected" at them; and (3) that young children sometimes report the details of a previous life, which upon checking turn out to be accurate and which they could not have known about in any other way than reincarnation. (302)

See also Honorton (1993) for his review of the evolution of claims made by several leading skeptics (i.e., Ray Hyman, James Alcock, and James Randi) about parapsychology research. He showed that for many years skeptics argued that psi effects had never been repeatedly demonstrated or were due to chance or fraud. However, Honorton noted, these skeptics now concede that at least some psi effects are "astronomically significant."

6. Noting that it had published a "string of articles" in the previous year that highlighted failures in the reproducibility of published research, *Nature* took the extraordinary step of publishing a special issue in April 2013 ("Challenges in Irreproducible Research") devoted to the topic.

7. In one joint "remote staring" study that seemed to highlight the influence of experimenter effects, psi proponent Marilyn Schlitz and psi skeptic Richard Wiseman used identical equipment and procedures and conducted their experiments in the same laboratory. Yet the participants observed by Schlitz showed a significant overall result, whereas those assigned to Wiseman showed no difference from chance (see Schmidt 2003).

8. As Utts (1999) points out, this method can often lead us to underestimate a relationship or effect because some smaller studies might produce results in a positive direction but do not reach significance only because they lack statistical power due to their small sample size. In a review that simply adds up the number of significant studies, the results from these smaller "nonsignificant" (although positive leaning) studies can be interpreted erroneously as evidence for the null hypothesis. If the data from these studies could have been included in a meta-analytic review, the combined data would more accurately reflect the real relationship or effect size.

9. Distant healing studies on simple organisms have in fact often revealed impressive effect sizes.

10. Although the studies we will review are only a sample from the literature on the Maharishi Effect, they are sufficiently representative for us to make a generalized assessment about the whole body of research. These studies include the highest profile research on the Maharishi Effect (having been published in the most prestigious journals), examine most of the categories of social indicators that have been measured in the series, and demonstrate most of the methodological controls that have been used to support the claims.

11. Note that I am not a TM teacher or practitioner, nor do I have close ties with the TM movement.

12. The original source of the TM-Sidhi technique was Patanjali's Yoga Sutras.

13. *Super Radiance Assemblies* was the term used to describe gatherings of advanced TM practitioners that exceeded the square root of 1 percent of any given population. They appear to be structured like spiritual retreats. Participants meditate twice daily, once in the morning and once in the late afternoon. Some participants

attend additional meditation sessions throughout the day. Other activities include watching videotaped lectures from Maharishi and helping with the maintenance of the Assembly itself (e.g., cooking or administration). Occasionally, participants maintain their ordinary work schedule between the meditations.

14. Park (2000) accuses Hagelin of scientific fraud, declaring the results from the Washington D.C. Demonstration Study a "clinic in data manipulation," although he provides little evidence or analysis to support that claim. Although time-series models are standard statistical tools used to predict future trends, Park calls the time-series analysis used in the study "technobabble" but does not suggest an alternative type of statistical analysis that should have been undertaken. In general, Park does not make a valid scientific critique according to the criterion of "testability" proposed by Radin (1997), that is, "the critic has to specify the conditions under which the research could avoid the criticism, otherwise the objection is just a philosophical argument that falls outside the realm of science" (218). Stenger (2009) similarly engages in a polemical and misleading attack on Hagelin and Maharishi, falsely linking Maharishi with a discredited unified field theory and misrepresenting Hagelin's highly regarded scientific publication record. For a withering response to Stenger's critique, see Scharf (2010).

15. Although I consider the theory behind the Maharishi Effect in detail in chapter 4, it can be briefly described as follows: The theory starts with the proposition that all violence, negativity, conflict, and other problems in society are a reflection of excessive stress in the collective consciousness. Collective consciousness is defined as "the wholeness of consciousness of the group" that is "more than the sum of the consciousness of all individuals comprising that group" (Orme-Johnson et al. 1988, 777). At the source of all individual and collective consciousness is a unified field of "pure consciousness." Through the practice of TM, individuals can directly experience this unified field, and such experiences are claimed to create "nonlocal, field-like effects of order and coherence in the environment" (Orme-Johnson et al. 1988, 778).

16. A striking example occurred during the terrorist attacks on New York on September 11, 2001. The deviation from random data registered by the GCP network was greater on September 11 than on any other day of the year. An analysis of the "intercorrelation" value between the various REGs (which measures the degree of similar behavior between the REGs) showed that September 11 had the largest intercorrelation of any day in 2001.

17. The article in *Nature* was by skeptical British psychologist David Marks (1986), who wrote, "Parascience has all the qualities of a magical system while wearing the mantle of science. Until any significant discoveries are made, science can justifiably ignore it, but it is important to say why: parascience is a pseudo-scientific system of untested beliefs steeped in illusion, error and fraud" (121).

The article in *Science* was by skeptical psychologist George Price in 1955. His article began in reference to Rhine's ESP findings:

> Believers in psychic phenomena . . . appear to have won a decisive victory and virtually silenced opposition. . . . This victory is the result of careful experimentation and intelligent argumentation. The best of

the card-guessing experiments of Rhine and Soal show enormous odds against chance, while the possibility of sensory clues is often eliminated by placing cards and percipient in separate buildings far apart. Dozens of experimenters have obtained positive results in ESP experiments, and the mathematical procedures have been approved by leading statisticians. . . . Against all this evidence, almost the only defense remaining to the skeptical scientist is ignorance. (359)

But Price then argued, "ESP is incompatible with current scientific theory" and asked: "If, then, parapsychology and modern science are incompatible, why not reject parapsychology? . . . The choice is between believing in something 'truly revolutionary' and 'radically contradictory to contemporary thought' and believing in the occurrence of fraud and self-delusion. Which is more reasonable?" (360). In other words, although Price found the evidence for ESP scientifically sound, he rejected it on the highly speculative grounds that all the parapsychologists involved must be lying.

CHAPTER FOUR: FOUNDATIONS OF SUBTLE ACTIVISM

1. Although the details of these developments are not important for the purposes of this book, the interested reader is referred to the comprehensive discussion of the history of cognitive psychology in Chapter 1 of E. Kelly and colleagues (2009).

2. *Qualia* is a technical term that refers to individual instances of subjective conscious experience, such as the pain of a sore tooth or the smell of a rose.

3. Although Maharishi Mahesh Yogi is the originator of the Maharishi Effect approach, a number of scientists associated with the TM organization have conducted extensive research on the phenomenon. Some of the leading researchers include John Hagelin, David Orme-Johnson, Michael Dillbeck, and Robert Oates. These researchers have worked closely with each other and with Maharishi and they tend to present a more or less uniform theoretical approach. Accordingly, although I sometimes refer to Maharishi as the author of the Maharishi Effect theory, at other times I refer to "Maharishi and the TM researchers" in that role. I also sometimes refer to individual TM researchers, especially in relation to aspects of the theory that draw from scientific disciplines in which they specialize.

4. I do not claim to have more than a layman's understanding of quantum physics; thus my description is inevitably a simplified summary of a highly complex discipline. For more in-depth discussions of these developments, see Capra (1975), Herbert (1985), Goswami (1993), Mindell (2000), or Oates (2002).

5. In a textbook first published in 1928, physicist Sir Arthur Eddington described preparing his lecture by drawing up his chair to write at his "two tables." The first was the solid, substantial object of everyday perception. The second was his "scientific table," which "is mostly emptiness. Sparsely scattered in the emptiness are numerous electric charges rushing about with great speed, but their combined bulk amounts to less than a billionth of the bulk of the table itself. . . . It makes all the difference in the world whether the paper before me is poised as it were on

a swarm of flies and sustained, shuttlecock fashion, by a series of tiny blows from the swarm underneath, or whether it is supported because there is substance below it; . . . all the difference in conception at least, but no difference to my practical task of writing on the paper" (Eddington 1958, 8).

6. Oates (2002) makes the valid point that, after the discovery of the quantum field, "particles" should be placed in inverted commas so that they are not mistakenly thought of as discrete, autonomous entities.

7. Note, however, that the movement toward a unified theory has evolved progressively from supersymmetry to supergravity to string theory.

8. The property of self-interaction or self-referral in the unified quantum field refers to the fact that, by its own self-interacting dynamics, the unified quantum field gives rise to all laws of nature and all manifest phenomena. In the context of Maharishi's Vedic Science, the self-referral state means the state where "knower, known, and knowledge" are seated one within the other, giving rise to the "immortal infinite dynamism at the unmanifest basis of creation" (Varma 1986, 27).

9. See also the discussion about quantum nonlocality in chapter 3.

10. For example, Sheldrake (1988) refers to an experiment by psychologist William McDougall that involved rats being required to learn which exit to use to leave a water maze without getting an electric shock. Subsequent generations of rats learned the skill more and more quickly. When researchers at Edinburgh University replicated the experiment, the rate of learning of the rats seemed to pick up approximately where McDougall's rats had left off. An Australian research team performing a similar experiment found that not only did subsequent generations of rats learn the skill faster, but so did a sample of control rats who were not descended from trained parents. All of these results are consistent with Sheldrake's hypothesis of learning through morphic resonance. For experiments related to human learning, see Sheldrake (1988, 182–196).

11. Whitehead (1979) articulated an innovative metaphysical framework that was, in part, a philosophical response to the collapse of Newtonian physics caused by Einstein's relativity theory and the discoveries of quantum physics. In contrast to the reductionistic and atomistic assumptions of mainstream science, Whitehead's philosophy embraces holism, organicism, and relationality.

12. For example, Sheldrake (1988) points out that the founders of modern sociology, August Comte and Saint-Simon viewed society as a developing organism that could be understood in the positivistic spirit of science. Emile Durkheim (also one of the "fathers" of modern sociology) similarly regarded society to be like an organism that had an existence of its own apart from the individuals in it. Durkheim proposed the existence of a "conscience collective" (collective consciousness) that was like the mind of a society, with a distinct reality, independent of individual actors, and passed down from one generation to the next. In the early twentieth century, theories of social Darwinism extended Darwin's metaphor of survival of the fittest among individual organisms to social groups as a way to explain the dominance of Western societies. After social Darwinism lost credibility, the most widely accepted framework until about the 1960s was known as functionalism. This approach explicitly adopted a physiological metaphor, comparing the functions of

social institutions and activities in relation to the maintenance of society as a whole with the role of physical systems like the heart, liver, and skin in relation to the whole organism. Structuralism, an approach that largely superseded functionalism, shared the latter's assumption that societies are organic wholes, but it attempted to identify the deep structures that underlie observable cultural phenomena, such as myths or systems of kinshi (see Sheldrake 1988, 243–246).

13. As Sheldrake notes, the concept of a group mind as the basis of society, although popular at the start of the twentieth century, became intellectually distasteful after World War II, in large part because of the horribly distorted version of this idea that took hold in Nazi Germany.

14. Although the notion of morphic fields shares certain qualities with the group mind concept, in my view they should not be equated. As Sheldrake concedes, morphic fields are inherently conservative—they make it more likely that patterns of behavior previously enacted will be repeated. However group or collective minds seem to be intrinsically creative. Most reports from people who experience themselves as being part of a group mind seem to describe rare states of peak creativity and performance.

15. An interesting implication of Sheldrake's proposal is the notion that this ultimate creative source could itself evolve as a consequence of the new patterns that emerge within it.

16. It is worth noting that the perinatal realm, as the doorway between the personal and transpersonal dimensions, combines elements of both in a complex way, so it is difficult to precisely define its boundaries.

17. One wonders here whether levels of intentionality and energy or power might also constitute relevant thresholds that, if surpassed, would enable individuals or small groups to impact collective levels. For example, it is conceivable that when an individual or small group consciously devotes the fruits of its spiritual practice to the transformation of collective levels of consciousness, it might enliven the collective field more directly than would practices performed without such an intention. Similarly, we could imagine that an individual or group might have to raise a certain amount of energy or power in a practice for it to affect the collective. Many ceremonial traditions, for instance, emphasize the art of containing and building the energy in a ritual until it reaches a critical peak of intensity (see, e.g., Starhawk's [1979] discussion of the "Cone of Power" exercise [159]). Dion Fortune (1993) claimed that, alongside spiritual practice, "some form of action and some form of sacrifice" is necessary to give a magical ritual sufficient power to see it through to manifestation (73). (In the context of the "Magical Battle of Britain," the sacrifice of Fortune's group was to not evacuate to her house in Glastonbury when the Battle of London began to get intense, but to remain in London. Fortune claimed that she would not have been able to put the same power into her letters and meditations had they chosen the safer option.) Although these may be general principles that apply to rituals of all kinds, it seems reasonable to speculate that if a practice is going to transform collective levels of consciousness, it might especially need to surpass a certain baseline level of energy or power.

18. Here is Bache (2000) on this point: "The fact that matter follows mind implies in principle the ability to control one's physical experience through the power

of 'coherent consciousness.' (Coherent consciousness is to ordinary consciousness what a laser, or coherent light, is to ordinary light)" (273).

19. For the other theorists, see, e.g., Capra (1975), Goswami (1995), and Laszlo (2006, 2007). For the critics, see Wilber (1984, 2006) and Gould (1983).

20. Wilber's more recent writings have significantly qualified his earlier endorsement of perennialism and the Great Chain of Being, calling for a move from metaphysics to "integral post-metaphysics" (Wilber 2006). For the purposes of explaining his criticism of those who would equate the findings of physics with mysticism, however, his use of the "Great Chain" is still relevant.

21. It is not possible to outline here the full breadth of Ferrer's thesis, but it is worth briefly referring to one further important aspect of his argument. Although he challenges perennialist notions of objective spiritual truth and affirms a radically pluralistic spiritual vision, Ferrer maintains that his approach does not fall into spiritual relativism or moral anarchy. Ferrer argues that while a comparison of spiritual teachings on the basis of a pre-established metaphysical hierarchy is incompatible with the participatory approach, this does not mean that "anything goes" in terms of the validity of spiritual insights and expressions. Rather, Ferrer proposes that spiritual truths should be assessed based on their emancipatory power for self and world, that is, their capacity "to free individuals, communities, and cultures from gross and subtle forms of narcissism, egocentrism, and self-centeredness" (Ferrer 2001, 168).

22. As religious studies professor William Barnard (2008) notes, although most contemporary neuroscientists are likely to dismiss the alternative perspective advanced by James (and others) out of hand, several theorists have been prepared to consider it quite carefully. For example, Barnard cites the case of George Wald, a Nobel-prize winning physiologist from Harvard, who wrote: "There is no way of knowing whether the brain contains consciousness in the sense that it is producing it or whether it is simply a reception and transmission mechanism which . . . has the function of selection and realization of conscious images and not the production of such images" (cited in Barnard 2008, 8).

23. His hypothesis was later corroborated by Grof's LSD research, in which hundreds of subjects in nonordinary states of consciousness induced by LSD (and later holotropic breath work) reported vivid experiences of Jungian archetypes (among other transpersonal phenomena), often involving accurate information about religious symbolism and mythical structures of various cultures of the world that the subject had not been familiar with before the LSD session.

24. In the case of Fortune's project, as seen in chapter 2, the archetypes that emerged were largely associated with the legend of King Arthur and the Holy Grail, a myth seen to be drawn from the depths of the English psyche.

25. Sheldrake (1988) himself points out that the notion of morphic resonance parallels one of two main principles listed by anthropologist James Frazer as the basis of magic (i.e., the "Law of Similarity"). The Law of Similarity is the idea that like produces like, or that an effect resembles its cause. According to Frazer (1911), "the magician infers [from the Law of Similarity] that he can produce any effect he desires merely by imitating it" (52).

CHAPTER FIVE: SUBTLE ACTIVISM AND THE
EMERGENCE OF PLANETARY CONSCIOUSNESS

1. In view of humanity's destructive effect on the biosphere, however, Russell (1983) wonders whether the human species might be more properly seen as some sort of malignant growth or planetary cancer. Russell speculates that we may be at a critical stage of evolutionary development that will require a radical transformation in how we relate to each other and the world in order to stop our malignant behavior and fulfill our role as a part of a planetary brain. Also note Paul Hawken's (2007) proposal that the collective activity of the hundreds of thousands of non-profit organizations working to protect and heal the Earth can be seen as humanity's immune response to toxins like political corruption, economic disease, and ecological degradation.

2. Howard Bloom (2000) also maintains that living beings have always been "modules of a collective thinking and invention machine" (2). He regards the proposed "worldwide neocortex" foreseen by Russell and others to be not a recent development seeded by the telecommunications revolution but a "phase in the ongoing evolution of a networked global brain which has existed for more than 3 billion years" (1). Some (e.g., Capra 1982) interpret the evidence underlying Gaia theory as additional support for the existence of an ancient planetary "mind."

3. Morin (1977) describes a process as recursive where "an active organization produces the elements or effects necessary for its proper generation or existence" (86). As S. Kelly (2010) notes, we see this principle in all forms of living organization, such as in the oxygen/carbon dioxide cycle where plants produce oxygen, which is consumed by animals, which produce carbon dioxide, which is consumed by plants. The hologrammatic principle is defined by Morin (1986) to mean that "the whole is in a certain way included (engrammed) in the part which is included in the whole" (419).

4. It is important to note that although we might sometimes conceive of this collective reality as a single organism (or a single "mind," such as a Gaian or species mind), that does not imply that this new whole has agency in the same way that we individual humans do, or that it could force its individual members to do things against their will. As Bache (2008) points out (in the context of group fields or minds), it is not like the Borg in *Star Trek* that assimilates the minds of other species into its own, reducing them to virtual automatons. Although our understanding of the precise nature of this kind of collective reality is necessarily speculative, it seems paradoxically to entail a field of influence that is greater than the sum of its individual members, yet which intrinsically supports their individuation.

5. In this context, it was striking that President Barack Obama was able to secure a commitment from the BP Oil Company in June 2010 to provide a $20 billion fund to pay for claims associated with the Deepwater oil spill in the Gulf of Mexico. Nonetheless, despite the fact that the spill represented an environmental catastrophe of unprecedented scope and that public outrage at BP created a rare political environment in which both parties were clamoring to demand that BP take full responsibility for the disaster, there were signs at the time that the business community did in fact withdraw its support for the Obama administration for this

and other relatively moderate attempts to rein in irresponsible corporate behavior (e.g., see Farnam and Kane 2010).

6. Teilhard himself appears to have anticipated something like the Internet emerging as the mechanical infrastructure of the noosphere:

> To an increasing extent every machine comes into being as a function of every other machine; and, again to an increasing extent, all the machines on the earth, taken together, tend to form a single, vast, organized mechanism. Necessarily following the inflexive tendency of the zoological phyla, the mechanical phyla in their turn curve inward in the case of man, thus accelerating and multiplying their own growth and forming a single gigantic network girdling the earth. And the basis, the inventive core of this vast apparatus, what is it if not the thinking-center of the noosphere? (Teilhard 1959c, 160)

7. To have an affect at a global level might require the involvement of very large numbers of people and/or highly skilled practitioners.

CHAPTER SIX: CONCLUSION

1. It has not been an aim of this book to provide evidence as to why an evolution of consciousness perspective is an appropriate framework for understanding our moment. For well-reasoned and evidence-based arguments in support of the concept of the evolution of consciousness, the best sources I am aware of are Jean Gepser (1985) and Ken Wilber (1995). My own attraction to this perspective is fundamentally based on a personal intuition, emerging from experience in spiritual practice, that the universe at a deep level inherently unfolds toward wholeness. It has been my experience that when I deeply relax and stop trying to manipulate my inner reality, I find myself in contact with a natural flow that unwinds and unfolds toward healing and wholeness. To me it seems that this flow is the natural condition of the universe, which I align myself with when I relax deeply and allow reality to be just as it is. Thus, it makes sense to me to think of this "optimizing force" (as spiritual teacher A.H. Almaas [2002] calls it) as always and everywhere present, naturally supporting an evolution of consciousness, whether in individuals, the collective human psyche, or the planet as a whole.

APPENDIX 2: SUBTLE ACTIVISM: SCIENCE, MAGIC, OR RELIGION?

1. This statement is an admittedly simplified view of a complex historical development involving many important exceptions. In addition to (and in tension with) the dualistic and otherworldly dimension of the Christian worldview, for example, one can also identify, from the beginning, a radically immanent and this-worldly spirit, as in the doctrine of Incarnation and the socially engaged orientation of much of Judeo-Christian culture. (See Tarnas 1991, 120–129, for a helpful discussion of these two significantly different aspects of the Christian vision and

Wink 1992, for a creative contemporary theological expression of the immanent and world-affirming dimension of Christianity.) Broadly speaking, however, with the erosion of religious authority in the modern domains of science and politics and the associated disenchantment of the modern cosmos, the optimistic and exultant side of Christianity—with its belief that, through Christ, Spirit had descended into flesh and was now immanent in humanity and the world—has tended to be sidelined or repressed by the dominant religious expression that has emphasized the separate and superior status of God from His creation. Again, important exceptions to this trend can be identified (see endnote 2).

2. Again, we could note a significant exception in the extensive charity and missionary work of the Judeo-Christian tradition, which clearly expresses a type of "this-worldly" orientation. However, whereas magic tends to use action on the subtle or spiritual plane to effect change in the material or social world, the dominant Judeo-Christian approach could be said to use action in the material or social world (charity work, good deeds, and so on) primarily to effect change on the spiritual plane (e.g., to achieve salvation, a place in heaven, etc).

3. For examples of magical activism, see Starhawk (1979) and Howell (2002). Although associating subtle activism with magic is in some ways a risky move given the historical antipathy of both science and religion toward magic, such a designation is arguably inevitable in light of the common perception of magic as an attempt to influence the external world through nonmaterial means. What is needed is not to deny an inevitable association between subtle activism and magic, but to reassert the legitimacy of a magical (or participatory) perspective in the context of an emerging integral epistemological approach that aims to honor multiple ways of knowing.

4. Panentheism refers to the belief that God or the Divine is both immanent in creation and transcendent to it.

BIBLIOGRAPHY

24-7 Prayer International 2009. Accessed October 16, 2014. http://www.24-7prayer. com.

Abe, R. 1999. *Weaving of Mantra: Kukai and the Construction of Esoteric Buddhist Discourse*. New York: Columbia University Press.

Abram, D. 1997. *The Spell of the Sensuous: Perception and Language in a More-than-Human World*. New York: First Vintage Books.

Aldridge, D. 2003. A Qualitative Research Perspective on Healing. In *Healing, Intention, and Energy Medicine: Science, Research Methods and Clinical Implications*, edited by B. Jonas and C. Crawford, 225–38. Edinburgh: Churchill Livingstone.

Almaas, A. H. 2002. *Spacecruiser Inquiry: True Guidance for the Inner Journey*. Boston, MA: Shambhala.

Alvarado, C. S. 1996. "The Place of Spontaneous Cases in Parapsychology." *Journal of the American Society for Psychical Research* 90:1–34.

Anderson, M. L., & White, R. A. 1956. "Teacher-Pupil Attitudes and Clairvoyant Test Results." *Journal of Parapsychology* 20:141–57.

Arendt, H. 1951. *Elements of Totalitarianism*. New York: Harcourt Brace Jovanovich.

Ariyaratne, V. 2005. Building a Culture of Nonviolence and Peace: The Sarvodaya Experience in Sri Lanka. In *Proceedings of the International Symposium Cultivating Wisdom, Harvesting Peace: Education for a Culture of Peace Through Values, Virtues, and Spirituality of Diverse Cultures, Faiths, and Civilizations*, editor S.H. Toh and V.F. Cawagas, 87–96. Brisbane, Queensland: Griffith University.

Aron, E., and Aron, A. 1986. *The Maharishi Effect: A Revolution Through Meditation*. Walpole, NH: Stillpoint.

Astin, J. 2003. Intercessory Prayer and Healing Prayer. In *Healing, Intention, and Energy Medicine: Science, Research Methods and Clinical Implications*, editors B. Jonas and C. Crawford, 13–22. Edinburgh: Churchill Livingstone.

Aurobindo, S. 1953. *Sri Aurobindo on Himself and on the Mother*. Pondicherry, India: Sri Aurobindo International University Centre.

Bache, C. 2000. *Dark Night, Early Dawn: Steps to a Deep Ecology of Mind*. Albany, NY: State University of New York Press.

———. 2008. *The Living Classroom: Teaching and Collective Consciousness*. Albany, NY: State University of New York Press.

Bachelard, G. 1934. *The New Scientific Spirit*. Translated by A. Goldhammer. Boston, MA: Beacon Press.

Barnard, G. 2008. "Entheogenic Mysticism: A Jamesian Assessment." Paper Presented at the Annual Meeting of the American Academy of Religion, Chicago, Illinois, October 31-November 3.

Barry, J. 1968. "General and Comparative Study of the Psychokinetic Effect on a fungus Culture." *Journal of Parapsychology* 32:237–43.

Bauwens, M. (nd). The Next Buddha Will be a Collective. Integral World. Accessed October 16, 2014. http://www.integralworld.net/bauwens4.html.

Begley, C. G., & Ellis, L.M. 2012. "Drug Development: Raise Standards for Preclinical Cancer Research." *Nature* 483(7391):531–33.

Benor, D. 2001. *Spiritual Healing: Scientific Validation of a Healing Revolution*. Bellmawr, NJ: Wholistic Healing.

Bem, D. J., and Honorton, C. 1994. "Does Psi Exist? Replicable Evidence for an anomalous Process of Information Transfer." *Psychological Bulletin* 115(1):4.

———, Palmer, J., and Broughton, R. 2001. "Updating the Ganzfeld Database: A Victim of Its Own Success?" *Journal of Parapsychology* 65(3):207–18.

Benson, H. J. A., Dusek, J.B., Sherwood, P., Lam, C. F., Bethea, W., Carpenter, S., Levitsky, S. et al. "2006. Study of the Therapeutic Effects of Intercessory Prayer (STEP) in Cardiac Bypass Patients: A Multicenter Randomized Trial of Uncertainty and Certainty of Receiving Intercessory Prayer." *American Heart Journal* 151(4):934–42.

Berman, M. 1981. *The Reenchantment of the World*. Ithaca, NY: Cornell University Press.

Berry, T. 2000. *The Great Work*. New York: Bell Tower.

———. 2003. Teilhard in the Ecological Age. In *Teilhard in the 21st Century: The Emerging Spirit of the Earth*, editors A. Fabel and D. St. John, 57–76. Maryknoll, NY: Orbis Books.

———. 2009. *The Sacred Universe: Earth, Spirituality, and Religion in the Twenty-first Century*. New York: Columbia University Press.

Berry, W. 2003. *The Long-Legged House*. New York: Counterpoint.

Bissell, M. 2013. Reproducability: The Risks of the Replication Drive. *Nature*, 503. Accessed October 16, 2014. http://www.nature.com/news/reproducibility-the-risks-of-the-replication-drive-1.14184

Bloom, H. 2000. *Global Brain: The Evolution of Mass Mind from the Big Bang to the 21st Century*. New York: John Wiley & Sons.

Bohm, D. 1980. *Wholeness and the Implicate Order*. New York: Routledge & Kegan Paul.

Borland, C., and Landrith III, G. S. 1976. Improved Quality of City Life Through the Transcendental Meditation Program: Decreased Crime Rate. *Scientific Research on Maharishi's Transcendental Meditation and TM-Sidhi Program: Collected Papers* 1:639–48.

Bosch, H., Steinkamp, F., Boller, E. 2006. "Examining Psychokinesis: The Interaction of Human Intention With Random Number Generators—A Meta-Analysis." *Psychological Bulletin* 132(4):497–523.

Bound 4 Life. (nd). "Our Story." Accessed October 16, 2014. http://bound4life.com/about-us.

Boyd, E. B. 2009. Life on Google Earth. Accessed May 20, 2009 (article now removed).http://commongroundmag.com/2009/01/googleearth0901.html.

Braud, W. 1988. Distant Mental Influence of Rate of Hemolysis of Human Red Blood Cells. In *Research in Parapsychology*, editors L. Henkel and R. Berger, 1–28. Metuchen, NJ: Scarecrow.

Briggs, J., and Peat, D. 1990. *Turbulent Mirror: An Illustrated Guide to Chaos Theory and the Science of Wholeness*. New York: Harper & Row.

Brooks, R. (nd). "An Oasis of Peace." https://mywebspace.wisc.edu/rsbrooks/web/oasis.html

Broughton, R. 1991. *Parapsychology: The Controversial Science*. New York: Ballantine Books.

Brown, C. L. 2005. "Overcoming Barriers to Use of Promising Research among Elite Middle East Policy Groups." *Journal of Social Behavior and Personality* 17(1):489.

Buddharakkhita, A. 1989. Metta: The Philosophy and Practice of Universal Love. *The Wheel*. Accessed October 16, 2014. http://www.accesstoinsight.org/lib/authors/buddharakkhita/wheel365.html.

Butterfly-Hill, J. 2001. *The Legacy of Luna: The Story of a Tree, a Woman, and the Struggle to Save the Redwoods*. New York: HarperOne.

Byrd, R. 1988. "Positive Therapeutic Effects of Intercessory Prayer in a Coronary Care Unit Population." *Southern Medical Journal* 81(7):826–29.

Campbell, J. 1991. *The Masks of God, Volume 1: Primitive Mythology*. New York: Penguin.

Capek, M. 1964. *The Philosophical Impact of Contemporary Physics*. New York: Van Nostrand.

Capra, F. 1975. *Tao of Physics*. New York: Bantam Books.

———. 1982. *The Turning Point*. New York: Simon & Schuster.

———. 1985. The Tao of Physics Revisited. In *The Holographic Paradigm and Other Paradoxes: Exploring the Leading Edge of Science*, editor K. Wilber, 215–48. Boston: Shambhala.

Carter, C. 2007. *Parapsychology and the Skeptics: A Scientific Argument for the Existence of ESP*. Pittsburgh, PA: Sterlinghouse Books.

Chalmers, D. 1996. *The Conscious Mind*. Oxford: Oxford University Press.

Chatwin, B. 1987. *The Songlines*. New York: Penguin Books.

Chaudhuri, H. 2002. "Yogic Potentials and Capacities." Accessed October 16, 2014. http://www.esalenctr.org/display/paper.cfm?ID=20.

Child, I. L. 1985. "Psychology and Anomalous Observations: The Question of ESP in Dreams." *American Psychologist* 40(11):1219–30.

Crawford, C., Jonas, B., & Sparber, A. 2003. "A Systematic Review of the Quality of Research on Hands-on and Distant Healing: Clinical and Laboratory Studies." *Alternative Therapies in Health and Medicine* 9(3):96–104

Dakers, A. (nd). *The Big Ben Minute—The History and Significance of the Big Ben Silent Minute Observation*. London: Andrew Dakers.

Dallapiccola, A. 2002. *Dictionary of Hindu Lore and Legend*. London: Thames and Hudson.

Daruna, J. 2004. *Introduction to Psychoneuroimmunology*. Burlington, MA: Elsevier Academic Press.

David-Neal, A. 1965. *Magic and Mystery in Tibet*. New York: University Books.

Davidson, D. 1984. *Inquiries into Truth and Interpretation*. New York: Oxford University Press.

Davies, J. L., & Alexander, C. N. 1989 (August). "Alleviating Political Violence Through Enhancing Coherence in Collective Consciousness: Impact Assessment Analysis of the Lebanon War." Paper Presented at the 85th Annual Meeting of the American Political Science Association, Atlanta, GA.

Devereux P., & Thompson I. 1979. *The Ley Hunter's Companion*. London: Thames and Hudson.

Dillbeck, M. C., Cavanaugh, K. L., Glenn, T., Orme-Johnson, D. W., & Mittlefehldt, V. 1987. "Consciousness as a Field: The Transcendental Meditation and TM-Sidhi Program and Changes in Social Indicators."*Journal of Mind and Behavior* 8(1):67–104.

———, Landrith III, G. S., & Orme-Johnson, D. W. 1981. "The Transcendental Meditation Program and Crime Rate Change in a Sample of forty-eight Cities." *Journal of Crime and Justice* 4:25–45.

Doronin, V. N., Parfentev, V. A., Tleulin, S. Zh., Namvar, R. A., Somsikov, V. M., Drobzhev, V. I., and Chemeris, A. V. 1998. "Effect of Variations of the Geomagnetic field and Solar activity on Human Physiological Indicators." *Biofizika* 43(4):647–53.

Dossey, L. 1997. "Notes on the Journey: The Return of Prayer." *Alternative Therapies in Health and Medicine* 3(6):10–21.

———. 1999. *Reinventing Medicine: Beyond Mind-Body to a New Era of Healing*. New York: HarperCollins.

Downey, G. D., and Lende, D. 2009. "The Encultured Brain: Why Neuroanthropology? Why Now? Neuroanthropology." Accessed October 16, 2014. http://neuroanthropology.net/2009/10/08/the-encultured-brain-why-neuroanthropology-why-now/.

Duane, T. D., and Behrendt, T. 1965. Extrasensory electroencephalographic induction between identical twins. *Science* 150:367–69.

Dunne, B. 1991. "Co-Operator Experiments With an REG Device." Accessed October 16, 2014. http://spiritualscientific.com/yahoo_site_admin/assets/docs/Cooperator_REG_experiments.123114148.pdf.

Duval R. 1988. TM or Not TM? "A Comment on 'International Peace Project in the Middle East.'" *Journal of Conflict Resolution* 32(4):813–17.

Eddington, A. 1958. *The Nature of the Physical World*. Ann Arbor, MI: Michigan University Press. Quoted in R. Oates, *Permanent Peace: How to Stop Terrorism and War—now and forever*. Fairfield, IA: Institute of Science, Technology, and Public Policy, 2002, 99.

Eliade, M. 1964. *Shamanism: Archaic Techniques of Ecstasy*. Princeton, NJ: Princeton University Press.

———. 1969. *Yoga: Immortality and freedom*. Princeton, NJ: Princeton University Press.

———. 1987. *The Sacred and the Profane: The Nature of Religion*. Orlando, FL: Harcourt.

Elgin, D. 1993. *Awakening Earth: Exploring the Evolution of Human Culture and Consciousness*. New York: William Morrow.

Emerson, R. E. 1887. War. Reprinted in *Emerson's Complete Works*, Vol. XI, Boston: Houghton, Mifflin & Co.

Epstein, S. 1980. "The Stability of Behavior: II. Implications for Psychological Research." *American Psychologist* 35(9):790.

Erdoes, R. 1976. *The Rain Dance People: The Pueblo Indians, Their Past and Present*. New York: Random House.

Ertel, S. 1998. "Cosmophysical Correlations of Creative Activity in Cultural History." *Biophysics* 43(4), 696–702.

———. (nd). Evolutionary Metaphysics. "The Second Annual Conference on Evolutionary Metaphysics, Dec. 9–14, 2007." Accessed October 17, 2014. http://www.esalenctr.org/display/evo_meta_sum2007.cfm.

Fabel, A., and St. John, D. 2003. *Teilhard in the 21st Century: The Emerging Spirit of the Earth*. Maryknoll, NY: Orbis Books.

Faivre, A. 1992. Ancient and Medieval Sources of Modern Esoteric Movements. In *Modern Esoteric Spirituality*, editors A. Faivre and J. Needleman, 1–70. New York: Crossroad.

Fales, E., and Markovsky, B. 1997. "Evaluating Heterodox Theories." *Social Forces* 76(2):511–25.

Farnam, T. W., and Kane, P. 2010. Democratic Campaign Committees Losing Big Wall Street Donors. *The Washington Post*, July 6. Accessed October 17, 2014. http://www.washingtonpost.com/wp-dyn/content/article/2010/07/05/AR2010070502913.html.

Ferrer, J. 1998. "Speak Now or Forever Hold Your Peace: A Review Essay of Ken Wilber's 'The Marriage of Sense and Soul: Integrating Science and Religion.'" *Journal of Transpersonal Psychology* 30(1):53–65.

———. 2001. *Revisioning Transpersonal Theory: A Participatory Vision of Human Spirituality*. Albany, NY: State University of New York Press.

———. 2003. "Integral Transformative Practice: A Participatory Perspective." *Journal of Transpersonal Psychology* 35(1):21–42.

———. nd. "Embodied Spirituality, Now and Then. Integral World." Accessed October 17, 2014. http://www.integralworld.net/ferrer2.html.

———, & Sherman, J. 2008. *The Participatory Turn: Spirituality, Mysticism, Religious Studies*. Albany, NY: State University of New York Press.

Festinger, L. 1957. *A Theory of Cognitive Dissonance*. Redwood City, CA: Stanford University Press.

Feyerabend, P. 1975. *Against Method: Outline of an Anarchistic Theory of Knowledge*. New York: New Left Books.

Flood, G., ed. 2003. *The Blackwell Companion to Hinduism*. Malden, MA: Blackwell.

Fortune, D. 1993. *The Magical Battle of Britain*. Bradford, Wiltshire: Golden Gates Press.

Frackowiak, R., Ashburner, J., Penny, W., Zeki, S., Friston, K., Frith, C., Dolan, R., and Price, C. 2004. *Human Brain function*, 2nd ed. San Diego, CA: Academic Press.

Frazer, J. G. 1911. *The Golden Bough: The Magic Art and the Evolution of Kings.* London: Macmillan. Quoted in R. Sheldrake. 1988. *The Presence of the Past: Morphic Resonance and the Habits of Nature.* New York: First Vintage Books; 314–15.

Freud, S. 1952. *Totem and Taboo.* In *The Origins of Religion,* editor A. Dickson, 1985, 221. Harmondsworth, U.K.: Penguin. Quoted in R. Sheldrake. 1988. *The Presence of the Past: Morphic Resonance and the Habits of Nature.* New York: First Vintage Books; 247.

Furst, P. 1972. *Flesh of the Gods: The Ritual Use of Hallucinogens.* New York: Praeger. Quoted in M. Harner. 1990. *The Way of the Shaman,* 41. New York: HarperOne.

Gaiamind 2009. Accessed November 21, 2014. http://www.gaiamind.com/invite.html

Gepser, J. 1986. *The Ever-Present Origin.* Athens: Ohio University Press.

Global Day of Prayer. nd. History. Accessed November 20, 2014. http://www.global-dayofprayer.com/index.php/about-us/history/.

Gilbert, R. A., ed. 1986. *Golden Dawn Companion.* London: Red Wheel Weiser.

Goswami, A. 1993. *The Self-Aware Universe.* New York: Tarcher/Putnam.

———. 1995. *The Self-Aware Universe: How Consciousness Creates the Material World.* New York: Jeremy Tarcher.

Gould, S. J. 1981. *The Mismeasure of Man.* New York: W.W. Norton.

———. 1983. Utopia (limited). Review of *The Turning Point: Science, Society, and the Rising Culture* by Fritjof Capra. *New York Review of Books,* March 3.

Greig, P. nd. "A History of 24-7 Prayer Down the Ages. 24-7 Prayer/Prayer, Mission, and Justice." Accessed October 17, 2014. http://www.24-7prayer.com/prayer/history.

Griffin, D. R. 1997. *Parapsychology, Philosophy, & Spirituality: A Postmodern Exploration.* Albany, NY: State University of New York Press.

Grigoryev, P., Rozanov, V., Vaiserman, A., Vladimirskiy, B. 2009. "Heliogeophysical factors as Possible Triggers of Suicide Terrorist Acts." *Health* 1(4), 294–97.

Grim, J., and Tucker, E. 2003. Introduction to *Teilhard in the 21st Century: The Emerging Spirit of Earth.* Edited by A. Fabel and D. St John. Maryknoll, NY: Orbis Books.

Grof, S. 1976. *Realms of the Unconscious: Observations from LSD Research.* New York: Viking Press.

———. 1985. *Beyond the Brain: Birth, Death, and Transcendence in Psychotherapy.* Albany, NY: State University of New York Press.

———. 1988. *The Adventure of Self-discovery: Dimensions of Consciousness and New Perspectives in Psychotherapy and Inner Exploration.* Albany, NY: State University of New York Press.

Habermas, J. 1971. *Knowledge and Human Interests.* Translated by J. J. Shapiro. Boston: Beacon Press.

———. 1987. *The Theory of Communicative Action, Vol. 2: Lifeworld and System: A Critique of functionalist Reason.* Translated by T. McCarthy. Boston: Beacon Press.

———. 1988. *On the Logic of the Social Sciences.* Translated by S. W. Nicholsen and J. A. Stark. Cambridge, MA: MIT Press.

Hagelin, J. 1998. *Manual for a Perfect Government: How to Harness the Laws of Nature to Bring Maximum Success to Governmental Administration.* Fairfield, IA: Maharishi University of Management Press.

———, Rainforth, M., Orme-Johnson, D., Cavanaugh, K., Alexander, C., Shaktin, S., Davies, J., et al. 1999. "Effects of Group Practice of the Transcendental Meditation Program on Preventing Violent Crime in Washington D.C.: Results of the National Demonstration Project, June-July 1993." *Social Indicators Research* 47, 153–201.

Hagerty, L. 2000. *The Spirit of the Internet: Speculations on the Evolution of Global Consciousness.* Tampa, FL: Matrix Masters.

Hall, M. 2008a. *The Secret Destiny of America.* New York: Jeremy Tarcher/Penguin.

———. 2008b. *The Secret Teachings of All the Ages: An Encyclopedic Outline of Masonic, Hermetic, Qabbalistic and Rosicrucian Symbolical Philosophy.* (no Listed Publishing Location): Forgotten Books.

Hanegraaff, W. 1998. *New Age Religion and Western Culture: Esotericism in the Mirror of Secular Thought.* Albany, NY: State University of New York Press.

Hansel, C. E. M. 1966. *ESP: A Scientific Evaluation.* New York: Charles Scribner's Sons.

———. 1980. *ESP and Parapsychology: A Critical Re-evaluation.* Buffalo, NY: Prometheus.

Hanh, T. N. 1994. "The Next Buddha May be a Sangha." *Inquiring Mind* 10(2).

Haraldsson, E., and Thorsteinsson, T. 1966. Psychokinetic Effects on Yeast: An Exploratory Experiment. In *Research in Psychology*, editors W. C. Roll, R. L. Morris, and J. D. Morris, 20–21. Metuchen, NJ: Scarecrow Press.

Harner, M. 1990. *The Way of the Shaman.* New York: HarperOne.

Harrington, A., ed. 1999. *The Placebo Effect: An Interdisciplinary Exploration.* Harvard, MA: Harvard University Press.

Harris, W. S., Gowda, M., Kolb, J. W., Strychacz, C. P., Vacek, J. L., Jones, P. G., Forker, A., et al. 1999. "A Randomized, Controlled Trial of the Effects of Remote, Intercessory Prayer on Outcomes in Patients Admitted to the Coronary Care Unit." *Archives of Internal Medicine* 159(19), 2273–78.

Hawken, P. 2007. *Blessed Unrest: How the Largest Movement in the World Came into Being and Why No One Saw It Coming.* New York: Viking.

Herbert, N. 1985. *Quantum Reality: Beyond the New Physics.* New York: Anchor Books.

Heron, J. 1998. *Sacred Science: Person-centered Inquiry into the Spiritual and the Subtle.* Herofordhire: PCCS Books.

———. 2006. *Participatory Spirituality: A Farewell to Authoritarian Religion.* Morrisville, NC: Lulu Press.

Higginbotham, R., and Higginbotham, J. 2009. *ChristoPaganism: An Inclusive Path.* Woodbury, MA: Llewellyn.

Hodge, D. 2007. "A Systematic Review of the Empirical Literature on Intercessory Prayer." *Research on Social Work Practice* 17(2):174–87.

Honorton, C. 1993. "Rhetoric Over Substance: The Impoverished State of Skepticism." *Journal of Parapsychology* 57:191–214.

————, and Ferrari, D. 1989. "Future Telling: A Meta-analysis of Forced-Choice Precognition Experiments, 1935–1987." *Journal of Parapsychology* 53:281–308.

Howell, F. 2002. *Making Magic With Gaia: Practices to Heal Ourselves and Our Planet.* York Beach, ME: Red Wheel.

Hufford, D. 2003. Challenges for Healing and Intentionality Research: Social Dynamics Involved in Entering the Mainstream. In *Healing, Intention and Energy Medicine: Science, Research Methods and Clinical Implications*, editors W. Jonas and C. Crawford, 293–306. Edinburgh: Churchill Livingstone.

Hyman, R. 1996. Evaluation of a Program on Anomalous Mental Phenomena. *Journal of Scientific Exploration*, 10:31–58. Quoted in Radin, D. 1997. *The Conscious Universe: The Scientific Truth of Psychic Phenomena*, 103. New York: HarperCollins.

————, and Honorton, C. 1986. "A Joint Communiqué: The Psi Ganzfeld Controversy." *Journal of Parapsychology* 50(4):351–64.

Ingram, P. 2007. *Buddhist-Christian Dialogue in an Age of Science.* Lanham, MD: Rowman & Littlefield.

International Day of Peace Vigil. 2008. Accessed November 24, 2014. http://www.idpvigil.com.

International Prayer Council. 2010. About the International Prayer Council. Accessed November 24, 2014. http://www.ipcprayer.org/about

Irwin, H. 1993. "Belief in the Paranormal: A Review of the Empirical Literature." *Journal of the American Society for Psychical Research* 87(1). Accessed October 17, 2014. http://www.aiprinc.org/para-ac05_Irwin_1993.pdf.

Jahn, R. G. 1982. "The Persistent Paradox of Psychic Phenomena: An Engineering Perspective." *Proceedings of the IEEE* 70(2):136–70.

Jahn, R. G., and Dunne, B. J. 1987. *Margins of Reality: The Role of Consciousness in the Physical World.* New York: Harcourt Brace Jovanovich.

Jaspers, K. 1951. *Way to Wisdom: An Introduction to Philosophy.* New Haven, CT: Yale University Press.

Johnson, G. 2014. New Truths that Only One Can See. *New York Times*, January 21. Accessed October 17, 2014. http://www.nytimes.com/2014/01/21/science/new-truths-that-only-one-can-see.html?_r=0.

Johnson, K., and Ord, D. R. 2012. *The Coming Interspiritual Age.* Vancouver, BC: Namaste Publishing.

Jonas, B., and Crawford, C. 2003. *Healing, Intention, and Energy Medicine: Science, Research Methods and Clinical Implications.* New York: Churchill Livingstone.

Jones, K., and Kraft, K. 2003. *The New Social Face of Buddhism: A Call to Action.* Somerville, MA: Wisdom.

Jung, C. G. 1952. *Synchronicity: An Acausal Connecting Principle*, Collected Works 8:438–39. Quoted in R. Tarnas. 2006. *Cosmos and Psyche: Intimations of a New World View* 51–52. New York: Viking; 2006.

————. 1955. *Modern Man in Search of a Soul.* Orlando, FL: Harcourt.

————. 1970. *The Collected Works of C. G. Jung, Vol. 10.* Princeton, NJ: Princeton University Press.

————. 1981. *The Archetypes and the Collective Unconscious.* Princeton, NJ: Princeton University Press.

Katz, S. 1978. Language, Epistemology, and Mysticism. In *Mysticism and Philosophical Analysis*, editor S.T. Katz, 22–74. New York: Oxford University Press.

Kawulich, B. 2005. "Participation Observation as a Data Collection Method." *Forum: Qualitative Social Research* 6(2):1–22.

Keepin, W. 1993. Lifework of David Bohm—River of Truth. *Revision* 16(1):32–46.

Keepin, W. 2007. *Divine Duality: The Power of Reconciliation Between Women and Men*. New York: Hohm Press.

Kelly, E. F., Kelly, E. W., Crabtree, A., Gauld, A., Grosso, M., Greyson, B. 2009. *Irreducible Mind: Toward a Psychology for the 21ˢᵗ Century*. Plymouth, UK: Rowman & Littlefield Publishers.

Kelly, S. 1993. *Individuation and the Absolute: Hegel, Jung, and the Path Toward Wholeness*. Mahwah, NJ: Paulist Press.

———. nd. "The Hidden face of Wisdom: Towards an Awakened Activism." Accessed November 20, 2014. http://www.earthrainbownetwork.com/FocusArchives/HiddenFaceWisdom.htm

———. 2010. *Coming Home: The Birth and Transformation of the Planetary Era*. Great Barrington, MA: Lindisfarne Books.

Kennedy, J. E. 2005. "Personality and Motivations to Believe, Misbelieve, and Disbelieve in Paranormal Phenomena." *Journal of Parapsychology* 69(2):263–92.

———, and Taddonio, J. L. 1976. "Experimenter Effects in Parapsychological Research." *Journal of Parapsychology* 40(1):33.

Krucoff, M., Crater, S. W., Gallup, D., Blankenship, J. C., Cuffe, M., Guarneri, M., Krieger, R. A., et al. 2005. "Music, Imagery, Touch, and Prayer as Adjuncts to Interventional Cardiac Care: The Monitoring and Actualisation of Noetic Trainings (MANTRA) II Randomised Study." *The Lancet* 366(9481): 211–17.

Kuhn, T. 1970. *The Structure of Scientific Revolutions* 2nd ed. Chicago, IL: University of Chicago Press.

Lachman, G. 2008. *Politics and the Occult: The Left, the Right, and the Radically Unseen*. Wheaton, IL: Quest Books.

Laszlo, E. 2006. *Science and the Reenchantment of the Cosmos: The Rise of the Integral Vision of Reality*. Rochester, VT: Inner Traditions.

———. 2007. *Science and the Akashic Field: An Integral Theory of Everything*. New York: Inner Traditions.

Lawlor, R. 1991. *Voices of the First Day: Awakening in the Aboriginal Dreamtime*. Rochester, VT: Inner Traditions International.

Lawrence, T. 1993. "Gathering in the Sheep and Goats: A Meta-analysis of forced-choice Sheep-goat ESP Studies, 1947–1993." *Proceedings of the Parapsychological Association* 36ᵗʰ *Annual Convention*. 75–86.

Lemert, C. 1991. "The End of Ideology, Really." *Sociological Theory* 9(2):164–72.

Leonard, G., and Murphy, M. 1995. *The Life We are Given: A Long-term Program for Realizing the Potential of Our Body, Mind, Heart, and Soul*. New York: Jeremy P. Tarcher/Putnam.

Lerner, M. 1997. *Politics of Meaning: Restoring Hope and Possibility in an Age of Cynicism*. Reading, MA: Addison-Wesley.

———. 2002. *Spirit Matters*. Charlottesville, VA: Hampton Roads.

Levenda, P. 2002. *Unholy Alliance: A History of the Nazi Involvement With the Occult*. New York: Continuum.

Levy-Bruhl, L. 1985. *How Natives Think*. Princeton, NJ: Princeton University Press.

Lipton, B. 2008. *The Biology of Belief: Understanding the Power of Consciousness, Matter, Mind, and Miracles*. San Rafael, CA: Mountain of Love.

Lovelock, J. 1979. *Gaia: A New Look at Life on Earth*. Oxford: Oxford University Press.

———. 1988. *The Ages of Gaia: A Biography of Our Living Earth*. New York: W.W. Norton.

Loy, D. 2003. *The Great Awakening: A Buddhist Social Theory*. Boston: Wisdom.

McDougall, W. 1920. *The Group Mind*. Cambridge: Cambridge University Press. Quoted in R. Sheldrake. 1988. *The Presence of the Past: Morphic Resonance and the Habits of Nature*. 248. New York: First Vintage Books, 1988.

Macy, J. 1991. *World as Lover, World as Self*. Berkeley, CA: Parallax Press.

———. 1998. *Coming Back to Life: Practices to Reconnect Our Lives, Our World*. Gabriola Island, BC: New Society.

———. 2002a. "Sarvodaya Means 'Everybody Wakes Up.'" *Earthlight Magazine* 45.

———. 2002b. "The Meditation that Can End a War." *Inquiring Mind* 19(1). Accessed October 17, 2014. http://www.joannamacy.net/resources/engaged-buddhism/106-sarvodaya.html.

Marks, D. 1986. "Investigating the Paranormal." *Nature* 320:119–24.

Masters, K., Spielmans, G., and Goodson, J. 2006. "Are There Demonstrable Effects of Distant Intercessory Prayer? A Meta-Analytic Review." *Annals of Behavioral Medicine* 32(1):21–26.

Matthews, C., and Matthews, J. 2003. *Walkers Between Worlds: The Western Mysteries from Shaman to Magus*. Rochester, VT: Inner Traditions.

May, E. C., Utts, J. M., Trask, V. V., Luke, W. W., Frivold, T. J., and Humphrey, B. S. 1988, March. Review of the Psychoenergetic Research Conducted at SRO International (1973–1988. SRI International Technical Report.

McDermott, R., ed. 1987. *The Essential Aurobindo: Writings of Sri Aurobindo*. Great Barrington, MA: Lindisfarne Books.

McLaughlin, C., and Davidson, G. 1994. *Spiritual Politics: Changing the World from the Inside Out*. New York: Ballantine Books.

Metzner, R. 2008. *The Expansion of Consciousness*. Berkeley, CA: Regent Press.

Michell, J. 1982. *Megalithomania*. London: Thames and Hudson.

Midgley, M., ed. 2007. *Earthy Realism: The Meaning of Gaia*. Exeter, U.K.: Societas Imprint Academic.

Mikulecky, M. 2007. "Solar Activity, Revolutions and Cultural Prime in the History of Mankind." *Neuroendocrinology Letters* 28(6):749–56.

Miller, H. 2014. "The Trouble With 'Scientific' Research Today: A Lot That's Published Is Junk." *Forbes*. Accessed October 17, 2014. http://www.forbes.com/sites/henrymiller/2014/01/08/the-trouble-with-scientific-research-today-a-lot-thats-published-is-junk/2/.

Milton, J., and Wiseman, R. 1999. "Does Psi Exist? Lack of Replication of an Anomalous Process of Information Transfer." *Psychological Bulletin* 125(4):387–91.

Mindell, A. 2000. *Quantum Mind: The Edge Between Physics and Psychology*. New York: Lao Tse Press.

Mitchell, D. 2000. "Assembling for Peace" *Yes Magazine*. Accessed October 17, 2014. http://www.yesmagazine.org/article.asp?ID=315.

Monbiot, G. 2006. *Manifesto for a New World Order*. London: New Press.

Monod, J. 1970. *Chance and Necessity: An Essay on the Natural Philosophy of Modern Biology*. New York: Knopf.

Montagnier, L., Aissa, J., Del Guidice, E., Lavallee, C., Tedeschi, A., Vitiello, G. 2011. "DNA Waves and Water." *Journal of Physics: Conference Series* 301: 6–10.

Morin, E. 1977. *La Méthode 1: La Nature De La Nature*. Paris: Seuil. Quoted in S. Kelly, *Coming Home: The Birth and Transformation of the Planetary Era* 133. Great Barrington, MA: Lindisfarne Books.

———. 1986. *La Méthode 3: La Connaissance De La Connaissance*. Paris: Seuil. Quoted in S. Kelly, *Coming Home: The Birth and Transformation of the Planetary Era* (Great Barrington, MA: Lindisfarne Books), 134.

———. 1991. *La Méthode 4. Les Idées. Leur habitat, leur vie, leur moeurs, leur organization*. Paris: Éditions du Seuil. Quoted in S. Kelly, nd. "Hidden Face of Wisdom: Toward an Awakened Activism." Accessed November 20, 2014. http://www.earthrainbownetwork.com/FocusArchives/HiddenFaceWisdom.htm

———. 1999. *Homeland Earth: A Manifesto for the New Millennium*. Cresskill, NJ: Hampton Press.

Musella, D. P. 2005. "Gallop Poll Shows that Americans' Belief in the Paranormal Persists." *Skeptical Inquirer* 29(5):5.

Nagel, T. 1974. "What Is It Like to be a Bat?" *Philosophical Review* 83, 435–50.

———. 2012. *Mind & Cosmos: Why the Materialist Neo-Darwinian Conception of Nature Is Almost Certainly False*. Oxford: Oxford University Press.

Nash, C. 1982. "Psychokinetic Control of Bacterial Growth." *Journal for the Society of Psychical Research* 51:217–21.

Nadeau, R., and Kafatos, M. 1999. *The Non-local Universe: The New Physics and Matters of the Mind*. New York: Oxford University Press.

Naess, A. 1989. *Ecology, Community and Lifestyle*. Cambridge, UK: Cambridge University Press.

Nelson, R. D. 1997. "Multiple field REG/RNG Recordings During a Global Event." *The Electronic Journal for Anomalous Phenomena (eJAP)* 97(2).

Nelson, R. D., Jahn, R. G., Dunne, B. J., Dobyns, Y. H., and Bradish, G. J. 1998. "FieldREG II: Consciousness Field Effects: Replications and Explorations." *Journal of Scientific Exploration* 12(3):425–54. Quoted in D. Radin, 2006. *Entangled Minds: Extrasensory Experiences in a Quantum Reality*. New York: Paraview.

———. 2001. "Correlation of Global Events With REG Data: An Internet-based, Nonlocal Anomalies Experiment." *Journal of Parapsychology* 65(3):247–72.

———. 2003. "Global Harmony. Global Consciousness Project Exploratory Analysis." Accessed October 17, 2014. http://noosphere.princeton.edu/groupmedit.html.

———, Dunne, B. J., and Jahn, R. G. 1984. *An REG Experiment With Large Data Base Capability. III: Operator Related Anomalies*. Princeton, NJ: Engineering

Anomalies Research Laboratory. School of Engineering/Applied Science, Princeton University.

————, and Radin, D. 2003. Research on Mind-matter Interactions (MMI): Group Attention. In *Healing, Intention, and Energy Medicine: Science, Research Methods and Clinical Implications*, editors W. B. Jonas and C. C. Crawford, 49–58. Edinburgh, Scotland: Churchill Livingstone.

————, and Bancel, P. 2011. Effects of Mass Consciousness: Changes in Random Data During Global Events. *Explore: The Journal of Science & Healing* 7:373–83.

————, Bradish, D. J., Dobyns, Y. H., Dunne, B. J., and Jahn, R. G. 1986. Field REG Anomalies in Group Situations. *Journal of Scientific Exploration* 10:111–42.

Nietzsche, F. 1974. *The Gay Science*. Edited by W. Kaufmann. New York: Vintage Books.

Novak, M. 1976. *The Joy of Sports*. New York: Basic Books. Quoted in R. Sheldrake. 2003. *The Sense of Being Stared at and Other Unexplained Powers of the Human Mind*. New York: Crown, 40.

Oates, R. 2002. *Permanent Peace: How to Stop Terrorism and War—Now and Forever*. Fairfield, IA: Institute of Science, Technology, and Public Policy.

O'Dea, J. 2005. Social Healing. In *Consciousness and Healing: Integral Approaches to Mind-body Medicine*, editors. M. Schlitz, T. Amorok, and M. Micozzi, 567–76. St. Louis, MO: Elsevier.

Orme-Johnson, D. 2009. "A Field-Theoretic View of Consciousness: Reply to Critics." *Journal of Scientific Exploration* 22(3):139–66.

————. nd-a. "List of Scientific Research on the Maharishi Effect." Accessed October 17, 2014. http://www.truthabouttm.org/truth/SocietalEffects/Rationale-Research/index.cfm.

————. nd-b. "Theory and Research on Conflict Resolution Through the Maharishi Effect." Accessed October 17, 2014. http://www.mum.edu/m_effect/th_and_res_doj.

————. nd-c. "Some Conceptual Precedents for a Field Theoretic View of Consciousness from the Perennial Philosophy, Social Sciences, and Quantum Physics. Truth about TM/Societal Effects." Accessed October 17, 2014. http://www.truthabouttm.org/truth/SocietalEffects/Rationale-Research/index.cfm#rationale.

————, Alexander, C. N., and Davies, J. L. 1990. "The Effects of the Maharishi Technology of the Unified Field: Reply to a Methodological Critique." *Journal of Conflict Resolution* 34:756–68.

————, Alexander, C. N., Davies, J.L., Chandler, H. M., and Larimore, W. E. 1988. "International Peace Project in the Middle East: The Effects of the Maharishi Technology of the Unified Field." *Journal of Conflict Resolution* 32(4):776–812.

————, and Dillbeck, M. C. 1987. Maharishi's Program to Create World Peace: Theory and Research. *Modern Science and Vedic Science* 1(2):207–59.

————., and Farrow J. T. 1977. (Editors.) *Scientific Research on the Transcendental Meditation Program: Collected papers, Volume 1*. Rheinweiler, W. Germany: MERU Press.

Palmer, J. 1971. "Scoring in ESP Tests as a Function of Belief in ESP. Part I. The Sheep-Goat Effect." *Journal of the American Society for Psychical Research* 66:373–408.

———. 1972. "Scoring in ESP Tests as a Function of Belief in ESP. Part II. The Sheep-Goat Effect." *Journal of the American Society for Psychical Research* 66:1–26.

Panentheism. nd. "In Stanford Encyclopedia of Philosophy." http://plato.stanford.edu/entries/panentheism.

Park, R. 2000. *Voodoo Science: The Road from Foolishness to Fraud.* New York: Oxford University Press.

Parker, A. 2003. "We Ask, Does Psi Exist? But Is This the Right Question and Do We Really Want an Answer Anyway?" *Journal of Consciousness Studies* 10(6–7):6–7.

Pearson, J. 2007. *Wicca and the Christian Heritage: Ritual, Sex, and Magic.* New York: Routledge.

Peat, D. 2008. *Gentle Action: Bringing Change to a Turbulent World.* New York: Pari.

———. nd-a. "Gentle Action: Surviving Chaos and Change." Accessed October 17, 2014. http://www.fdavidpeat.com/bibliography/essays/gentle.htm.

———. nd-b. "Gentle Action for a Harmonious World." Accessed October 17, 2014. http://www.fdavidpeat.com/bibliography/essays/edges.htm.

Persinger, M. A. 1987. "Spontaneous Telepathic Experiences from Phantasms of the Living and Low Global Geomagnetic Activity." *Journal of the American Society for Psychical Research* 83:23–36.

———. 1995. "Sudden Unexpected Deaths in Epileptics following Sudden, Intense Increases in Geomagnetic Activity: Prevalence of Effect and Potential Mechanisms." *International Journal of Biometeorology* 38(4):180–87.

———. 2008. "On the Possible Representation of the Electromagnetic Equivalents of All Human Memory Within the Earth's Magnetic field: Implications of Theoretical Biology." *Theoretical Biology Insights* 1:3–11.

———, and Gearhart, L. 1986. "Geophysical Variables and Behavior: Onsets of Historical and Contemporary Poltergeist Episodes Occurred With Sudden Increases in Geomagnetic Activity." *Perceptual and Motor Skills* 62:463–66.

———. Lewicki, D., and Schaut, G. 1987. "Geophysical Variables and Behavior: Days of Subjective Precognitive Experience and the Days Before the Actual Events Display Correlated Geomagnetic Activity." *Perceptual and Motor Skills* 65:173–74.

Pio, E. 1998. *Buddhist Psychology: A Modern Perspective.* New Delhi, India: Abhinav.

Pobachenko, S. V., Kolesnik, A. G., Borodin, A. S., and Kalyuzhin, V. V. 2006. "The Contingency of Parameters of Human Encephalograms And Schumann Resonance Electromagnetic fields Revealed in Monitoring Studies." *Complex Systems Biophysics* 51(3):480–83.

Popper, K. R. 1968. *The Logic of Scientific Discovery.* New York: Harper & Row.

———, and Eccles, J.C. 1977. The Self and Its Brain. Berlin, Germany: Springer. Quoted in R. Sheldrake. 1991. *The Rebirth of Nature: The Greening of Science and God,* 88. New York: Bantam Books.

Priests for Life. nd. "Prayer Campaign." Accessed November 24, 2014. http://www.priestsforlife.org/prayercampaign.

Pratiss, I. nd. "Meditation for Gaia." Accessed October 17, 2014. http://www.ianprat-tis.com/pdf/meditationforgaia.pdf.

Pratt, J. G., Rhine, J.B., Smith, B. M., Stuart, C. E., and Greenwood, J. A. 1966. *Extra-sensory Perception After Sixty Years*. Boston: Bruce Humphries.

Price, G. R. 1955. "Science and the Supernatural." *Science* 122:359–67.

Prigogine, I. 1980. *From Being to Becoming: Time and Complexity in the Physical Sciences*. San Francisco, CA: W.H. Freeman

Primavesi, A. 2000. *Sacred Gaia: Holistic Theology and Earth System Science*. New York: Routledge.

Radin, D. 1997. *The Conscious Universe: The Scientific Truth of Psychic Phenomena*. New York: HarperCollins.

———. 2006. *Entangled Minds: Extrasensory Experiences in a Quantum Reality*. New York: Paraview.

———, and R. Nelson. 1989. "Evidence for Consciousness-related Anomalies in Random Physical Systems." *Foundations of Physics* 19:1499–514.

———, and Nelson, R. 2003. A Meta-analysis of Mind-Matter interaction Experiments from 1959 to 2000. In *Healing, Intention, and Energy Medicine: Science, Research Methods and Clinical Implications*, editors. W. B. Jonas and C.C. Crawford, 39–48. Edinburgh: Churchill Livingstone.

———, Nelson, R., Dobyns, Y., and Houtkooper, J. 2006. "Re-examining Psychokinesis: Comment on Bosch, Steinkamp, and Boller 2006." *Psychological Bulletin* 132(4):529–32.

Radin, D. I., and Ferrari, D. C. 1991. "Effects of Consciousness on the Fall of Dice: A Meta-analysis." *Journal of Scientific Exploration* 5(3):61–84.

Rao, K. 2002. *Consciousness Studies: Cross-cultural Perspectives*. Jefferson, NC: McFarland & Co.

Rhine, J. B. 1964. *Extra-sensory Perception*. Boston, MA: Braden Publishing.

———, and Pratt, J. G. 1954. "A Review of the Pearce-Pratt Distance Series of ESP Tests." *Journal of Parapsychology* 18:165–77.

Rhine, L. E. 1961. *Hidden Channels of the Mind*. New York: William Sloane Associates.

———. 1981. *The Invisible Picture: A Study of Psychic Experiences*. Jefferson, NC: McFarland & Co.

Ridley, J. 2000. *The Freemasons*. London: Robinson.

Robb, J., and Wilson, J. 2000. "Prayer Is Social Action." Accessed October 17, 2014. http://www.urbana.org/articles/prayer-is-social-action.

Roesch, M. 2009. "Harmonic Convergence." Accessed October 17, 2014. http://www.siskiyous.edu/shasta/fol/har/index.htm.

Rorty, R. 1979. *Philosophy and the Mirror of Nature*. Princeton, NJ: Princeton University Press.

Rosary Bowl Web Site. "A World at Prayer Is a World at Peace: A Rosary Celebration." http://www.rosarybowl.org/about-faq.html.

Roszak, T. 1999. *The Gendered Atom: The Sexual Psychology of Science*. New York: Green Books.

Rothberg, D. 1993. "The Crisis of Modernity and the Emergence of Socially-engaged Spirituality." *ReVision* 15(3):105–14.

———. 1994. "Spiritual Inquiry." *ReVision* 19(2):41–42.

————. 2006. *The Engaged Spiritual Life: A Buddhist Approach to Transforming Ourselves and the World*. New York: Beacon Press.

————. 2008. Connecting Inner and Outer Transformation: Toward an Expanded Model of Buddhist Practice. In *The Participatory Turn: Spirituality, Mysticism, Religious Studies*, editors J. Ferrer and J. Sherman, 349–70. Albany, NY: State University of New York Press.

Russell, P. 1983. *The Global Brain: Speculations on the Evolutionary Leap to Planetary Consciousness*. Los Angeles: J.P. Tarcher.

Sagan, C. 1995. *The Demon Haunted World*. New York: Random House. Quoted in D. Radin. 1997. *The Conscious Universe: The Scientific Truth of Psychic Phenomena*, 3 New York: HarperCollins.

Salzberg, S. 1995. *Lovingkindness: The Revolutionary Art of Happiness*. Boston: Shambala.

Satchidananda, S. 1990. *The Yoga Sutras of Patanjali*. Buckingham, VA: Integral Yoga.

Scharf, D. 2010. "Pseudoscience and Victor Stenger's Quantum Gods: Mistaken, Misinformed and Misleading." *NeuroQuantology* 8(1):77–100.

Schlitz, M., and Braud, W. 1997. "Distant Intentionality and Healing: Assessing the Evidence." *Alternative Therapies in Health and Medicine* 3(6):62–73.

————, and Radin, D. 2003. Nonsensory Access to Information: The Ganzfeld Studies. In *Healing, Intention, and Energy Medicine: Science, Research Methods and Clinical Implications*, editors B. Jonas and C. Crawford, 75–82. Edinburgh: Churchill Livingstone.

Schmeidler, G. R., and McConnell, R. A. 1973. *ESP and Personality Patterns*. Westport, CT: Greenwood Press.

Schmidt, S. 2003. Direct Mental Interactions With Living Systems (DMILS). In *Healing, Intention, and Energy Medicine: Science, Research Methods and Clinical Implications*, editors B. Jonas and C. Crawford, 23–38. Edinburgh: Churchill Livingstone.

————, Schneider, R., Utts, J., and Walach, H. 2004. "Distant Intentionality and the Feeling of Being Stared At: Two Meta-Analyses." *British Journal of Psychology* 95:235–47.

Schoch, R., and Yonavjack, L. 2008. *The Parapsychology Revolution: A Concise Anthology of Paranormal and Psychical Research*. New York: Tarcher.

Schrodt, P. 1990. "A Methodological Critique of a Test of the Effects of the Maharishi Technology of the Unified Field." *Journal of Conflict Resolution* 34(4):745–55.

Schouten, S. 1979. "Analysis of Spontaneous Cases as Reported in *Phantasms of the Living*." *European Journal of Parapsychology* 2:408–55.

————. 1981. "Analyzing Spontaneous Cases: A Replication Based on the Sannwald Collection." *European Journal of Parapsychology* 4:8–48.

————. 1982. "Analyzing Spontaneous Cases: A Replication Based on the Rhine Collection." *European Journal of Parapsychology* 4:114–58.

Searle, J. 1997. *The Mystery of Consciousness*. New York: The New York Review of Books.

————. 2000. "Consciousness, free Action, and the Brain." *Journal of Consciousness Studies* 7(10):3–22.

Sellars, W. 1956. Empiricism and the Philosophy of Mind. In *Minnesota Studies in the Philosophy of Science: Vol. 1. The foundations of the Science and the Concepts of Psychology and Psychoanalysis*, editors H. Feigl and M. Scriven, 253–329. Minneapolis: University of Minnesota Press.

Sheldrake, R. 1981. *A New Science of Life: The Hypothesis of Morphic Resonance*. Rochester, VT: Park Street Press.

———. 1988. *The Presence of the Past: Morphic Resonance and the Habits of Nature*. New York: First Vintage Books.

———. 1991. *The Rebirth of Nature: The Greening of Science and God*. New York: Bantam Books.

———. 2003. *The Sense of Being Stared At: And Other Unexplained Powers of the Human Mind*. New York: Crown.

———. 2005. "Sheldrake and His Critics: The Sense of Being Glared At." *Journal of Consciousness Studies* 12(6).

Sherwood, S., and Roe, C. A. 2003. "A Review of Dream ESP Studies Conducted Since the Maimonides Dream ESP Programme." *Journal of Consciousness Studies* 10(6–7):6–7.

Sicher, F., Targ, T., Moore, D., and Smith, H. 1998. "A Randomized Double-blind Study of the Effect of Distant Healing in a Population With Advanced AIDS. Report of a Small Scale Study." *Western Journal of Medicine* 169(6):356–63.

Sloman, A. 1991. "Developing Concepts of Consciousness." *Behavioral and Brain Sciences* 14(4):694–95.

Spangler, D. 1984. *The Rebirth of the Sacred*. London: Gateway Books.

———. 2008. *World Work*. Everett, WA: Lorian Press.

Spretnak, C. 1999. *The Resurgence of the Real*. New York: Routledge.

Sri Lankan Government. 2002. "Massive Gathering in Anuradhapura for Peace Meditation Programme." http://www.priu.gov.lk/news_update/Current_Affairs/ca200203/20020315peace_meditation.htm.

Stanczak, G. C., and Miller, D. E. 2002. *Engaged Spirituality: Spirituality and Social Transformation in Mainstream American Religious Traditions—Report Supplement*. Center for Religion and Civic Culture, University of Southern California. Accessed November 20, 2014. http://crcc.usc.edu/docs/Engaged SpiritualityAppendix.pdf. Quoted in S. Kelly, nd. "The Hidden face of Wisdom: Towards an Awakened Activism." Accessed November 20, 2014. http://www.earthrainbownetwork.com/FocusArchives/HiddenFaceWisdom.htm

Stapp, H. 1988. Quantum Physics and the Physicist's View of Nature: Philosophical Implications of Bell's Theorem. In *The World View of Contemporary Physics*, editor R. Kitchener, 40. Albany: SUNY Press. Quoted in Nadeau, R. and Kafatos, M. 1999. *The Non-local Universe: The New Physics and Matters of the Mind*, 80. New York: Oxford University Press, 1999.

Starhawk. 1979. *The Spiral Dance: A Rebirth of the Ancient Religion of the Great Goddess*. San Francisco, CA: HarperSanFrancisco.

Steinkamp, F., Milton, J., and Morris, R. L. 1998. "Meta-analysis of forced-choice Experiments Comparing Clairvoyance and Precognition." *Journal of Parapsychology* 62:193–218.

Stepan, N., and Gilman. S. 1993. Appropriating the Idioms of Science: The Rejection of Scientific Racism. In *The "Racial" Economy of Science: Toward a Democratic Future*, editor S. Harding, 170–93. Bloomington, IN: Indiana University Press.

Stevenson, I. 1970. *Telepathic Impressions*. Charlottsville, VA: University of Virginia Press.

Stenger. V. 2009. *Quantum Gods: Creation, Chaos, and the Search for Cosmic Consciousness*. Amherst, NY: Prometheus Books.

Stokes, D. 1997. *The Nature of Mind: Parapsychology and the Role of Consciousness in the Physical World*. Jefferson, NC: McFarland & Co.

Swimme, B. 1999. *The Hidden Heart of the Cosmos: Humanity and the New Story*. New York: Orbis Books.

———. 2003. The New Natural Selection. In *Teilhard in the 21ˢᵗ Century: The Emerging Spirit of Earth*, editor A. Fabel and D. St. John, 127–37. Maryknoll, NY: Orbis Books.

Tambiah, S. 1990. *Magic, Science, Religion and the Scope of Rationality*. Cambridge, UK: Cambridge University Press.

Targ, E., and Thomson, K. S. 1997. "Can Prayer and Intentionality be Researched? Should They Be?" *Alternative Therapies Health Medicine* 3(6):92–96.

Tarnas, R. 1991. *The Passion of the Western Mind: Understanding the Ideas that Have Shaped Our World View*. New York: Ballantine Books.

———. 2001. "Is the Modern Psyche Undergoing a Rite of Passage?" Accessed October 17, 2014. http://cosmosandpsyche.com/Essays/php.

———. 2006. *Cosmos and Psyche: Intimations of a New Worldview*. New York: Viking Penguin.

Tart, C. 2009. *The End of Materialism: How Evidence of the Paranormal Is Bringing Science and Spirit Closer Together*. Oakland, CA: Noetic Books.

Taylor, C. 1987. Overcoming Epistemology. In *After Philosophy: End or Transformation?*, editor K. Baynes, J. Bohman, and T. McCarthy, 464–85. Cambridge: MIT Press.

Tedder, W., and Monty, M. 1981. Exploration of Long Distance PK: A Conceptual Replication of the Influence on a Biological System. In *Research in Parapsychology 1980*, editors W. G. Roll and John Beloff, 90–93. Metuchen, NJ: Scarecrow.

Teilhard De Chardin, P. 1959a. *The Phenomenon of Man*. New York: Harper & Row

———. 1959b. Life and the Planets: What Is Happening at This Moment on Earth. In *The future of Man*, Translated by N. Denny, 90–116. New York: Image Books.

———. 1959c. A Great Event foreshadowed: The Planetization of Mankind. In *The future of Man*, Translated by N. Denny, 117–132. New York: Image Books.

Thompson, W. I. 1985. It's Already Begun: The Planetary Age Is an Unacknowledged Daily Reality. *In Context*, 86:26.

Tikkun. "America Needs Repentance." Accessed November 24, 2014. http://www.tikkun.org/fmd/files/2009_high_holiday.pdf.

Truzzi, M. 1987. On Pseudo-skepticism. *Zetetic Scholar* 12(13):3–4.

———. 1998. On Some Unfair Practices Towards Claims of the Paranormal. In *The Parapsychology Revolution: A Concise Anthology of Paranormal and Psychical*

Research, editors R. Schoch and L. Yonavjak, 256–265. New York: Jeremy Tarcher/Penguin.

Turnbull, J. 2007. Can We Get There from Here? Why the Gaian Worldview Will Struggle. In *Earthy Realism: The Meaning of Gaia*, editor M. Midgley, 38–44. Charlottsville, VA: Societas Imprint Academic.

Tyler, P. 2003. A New Power in the Streets. *New York Times*, February 17. Accessed October 17, 2014. http://www.nytimes.com/2003/02/17/international/middleeast/17ASSE.html?pagewanted=all.

Utts, J. 1995. "An Assessment of the Evidence for Psychic Functioning." *Journal of Parapsychology* 59(4):289–320.

———. 1999. "The Significance of Statistics in Mind-matter Research." *Journal of Scientific Exploration* 13(4):615–38.

———. 2003. Statistical Issues in Healing Research. In *Healing, Intention and Energy Medicine: Science, Research Methods and Clinical Implications*, editors B. Jonas and C. Crawford, 239–50. Edinburgh: Churchill Livingstone.

Van Baal, J. 1963. Magic as a Religious Phenomenon. *Higher Education and Research in the Netherlands* 7:10–21. Quoted in W. Hanegraaf. *New Age Religion and Western Culture: Esotericism in the Mirror of Secular Thought*, 83. Albany, NY: State University of New Press.

Varela, F. 1996. «Neurophenomenology: A Methodological Remedy for the Hard Problem.» *Journal of Consciousness Studies* 3:330–49.

———, and Shear, J. 1999. *The View from Within: First-Person Approaches to the Study of Consciousness*. Thorverton, UK: Imprint Academic.

———, Thompson, E., and Rosch, E. 1991. *The Embodied Mind: Cognitive Science and Human Experience*. Cambridge, MA: MIT Press.

Varma, Mahesh Prasad [Maharishi Mahesh Yogi]. 1972. *Science of Creative Intelligence: Knowledge and Experience* [Course Syllabus]. Los Angeles: Maharishi International University Press.

———. 1980. The Structure of Pure Knowledge. In *Science, Consciousness and Ageing: Proceedings of the International Conference*, 73–80. Rheinweiler, Germany: MERU Press.

———. 1986. *Maharishi's Program to Create World Peace*. Washington, D.C: Age of Enlightenment Press, 27. Quoted in D. Orme-Johnson and M. Dillbeck. 1987. Maharishi's Program to Create World Peace: Theory and Research. *Modern Science and Vedic Science* 1(2):3.

———. 1996. *Maharishi's Absolute Theory of Defence: Sovereignty in Invincibility*. India: Age of Enlightenment.

Vaughan-Lee, L. 2005. *Spiritual Power: How It Works*. Inverness, CA: Golden Sufi Center.

———. 2009. *The Return of the feminine and the World Soul*. Inverness, CA: The Golden Sufi Center.

Velmans, M. ed. 2000. *Investigating Phenomenal Consciousness: New Methodologies and Maps*. Amsterdam: John Benjamins.

Versnel, H. S. 1991. "Some Reflections on the Relationship Magic—Religion." *Numen* 38(2):177–97.

Von Franz, M. 1985. "The Transformed Beserk: Unification of Psychic Opposites." *ReVision* 8(1):17–26.

Wallace, R. 2005. *Victory Before War: Preventing Terrorism Through the Vedic Peace Technologies of His Holiness Maharishi Mahesh Yogi.* Fairfield, IA: Maharishi University of Management Press.

Walsh, R. 2007. *The World of Shamanism: New Views of an Ancient Tradition.* Woodbury, MN: Llewellyn.

Walton, K. G., Cavanaugh, K. L., and Pugh, N. D. 2005. "Effect of Group Practice of the Transcendental Meditation Program on Biochemical Indicators of Stress in Non-meditators: A Prospective Time Series Study." *Journal of Social Behavior and Personality* 17(1):339.

Waskow, A. 2003. "What Is Jewish Renewal?A Definition in Process." Accessed October 17, 2014. http://www.shalomctr.org/node/167.

Watkins, A. 1970. *The Old Straight Track.* London: Garnstone Press.

Wax, R. and Wax, M. 1962. "The Magical World View." *Journal for the Scientific Study of Religion* 1(2):179–88.

West, C. 1982. *Prophesy Deliverance! An Afro-American Revolutionary Christianity.* Philadelphia, PA: Westminster Press.

What Is the Earth Charter? (nd). Accessed November 24, 2014. http://www.earth-charterinaction.org/content/pages/What-is-the-Earth-Charter%3F.html.

White, R. 1992. "Review of Approaches to the Study of Spontaneous Psi Experiences." *Journal of Scientific Exploration* 6(2):93–126.

Whitehead, A. N. 1979. *Process and Reality (Gifford Lectures Delivered During the Session 1927–28).* New York: The Free Press.

Wilber, K. 1984. *Quantum Questions: Mystical Writings of the World's Greatest Physicists.* Boston: Shambhala

———. 1995. *Sex, Ecology, Spirituality: The Spirit of Evolution.* Boston: Shambhala.

———. 1997a. *The Eye of Spirit: An Integral Vision for a World Gone Slightly Mad.* Boston: Shambhala.

———. 1997b. "An Integral Theory of Consciousness." *Journal of Consciousness Studies* 4(1):71–92.

———. 1999. *The Marriage of Sense and Soul: Integrating Science and Religion.* New York: Random House.

———. 2000. "Integral Transformative Practice: In This World or Out Of It?" *What Is Enlightenment* 18:34–39.

———. 2006. *Integral Spirituality: A Startling New Role for Religion in the Modern and Postmodern World.* Boston: Integral Books.

Wilbert, J. 1972. Tobacco and Shamanistic Ecstasy among the Warao Indians of Venezuela. In *Flesh of the Gods: The Ritual Use of Hallucinogens,* editor P. T. Furst, 55–83. New York: Praeger.

Wilford, H. 2008. *The Mighty Wurlitzer: How the CIA Played America.* Cambridge, MA: Harvard University Press.

Williams, B. 2014. "GCP Technical Note: Global Harmony 1998–2014." Accessed November 20, 2014. http://global-mind.org/papers/pdf/global.harmony.2014-Williams.pdf

Williamson, M. 2000. *Healing the Soul of America: Reclaiming Our Voices as Spiritual Citizens*. New York: Touchstone.

Wink, W. 1992. *Engaging the Powers: Discernment and Resistance in a World of Domination*. Minneapolis, MA: Augsburg Fortress.

World Scientists' Warning to Humanity. 1992. "Union of Concerned Scientists." Accessed November 24, 2014. http://www.ucsusa.org/about/1992-world-scientists.html.

York, M. 1996. New Age and Paganism. In *Paganism Today: Wiccans, Druids, the Goddess and Ancient Earth Traditions for the Twenty-first Century*, editor C. Hardman and G. Harvey, 157–65. London: Thorsons.

INDEX

Made in the USA
San Bernardino, CA
27 April 2017